SUNRISE OVER BEIRUT

SUNRISE OVER BEIRUT

PART THREE
OF A
TRILOGY

SANDY SIMON

The Cedars Group
Delray Beach, Florida
2013

Copyright © 2013 by Sandy Simon

ISBN 0-9669625-6-7
Printed in the United States of America

This book is a work of fiction. Names, characters, places, and incidents either are products of the author's imagination or are used fictitiously. Any resemblance to actual events or locale or persons, living or dead, is entirely coincidental.

Published by
The Cedars Group
220 MacFarlane Drive, Suite PH-6
Delray Beach, Florida 33483

www.sandysimon.com

This book is dedicated…

to my father, Alexander Eassa Simon Chalhoub and my mother, Linda Helen Zaine Thomé Simon whose lives inspired this book.

to all those tenacious, resilient, and dedicated immigrants from Lebanon and Syria who, since 1850, have sought freedom and opportunity in America, and have contributed their heritage, culture, and wealth to the fabric of their adopted country.

and, finally, to St. Jude Children's Research Hospital in Memphis, Tennessee, which will receive a portion of the proceeds from sales of this book.

ACKNOWLEDGEMENTS

First and foremost, I acknowledge and thank Christiane Collins for her remarkable feat of not only typing and retyping this entire manuscript that I wrote in long hand, but more importantly, for researching, editing, and offering numerous excellent suggestions that added so much to this book; and to Mary Strobel, the finest professional editor who led me through the difficult task of editing and rewriting of this novel.

I thank my cousin, Dr. Robert George, for his medical knowledge and insight that he generously shared.

I am also grateful to cousins Habib Zein, Ibrahim Chalhoub, and Maha Zein for their excellent interpretations of idioms, words, and culture of Lebanon and Syria.

This book is a romantic, historically accurate novel based on extensive research into the history of the Middle East, but also includes important Biblical history. So, I thank my rector, The Reverend William "Chip" Stokes, at St. Paul's Episcopal Church in Delray Beach, for the many studies he led on the Old and New Testaments of the Holy Bible which have been a vital source of the information herein.

Others who helped me include my dear friends Jean Goode, Peter Tanous, the late Richard Shadyac, Sally Benson, Dan Murtaugh, Associate English Professor, Florida Atlantic University, and George Cody of The American Task Force for Lebanon.

I am grateful to those Israeli, Palestinian, and Lebanese writers and to Haa'ertz newspaper archives who have contributed so much to the written knowledge of the events surrounding the Six Day War, which changed the politics and character of the Middle East forever. And to Lt. James Ennis for his eye witness chronicle, "Attack on the USS Liberty", the most decorated ship in the U.S. Navy.

I am also grateful for Sarah Collins Laffer for her excellent cover and book design.

Author's Note

Sunrise Over Beirut is the result of extensive research into the events of the Six Day War, June 5-11, 1967, during which the state of Israel invaded, occupied and drove out citizens of Gaza, the West Bank, East Jerusalem and Syria's Golan Heights.

It is also a historically accurate novel that includes a love story about two lovers, beautiful Leah Wolsinski, a Polish-Jewish refugee living in an Israeli Kibbutz in the Galilee and Francois DuBois, a French-Lebanese banker in Beirut.

My account of the assault on the USS Liberty, which occurred after many hours of aerial surveillance by Israeli planes, killed 34 U.S. Navy men and wounded 171, and is based on eyewitness accounts, military reviews by retired U. S. Admirals and Israeli archives. "…Nevertheless, to this day the American public does not know why the attack took place and who was involved overall." (Thomas H. Moorer, Admiral, U. S. Navy (Ret).

Commander William L. McGonagle, Captain of the Liberty was awarded the Purple Heart, a Silver Star Medal and, later, the Congressional Medal of Honor, a rare award, for his heroism and leadership. Because of White House political influence, Commander McGonagle's last award was reported to have been presented to him in secret and he was sworn never to tell anyone of his award under the threat of life imprisonment.

The Liberty is the most decorated ship in the history of the U.S. Navy, yet, all crew members were sworn to absolute silence for ten years under the threat of court martial and imprisonment for life. To this date, some forty-five years later, not one senator or congressman have ever called for an investigation of the assault on the USS Liberty, although it is the first time in the history of the United States its servicemen were left behind.

Why?

TABLE OF CONTENTS

Chapter 1	Beirut, June 5, 1967, The Attack	1
Chapter 2	June 5, 1967 The Six Day War Begins	7
Chapter 3	Leah	10
Chapter 4	Beirut: Day One, Late Morning; June 5, 1967	17
Chapter 5	Cabinet Meeting, Beirut, Lebanon; June 5, 1967	21
Chapter 6	Beirut; June 12, 1967	26
Chapter 7	Attack on the USS Liberty; Beirut	32
Chapter 8	Malta; June 11, 1967	38
Chapter 9	June 14, 1967; Beirut: Attack Follow-up	45
Chapter 10	Leah; Tel Aviv	48
Chapter 11	Paris	54
Chapter 12	Paris, Love, Memories and Escape	62
Chapter 13	Paris to Beirut	68
Chapter 14	Leah's Arrival in Beirut	74
Chapter 15	Tyre	83
Chapter 16	Tyre Emergency Conference	89
Chapter 17	Leaving Tyre	100
Chapter 18	Baalbek	106
Chapter 19	Beirut	112
Chapter 20	St. George Hotel; Beirut	118
Chapter 21	Beirut	125
Chapter 22	Douma	129
Chapter 23	Figarie	133
Chapter 24	Alexander and François	138
Chapter 25	Cedars Foundation Meeting in Beirut	143
Chapter 26	Damascus, Syria	154
Chapter 27	The Souk	164
Chapter 28	Return from Palmyra	174
Chapter 29	Paris	178
Chapter 30	Venice, Italy	184
Chapter 31	Venice: The Encounter	194
Chapter 32	Venice	201

The Art of War is of vital importance to the state.
It is a matter of Life and death,
a road either to safety or to ruin.
Appear where you are unexpected.
Attack your enemy where he is unprepared.
Sun Tzu

CHAPTER 1

Beirut, June 5, 1967
The Attack

"What the hell? What the hell is that?"

François DuBois, startled by an ominous sight low in the western skies, rose from his chair behind his large, polished mahogany desk, and warily looked out his floor-to-ceiling office window on the thirtieth story. He stepped around his desk to get closer to the window and squinted to focus on a distant row of distinct dots above the eastern Mediterranean Sea.

As he did each day, this Monday morning he arrived in his office at exactly 7:30 a.m. He enjoyed his early mornings, the quiet time to clear his mind before the busy day began. It gave him time to review his day's agenda and organize his thoughts. And he loved watching the sun's impact on the city and the sea, marveling at the color changes of the skies and the sea at sunrise. But this morning in Beirut was different.

François couldn't take his eyes off the western sky, still squinting while staring at the dots moving low in the sky that kept getting larger. Frowning, he looked at his wrist watch. It was now ten minutes before nine o'clock.

"Hanna!" he shouted over his shoulder, impatiently, "Come in here. Quickly! Now!"

Hanna, his devoted and trusted, bespectacled assistant, rushed in, alarmed by the sharp sound of his employer's voice that was filled with unfamiliar urgency.

"Hanna! Look!" He anxiously motioned west toward the horizon.

As they both stood side by side near the glass windows, cupping their hands above their eyes, François pointed to the distance. "What do you see, Hanna?

There," he pointed again.

"Dots," Hanna replied excitedly, "yes, I see small dots, in a line."

"Those dots are growing larger and larger. Look carefully, Hanna," François urged.

"Yes, sir, they are." Hanna, frightened and concerned now, spoke softly and with a deeply furrowed brow. "What are they, Monsieur DuBois? What do you think they are, sir?"

"I'm not sure, Hanna, but I want you to get President Helou on the telephone," François ordered quickly, then blurted out, "Yes! Now I can see that they are jet fighters flying directly toward Beirut. And they are flying dangerously low." He began to hear the faint drone of jet engines. The jet fighters were becoming well-defined as they droned closer and closer toward them at supersonic speeds.

François took a closer look, unsure exactly what he was watching, nervously waiting for Hanna's voice, which felt like many minutes, but was really just a few short moments.

"I have the President's secretary on the telephone, sir."

"They're coming closer, Hanna! Get me the President, not his secretary!" he yelled impatiently. "Hurry!"

Seconds later he saw Hanna's head signal to him. François quickly reached for the phone.

"Mr. President, are you still east of Beirut in Baabda today?"

"Yes, François, I'm still here in Baabda. What's happening?"

"I am in my downtown office, and at this moment I am watching what appears to be a squadron of jet fighters coming directly toward Beirut, flying very low, beneath my offices. I'd say maybe less than two hundred feet above the sea at most."

"Two hundred feet, you say, François?" President Charles Helou asked incredulously.

"Yes, sir, very low. They are below my feet!"

"That means they are intending to be unseen, even by radar and our defense system."

The noise of the fighters' engines was growing louder, increasing the sense of urgency and danger by the second, disturbing François all the more.

"Yes, sir, it appears that way to me also. That is why I called you first."

"Just a moment, François. Hold on while I call the Defense Minister."

"I'll hold, of course, Mr. President, but as you know, if they are Israeli jets, they will be over Beirut in less than a couple of minutes, and in less than twelve minutes they will cross the Bekaa Valley and be on the outskirts of Damascus."

"If they were sent to attack Beirut, they should be firing rockets and their guns any second now. Hold on. I will be right back to you, but you must immediately take cover, François, and get out of your office!"

"Monsieur Dubois," Hanna turned and cried out, frightened for his family, "Are we going to die?"

"It's a little too late for us, Hanna. By the time it would take us to get to the elevators, they will have already attacked us."

"I believe we are not their target, Hanna," Francois said a moment later to Hanna who felt a flash of relief. The telephone receiver remained glued to François' ear, his forehead creased, frowning as he continued to stay visually focused on the dots as they morphed into frontal profiles of a squadron of nearly thirty fighter jets fully loaded with air-to-ground missiles under each wing.

"They are French Mystères, Monsieur DuBois," Hanna said angrily. "Israeli French Mystère fighters!"

"They are not attacking us, Hanna," François blurted out. "See how they are climbing in altitude as they near our beaches? They have to rise above our mountains east of the city. They are flying beyond Beirut."

"Maybe they are going to attack Baalbek in the Bekaa Valley, sir."

"No, Hanna. The Bekaa is harmless to them. They are going after the Syrians! With all that has been going on between Israel and Egypt's Gamal Abdel Nasser, I believe these planes are going to attack Syria…not Beirut…from the west, not from the south as the Syrians expect. It is well known that Syria's President Nur Al-Din Al-Atassi, his Defense Minister Hafez Al Assad, and Egypt's Gamal Abdel Nasser have been negotiating a mutual defense treaty. Israel and Syria have been shooting at each other for weeks. And since Nasser recently closed the Strait of Tiran in the Gulf of Aqaba to Israeli shipping, the situation has really gotten tense. Even Jordan's King Hussein, I believe, has joined with Nasser."

As the jets' engines' roar grew more deafening, Hanna raised both arms in fury at the planes, and angrily shouted in Arabic, *"Y'harah Deanek*! Goddamn you!"

François gripped the telephone hand piece tighter as he conversed with his assistant while watching the jet fighters scream ever closer now, rising and illegally entering Lebanon's air space.

"François are you still there?" the president's familiar voice asked.

"Yes, Mr. President, I am here," François responded, with growing concern.

"Good. I just spoke with General Bustani. He has confidential information that Israel has dispatched all its crack squadrons, nearly four hundred planes!" He repeated for emphasis, "Four hundred jet fighters that are heavily armed with the latest French and advanced American technology, rockets and guns, and, at this very moment, are attacking airfields in Egypt and Jordan. We believe the planes you are monitoring are assigned to attack Syria's airfields. This is terrible news. Terrible. What the hell is Israel doing? What do they want now?"

The president, by asking what most Arabs wanted to know, was keenly aware of the events leading up to these attacks by Israel.

Since the early 1900s, European Jews, encouraged by a new movement called Zionism, were immigrating into Palestine. Their numbers increased from 15,000 per year, as originally arranged by the British in their agreement with the Palestinian leadership, to over 100,000 every year, a number urged by President Harry Truman during his 1948 presidential campaign seeking the U.S. Jewish vote.

Confrontation was the choice of all sides. From Israel's perspective, now unilaterally seeking to take Gaza and the West Bank, even if contrary to civil societies and international law, was important to their goals of a "Greater Israel" and ill-perceived security. The relocation of refugees out of Gaza was actually carefully planned by Israel even before the war began. Egypt's closing of the Strait of Tiran was the raison d' etre they were looking for.

In 1948 the Arab-Israeli War, known as *Al Nakbah*, "The Disaster," over 700,000 Palestinians were forced from their homes in contravention of the Balfour Declaration.

This was followed by the 1956 Israeli invasion to take over the Suez Canal from Egypt.

"I cannot imagine what they want this time, sir," François replied. "I'm just glad that Lebanon did not participate in the 1956 war. We all feel badly about the treatment the Jews endured from the Nazis and what they're going through as refugees. With so many coming into such a small place, one where people live and have lived for centuries is a recipe for long term problems in my opinion, sir."

"Despite all that has come before," the president nodded his concurrence, "for more than a decade, the Lebanese have lived in relative peace. We have endured mostly Syrian, Egyptian, and Israeli exchanges of political polemics, verbal outrage, and sporadic Israeli aerial dog fights against Egyptian and Syrian jets over the Sinai, the Golan and South Lebanon. Will it ever end?" he asked rhetorically, comfortable discussing these issues with his friend François.

"Mr. President, Lebanon doesn't want to be at war with anyone. Not since the Arab-Israeli War of 1947 have we allowed ourselves to be drawn into the Arab-Israeli conflict. And we must stand strong and not be tempted to join into this current situation."

"François, Lebanon has not closed its doors to the Palestinian refugees and, as a consequence, several hundreds of thousands have settled in Lebanon, mostly in the south. They are now nearly twenty percent of our population, tilting the Christian majority to a minority of forty percent and the poor Shiia Muslim and Palestinian population to more than one third. This is a terrible financial burden on our citizens. Of course, in addition, many refugees have given birth to babies within Lebanon and they have therefore may become eligible to become citizens who are in dire need of housing, food, medical and utility services. It's too much for us."

"And one day, Mr. President, our government must seriously address this problem because there is so much poverty and despair in the south."

"You are correct, François, but now, with these new Israeli attacks, there is no telling what is going to happen next. We don't know and must find out for certain the position of the United States, our friend and Israel's benefactor."

"Yes, sir, we must, but we all know President Lyndon Johnson's sympathies are completely with Israel."

"Do you think he is supporting these actions?"

"We do not know as yet. I am waiting now to hear from our ambassador in Washington. It is only 2:30 in the morning there. We may have to wait until this afternoon to learn exactly what is happening and what our options are, if any.

"However, François, Israel's multiple attacks today are unprecedented and extremely dangerous. This, of course, means war, and it will be hell for all of us throughout the region. François, as we confirm what I have been told, which should not take long. I must call an emergency meeting of the *Majlis al Nuwab*, the Parliament. I need you to be available." After a brief moment of thought, he added, "You're right. Thank God Lebanon was not involved in any of these recent battles and the last war in 1956, or our airport and this very city would now be under attack."

François stepped around his desk and slowly sank down into his chair. His brow furrowed with concern and fear of what appeared to be a catastrophic upheaval on the people of Lebanon and its neighbors.

"What is to become of our beloved Lebanon?" the president asked rhetorically. "We are a beautiful but tiny democratic country with open borders, a *laissez-faire* culture, and an ineffective army. We are a land that thrives on free trade."

François replied. "I pray the land of my father is not caught in this war and have to face enormous destruction by heavily armed Israel and its battles with Syria and Egypt. We have so little to protect our way of life…a way of life coveted by people of every state in the Middle East…Syria, Israel, and Egypt. Even the Gulf States envy Lebanon. Lord knows we can only watch and wait, hoping they do not draw us into the fray."

Hanna Saba, François' executive assistant for more than ten years, usually at his desk by at least 7:30 a.m., stood ready to be of service the moment his energetic and very actively involved superior needed him, especially after speaking with the president. Often, Hanna provided what François needed even before he asked. They were a very good team, and trusted each other completely. Hanna knew his future employment and prosperity were tied to François Dubois' rising career.

It had been Hanna's good fortune to be selected by François immediately after Monsieur DuBois, already senior vice-president at Credit Suisse, Beirut, Regional Manager of the Middle East, was appointed Vice Minister of Finance of Lebanon, the legendary "Switzerland of the Middle East," and Beirut, "Paris of the Middle East."

François' extensive educational background at The American University of Beirut, AUB, the Sorbonne in Paris, and the London School of Economics served him well. He carefully groomed his friendships in France, England and the

Middle East, and spoke fluent Arabic, Italian, English and French, with accents that conveyed excellent breeding, grooming, and upper class cultures. Hanna's work ethic and his success at AUB impressed François.

Recalling his life's events, he told Hanna one day, in total confidence, the story of his background.

"My mother, Madeleine DuBois Moreau," he began, remembering, "brought me to Beirut from Marseille, France. In 1940, I was nearly twenty years old. My mother feared I might be conscripted into the German army or worse, killed along with thousands of other Frenchmen. We fled Marseille in the dead of night on a Lebanese fishing boat, which brought us to Beirut. But it was not safe here for us, so we went north to my father's village, Douma. My stepfather, Philippe Moreau, had become the Director of the French Resistance during the war.

"My mother later learned that her husband had been commissioned by the president of France to organize the three principle disparate bands of partisans. At first these loyal partisans merely irritated the occupying Germans with such acts as spilling red wine on the Germans' uniforms while serving them in the cafes and other minor gestures until Moreau became their director in 1939. After several years under his convincing leadership, a dramatically more effective resistance emerged. His meticulously coordinated programs of bombing bridges, railroads and surprise commando attacks significantly thwarted the planned movements of German equipment and armed personnel, causing the German occupiers significant delays, upsetting their movements and effectiveness.

"In 1940, after the Germans invaded France, he arranged for my mother and me to flee in the middle of the night.

"As a result, he infuriated the German High Command, became a wanted man by the Germans and their allies, the puppet Vichy French government, and, as we learned after the war, he was assassinated in 1944.

"In 1945 we were befriended by and taken in by Monsieur Kabbani, Director of Kabbani Brothers through an arrangement by my Uncle Milhelm. I later attended AUB and then the Sorbonne. Monsieur Kabbani has been my mentor since those days. He was very kind to us, and shares his wisdom with me to this day.

"And I will honor him by doing all I can for Lebanon in the coming days. You will see this in the days to come, Hanna."

There is no instance of a country having benefited from prolonged warfare.
Sun Tzu

Chapter 2

The Six Day War Begins
June 5, 1967

By now, the deafening sounds of the jet fighters' roaring engines threw the city's population into a fit of fear, terrorizing everyone as they craned their necks looking up toward the skies, trying to see what was making all that fearful noise. The apprehension felt palpable. For weeks, even months, the entire region learned to live with tension and high alert with sporadic attacks on Syria by the Israelis, and saber-rattling from Israel and Egypt's Nasser. All sides kept poised for battle while testing the boundaries of the other side. Syria's guns on the Golan Heights were fired into Israeli northern villages below mostly by angry Palestinian refugees. Israel's jet fighters constantly invaded Syrian air space, shooting at Syrian farmers on the ground, and shooting down Syrian planes. Tensions built day after day with Israel threatening Egypt's ally, Syria so much that Egypt concluded it was forced to act. There was enough warrior mentality to go around. The only leader, aside from Lebanon's clearly not wanting war, was Jordan's "Little King" Hussein, as Israel's Rabin cynically called him. But then, he was reluctantly forced by Israel's intransigence and attacks to join Egypt and Syria in their mutual defense treaties. The Middle East became a powder keg of dynamite whose fuse now had been lit. War might have been prevented, as Hussein, Ben-Gurion and nearly half of Israel believed, but not likely, considering the twenty-five years of anger and hatred on both sides.

Since the 1947 war, known as The Catastrophe *Al Nakbah*, Palestinians found themselves displaced by the hundreds of thousands of European immigrants brought by the Zionist Agency which declared a "return to their homeland" and, consequently, pushed out the natives from their homeland. While they used as their justification the Balfour Declaration by the British in 1917, others believed it was intended that only a part of Palestine become Jewish. Still everyone knew that the Declaration included the statement that the rights of the indigenous population would not be prejudiced. But their rights were indeed being severely prejudiced.

The Zionist governments long hoped to expand northward throughout south Lebanon to harness for themselves the clear, abundant flowing waters of the Litani River, Lebanon's snowmelt-fed river that flows into the sea just a few short miles north of the Israeli border, copious waters the Israeli government long coveted dearly along with the significant snowmelt and waters of the Golan Heights that flow down into the Sea of Galilee.

François found himself torn emotionally. The only woman he ever loved, Leah, was always on his mind, and, naturally, his first thoughts invariably went to her, his love, living in Israel, then to the safety of the Lebanese people, to concern about the future of his adopted country.

By 1967, Beirut and Lebanon itself entered its second decade of unparalleled prosperity and worldwide appeal. The Treasury brimmed from wealth provided by the incredible dynamics of the envied Lebanese private enterprises of banking and trade, the substantial financial windfalls of unprecedented tourism from the Gulf States and the Lebanese diaspora that arose because Lebanese all over the world returned to revisit their homeland and families, re-experience the unique culture of Lebanon, enjoy Lebanon's beautiful weather during most of the year, and the *joie d' vivre* of the people of Lebanon, a small, *laissez-faire*, free market, and Western-aligned democracy always thrived during peaceful times. The postwar ballooning demands for Western products by Saudi Arabia, Iraq, Kuwait, and the Gulf oil emirates flowed through Beirut's banks and its ports. And François DuBois participated as he managed the extraordinarily profitable Credit Suisse banking center of that massive whirlwind flow of petrodollars and resulting profitable investments through his dynamic and productive offices.

François' leadership, business acumen, integrity, and diplomacy reflected the character of his parentage. His successes and cultural background enabled him to become well-respected in both the Lebanese political and business worlds. François was not a Maronite Catholic, the religion necessary for the president and high appointees, but that of his father, an Antiochan Orthodox Christian, a well-respected but rarely a political power sector. He became an important adviser to the ruling party and was considered a favorite friend and advisor of President Charles Helou, the Maronite president who was elected in 1964. Charles, of the powerful Helou family, remained prominent in Beirut politics and society for many years.

François established an excellent reputation by recommending lucrative investments and arranging beneficial mergers and acquisitions. He made many powerful wealthy and influential friends throughout the banking, business and political circles of the city and Europe. Because he was Antiochan Orthodox and not Muslim, he was not considered a political threat in the unique world of Lebanon's politics. Due to his loyalty to his Lebanese-American father, François remained staunchly pro-Lebanon and pro-American.

François, still a handsome bachelor at forty-seven years, often escorted beautiful ladies from prominent families, which did no harm to his career. But his heart belonged to Leah, his love from when they first met at the Sorbonne, twenty years earlier, now a beautiful Israeli whose love didn't leave his mind even today, watching the menacing Israeli jets overhead. But the planes created a conflict he would have to confront, and very soon.

Expectations are the breeding ground for resentment
Anonymous

Chapter 3

Leah

My Love,

I always have this beautiful image of you in my mind, François. I remember the first moment you entered my life. Paris...at the Sorbonne...we were so young in 1947. We had, as they say, strong chemistry. You became my first true love. And I was your first love. How lucky we were to find each other, just as your mother was and remains your father's first true love. We did not anticipate that during those magnificent moments together we would ever be separated. Twenty years later, here I am in Israel, and you are in Beirut. What is going to happen now? Must we leave the region to be together? God knows you cannot be with me in Israel. And because of your position, you may not be able to have me with you in Beirut, although Lebanon has been safe and pleasant for Jews, until now. Lebanon is such an amazing and unique mixture of peoples of different religions...Druze, Shiia Muslims, Sunni Muslims, Maronite Christians, Orthodox Christians, Greeks, Armenians and Jews.

Maybe you'll find a way that I can join you in Beirut. Or, maybe we'll have to go somewhere else. I just want us to be together, my love, forever.

I'll never forget that painful moment as we walked along the Seine when I had to tell you, which was the most difficult decision I have ever made, that I must leave you and Paris to help build a homeland for my people in Palestine. Part of me died that night and I have missed you terribly ever since.

I still think about you every day and long for the time we can be together again.

I send you all my love and wish you peace.

Shalom, my love,

Leah

After reading her letter over and over, François picked up his pen and began writing his reply.

> Leah, I know I should not, at this moment, reply to your beautiful letter, which I think I have read and reread lovingly a hundred times. And while I know I shouldn't write you now, because I am so angry at you and your damned extremist government, I am going to write you now anyway. I am so angry, so frustrated, I can't help myself. But I want you to know how I feel.
>
> I just watched your damned Israeli squadron of heavily armed fighter jets flying low, directly at my office. You cannot imagine the sense of terror their presence brought to me, to my staff, the people of Beirut and to my country for no reason whatever! I want you to know how frustrated I am because you insist on staying in that country instead of with me. Each time I've read your letter, I remember the love and joy we shared in Paris. We were so happy. You filled my heart with your love, so much there has been no room for anyone else. And then, I ache inside because we have been apart all these years. I am lonely for you because I still love you so much. But that love is sharing a growing anger at you and your damned difficult government. Each time I read your letter I always feel a mix of contradicting emotions. I know I still love you with all my heart, but I live with enormous frustrations nearly to the point of being so angry with you that I am beginning to think we should not see each other again. I am so sorry, but I cannot continue to live this way.
>
> François

Moments after he finished writing the letter to her and once again aware of the sound of Israeli jets overhead, he crumpled both letters in his hands. He rested his head with both his hands trying to shake off the range of emotions coursing through him. At that precise moment of despair, his private telephone buzzed startling him from his thoughts. He reached quickly for the receiver and spoke sharply, "François DuBois speaking."

"*Allo*, François," the familiar feminine voice of Leah once again caused his mind to race and his body to shiver.

"Leah, is that you? I haven't heard from you for a long time. Are you still in the kibbutz in Galilee? Why are you calling me now?" he asked abruptly, frustrated at the events enveloping his world and irritated that only if she contacted him could he speak with her.

While he loved hearing Leah's distinctive voice, he was deeply engrossed with fears of possible war, of Lebanon's safety and concern that a regional war would soon erupt, reaping massive destruction of his beloved Lebanon. And, he was angry with Leah's insistence on remaining in Israel. Especially now.

"Yes, my darling, it is Leah. And I miss you so much. But that is not why I called, François. Something terrible is happening." Her voice was shaking.

He quickly grabbed her letter, shook it and replied angrily, "How can you write to tell me you love me and be part of that crazy, aggressive country, Leah? Yes, there is something terrible happening! Israel is attacking three Arab counties. Right now! As we speak! Your damned Israeli fighter jets just flew over my offices loaded with rockets! I am so angry, Leah, and I'm very frustrated with you too! How can you write me such a letter, professing your love for me and continue to choose to live there. What the hell is going on? Has your government gone mad?"

"Are you safe, François?" she asked nervously.

"What kind of a question is that? How can I know, Leah? Israel's heavily armed planes are flying over Beirut, to who knows where, likely en route to Damascus... unless they intend to attack Baalbek or Zahle in the Bekaa Valley! They have invaded Lebanon's air space. And, of course, Lebanon has no Air Force or any true defenses against Israel's Air Force. We wonder if there will be more, and if they plan to attack Beirut. And you, Leah. How can you remain there and profess your love for me? Are you safe? And where are you? What is going on in Israel?" He peppered questions at her while being tossed by feelings of resentment, anger, deep concern, impotence and yet, his enduring love for Leah.

"It's so complicated, my love, and so difficult to explain. I'm in Tel Aviv at a pay phone...only to call you. I have to be very careful. But the immediate issue has more to do with the communications breakdown between Israel's hardliners and Egypt's Gamal Abdel Nasser. As you must know, Nasser closed Aqaba to Israel's shipments, a blockade that is interpreted here as an act of war, emboldening our right wing. That's all they needed. It's an excuse to initiate attacks and invasions they have planned for months! Most Israelis are afraid, François. Some, like I, who have been seeking peace among our neighbors, have been fruitlessly opposing any retaliatory action against Egypt. Even Ben-Gurion, now retired, is totally against this action. But his opinion is no longer considered important, I am so afraid. Many Israelis, I believe, are concerned about Israel's very survival, and, as a result, the right wing won out in the government, pressing a 'go for broke' action. That is why Israel is taking this preemptive action. I am calling you because I love you and urge you to be aware that Israel's government is not listening to reason anymore — at least not after Jordan and Syria signed the mutual defense agreements with Nasser. We have no quarrel with Lebanon as long as Lebanon's government does not join in. But we don't know if the hardliners like General Dayan want to bring Lebanon and its waters into the fight."

"Leah, are you saying that Israel is now preemptively attacking Egypt, Syria and Jordan? All three nations? Today? This morning?" he asked, not trying to hide the edge in his voice.

"Yes, my darling. That is why I called you. Israeli radio has been falsely broadcasting all last night and this morning announcing to everyone in the world that we are under attack from Egypt and Syria and that now we must defend ourselves! But there have been no attacks on Israel! You must get out of Beirut immediately! For your safety, I urge you to go north to the mountains. Perhaps to Douma…where your mother took you when you were young."

"But I cannot do that, Leah. I'm no longer a boy. You know it is not in my blood to run away from danger. I must remain in the city. The president has asked me to be available for the emergency meetings. He's calling them now as we speak."

"I understand, François. Of course I understand, knowing you, and knowing the stories of your father and mother. But please be careful."

"My mother and father are here…in Beirut now, Leah. I was hoping I could introduce you to them so they could love you as I do. But now, that is out of the question. This is not the time for such a meeting," he nearly yelled into the phone as he pounded her now crumpled letter on to the desk, furious.

"Please, Francois, Please do not be so angry with me. I do not agree with what is happening here, but I truly believe if I stay here, at least for the time being, I can help calm the Israeli waters."

"But, Leah, you are not going to be heard. You may even be in danger. You must get out of there. Or stop writing me love letters. You can't have it both ways. I'm getting tired of this separation, and your insisting you must stay in Israel.

"And what about you, Leah? What is Israel's objective, Leah? Do you know what they seek? Is it power over their neighbors alone? Or is it the entire Middle East…to the Euphrates? Is this the moment Israel intends its expansion that the Arab world has long feared?"

"I don't know…I…cannot talk too long, François. My position leaves me vulnerable to those who oppose my efforts of seeking peace. I am probably being watched even now. But I can say that we have asked that very question of Nasser. What does Nasser want? Does he want to destroy Israel?" After a moment, she blurted, "I must go now, but soon, darling, soon we must meet again…alone. I will call you as soon as I can. Please, please consider my message. I don't know how long or how big this will be. But it is a regional problem. And it will be devastating and, please, my love, please know I love you with all my heart."

"Don't say that, Leah, unless you mean it. And you can't mean it and stay there.

"As for Lebanon, depending on Israel's treatment of Lebanon, I will urge that we stay out of this war. We will see what role Lebanon can take, Leah. Hopefully, we will stand aside. We are so small and vulnerable. We are much smaller than Israel!"

"You must leave there and come to me. We should arrange to meet in Italy like last time. And it needs to be soon or not at all. I mean it, Leah. I've said all I can right now. I'm very angry…at Israel, and at you," he nearly yelled, exhausted and stressed.

"*Shalom*, darling," she whispered, worried and frightened at his words.

François slowly, silently but firmly replaced the handset on the telephone as he contemplated the situation. He smiled slightly then frowned, as he experienced the absurdly combined emotions of love and anger at the same time. He could feel his muscles relax for a moment as he sat back in his chair and looked out the large windows of his office overlooking the Mediterranean Sea, thinking... remembering what his mother had said: "Life is a series of cycles, my son. We are doomed to repeat history." *Yes*, he thought to himself, *as long as our leaders continue doing the same things we will continue to reap the same results. To continue is insanity on both sides.*

A few minutes later, Hanna entered his office and interrupted his thoughts. He silently stood opposite François, papers in his hands, but refrained from speaking as François glanced up at him briefly then lowered his eyes, obviously deep in thought.

"So here we are again," François muttered angrily, "neighbors fighting neighbors. Over what? Power? Land? Control? Over all of Palestine? This region has been the battleground now for too many years...first the Canaanites, then the Israelites, the Babylonians, Assyrians, Persians, the Greeks, Romans, the Crusades, then the Ottomans for five-hundred years. And now, the Israelis! Will it never end?"

"Sir, we all know that for hundreds of years, Palestine was a land of relative peace. Christian villages like Bethlehem, Nazareth, and Ramallah lived peacefully, side by side with Jews in their own villages. Then the Muslims came to Palestine the 700s, there was calm in Palestine for several centuries." Hanna smiled, thinking of good times. "Muslim villagers took their places in Palestine and for hundreds of years they lived in peace with the Christians and the Jews."

"However," François interjected, "don't forget that in the eleventh century, Pope Urban II, believing that his realm needed to remove the fighting, disenfranchised knights and poor suffering serfs of Europe, directed them to Jerusalem on the Crusades to free the Holy Land from the infidels, the Muslims. They came, claiming the Holy Land for themselves even though everyone, Christian, Jew and Muslim, were relatively happy, peacefully living together.

Ironically, during those two hundred years from 1099 to 1200, the Muslims protected the indigenous Jews and indigenous Christians from the invaders."

"But the Europeans slaughtered tens of thousands of Arab Muslims and Jews, didn't they?"

"Regrettably, Arabs to this day, look on the Crusades as a Western/European invasion meant to convert and destroy the Eastern/Muslim world, its culture, its religion and to take its lands. They succeeded for a long time, until Saladin and his Muslim forces drove them out.

"And now, the Arabs believe Zionist Israel, which has been flooded by hundreds of thousands of immigrants from Europe, have brought with them a totally different culture, strange foods and strange concepts like political and labor unions, to be another massive European/Western assault on their way of life, their culture, and their religion and, once again, intent on taking their lands."

"Monsieur DuBois, the Arabs are going to do all in their power not to allow any more taking of their land of Palestine, destruction of their homes, their culture, their religion, and their world by the West. Even resilient Lebanon's mix of Western-oriented culture, French influence, and Christian leadership angers many Muslims."

"And now, Hanna, it appears Israel insists on being the major armed power in the Middle East. Many Arabs believe it is Israel's intent to actually settle and occupy all the lands 'from the Euphrates to the Nile,' as described in their Torah."

"But all of us are children of Abraham, not just Jews!" Hanna interrupted angrily.

Francois continued, "Meaning they plan to take all of Lebanon, Jordan, most of Syria, significant parts of Iraq and Egypt's Sinai Peninsula. All, some believe, will become swallowed by Israel, with European and American support. The Israeli right wing extremists blatantly and stubbornly say bringing all Jews from all over the world to Palestine is indeed their goal."

"God help us, Monsieur DuBois. It certainly looks like the hardline Israelis believe it is now the time for them to conquer to the Euphrates…from the Nile. It looks very bad. Certainly Israel's powerful, well-trained Air Force and Western weaponry outmatch all the Arab countries' armies combined."

"And, Hanna, I worry all the time about Lebanon's security and Leah's safety."

Silently, he returned into silent thought, convinced he had to do something, but what?

As soon as Leah Wolsinski softly placed the telephone receiver back on the public telephone, she carefully looked around to find out if she was being watched. She knew she had to be careful as she stepped from the phone booth along the busy sidewalk and sat down at a small, metal table outside a nearby coffee house.

She heard the incessant shrill government air raid sirens and loudspeaker warnings to take cover, even though so far there had been no enemy planes overhead, no bombs, and no attacks on Israel. Leah felt the government was creating a false impression that Israel was under attack as a subterfuge so Jews and Israeli supporters, everywhere, believing their claims, would strongly support them as weak defenders and as the underdog once again.

She needed time to think…to remember. This urge to recall her being with François in Paris always overcame Leah after she spoke with her love, François DuBois, successful banker, Special Advisor to Lebanon's President, and quite likely, soon to be named Minister of Finance. And after that? Who knows? Leah sipped the hot, thick Turkish coffee from her demitasse cup brought by the waiter in response to her gesture. She lit a cigarette, a salve she sought when she was anxious, nervous, and worried. Her frown soon left her forehead as she recalled their wonderful times at the Sorbonne in 1947, especially when she was with François, that delicious, handsome young man full of vitality, grace and charm. And, refreshingly, so willing to be vulnerable!

After Paris, Leah did go to Palestine, full of youthful, naïve commitment to help build a homeland for the Jewish people in Palestine, living in peace side by side with the Arabs, both Christian and Muslim. The only place for someone thinking as she did, was in a socialist kibbutz where she worked in the farms, away from politics, angry Zionists and anti-Arabs.

She lived for nearly twenty years the life of a settler in northern Palestine in a kibbutz on the shores of the Sea of Galilee near Tiberius. She thrived living her life in kibbutz Ra'agan, a commune where all individuals gave up ownership of anything. Collectively, all owned everything, even one's individual inheritance. Most kibbutzim thrived in this environment and felt fulfilled because they were agricultural, non-political Socialists living in peace in the rural areas. She loved working the earth, growing crops, and even fishing in the Sea of Galilee "as did Peter and his brothers."

Leah felt enriched by accomplishing something good, like growing healthy vegetables for the markets…and not getting involved in the politics of Tel Aviv or Orthodox Jerusalem. She was certainly Jewish, raised by her now deceased parents to respect and follow her religion. More secular Jewish than a nationalist Zionist, she never felt comfortable with those who demanded, like Ben-Gurion, that all Arabs must eventually leave Palestine and that all of Palestine should become totally Jewish. In contrast, she believed the Arabs had rights and could live side by side with the Jews. She respected the rights of all human beings. A free spirit, Leah fully believed that helping build a homeland was her purpose in Palestine, her purpose in life. She wanted to live freely as a Palestinian Jew…free to choose, to believe, to simply be a Jew. As one who experienced growing up in Europe during the 1930s and 1940s, a place where many rights were taken away from so many people, especially Jewish people, she did not want her religion or anyone else's to be an issue. She wondered why all Jews in Palestine didn't understand that the whole idea was to build a nation within Palestine where everyone was free to work, free to worship, free to play, and free to think. That is what the early leaders, including Ben-Gurion, professed until after the British left.

Then he, along with so many other ardent Zionists changed his public position to demand that all of Palestine be for Jews only, and that all Arabs be removed from their land.

Even if it meant others would strongly disagree, Leah decided she had to do something.

All Warfare is Based On Deception
Sun Tzu

CHAPTER 4

Beirut: Day One, Late Morning
June 5, 1967

"All hell is breaking loose, François!" The president was back on the phone. "The entire Air Forces and airports of Syria and Egypt are being totally destroyed on the ground, as we speak. Thousands of mechanics, firemen, emergency workers, support personnel and pilots have all been killed! Planes, fire trucks, ambulances and car fleets have been destroyed. Nothing is left! The Israelis have surprised everyone. Their American weaponry is so accurate, so advanced," yelled the president into his telephone. "The American missiles never miss! All is lost for the Arabs. All their military capability is wiped out. So much is gone," he said sadly. "We are all totally vulnerable to whatever they want to do to us. It is, may I say, the equivalent of the hated German blitzkrieg of Poland, England, and France! So destructive! So uncivilized!" he continued, his high-pitched voice filled with anxiety.

"Mr. President, we need to take steps to stay out of this," François interjected. "Nasser and his thousands of soldiers are now powerless. Do you think it's possible to propose peace before Lebanon is attacked?"

"I don't know, François, it is another 'Western Invasion,' a new age of European Crusades as they were called nine hundred years ago. Those Europeans literally butchered hundreds of thousands of Muslims and everyone else except for the Christians, who were later tracked down in Lebanon's northern mountains where they were in hiding and killed by revenge-filled Muslims after the Europeans departed. Who can forget the atrocities of those damned Crusades? Oh yes," the Maronite Christian President added with a visceral sense of cynicism, "they always called it a Christian Crusade. But the Arab World calls it 'The Western Invasion.' Your Eastern Orthodox Church was correct when it urged the pope not to invade Palestine. After all, they said, and it was true, Constantinople, Europe's largest and wealthiest city, knew that in those days all people lived in peace in the Holy Land: Muslims, Christians, and Jews. But Rome had its own problems and Pope Urban II thought his Crusades were the answer for his Europeans who couldn't get along with anyone, even each other!"

"Yes," added François, "Europe was still in the Dark Ages while the Arabs were advancing in many ways. It is sad," François continued with his mentor, the president. "Arabs are given credit for advancing the Renaissance in Europe. Even today, centuries later, Muslims throughout the entire Arab world cannot forget those Crusades. Imagine, America, mostly a Christian nation, is financing the destruction of the Christians of Palestine."

"I don't get it," responded the president, "I just don't understand why the United States is financing this complete destruction of Palestine, which, like Lebanon, with all three religions has been living in peace."

"I pray we can continue our internal peace, Mr. President, but the more Palestinian refugees we absorb, the more likely we will descend into internecine disputes." "Forgive me, my dear friend, for elaborating on these issues so deeply and so passionately, but you and I have a very special relationship. You bring the French and American views to me, which I count on so much. I cannot speak of these things to others in my political circles, not even to my family. I have to hold it inside.

"The Zionists are alienating the entire Arab world. I hate to say this," the Christian president added, "but it appears that the supporters of Israel in America are in control of the White House, the Senate, and their House of Representatives. Those political leaders seem to be willing to turn their backs on America's own best interests in the Middle East for their own expediency, solely to ensure their reelection. In fact, I understand America's Senate and House members enjoy more than ninety percent likelihood of reelection, far more even than those reelected in communist Soviet Union. Astounding!

"François, I am calling for an immediate emergency meeting of the Arab League. It will likely be held away from the confrontation states, perhaps in Dubai. I will keep you informed so that you may be by my side, my friend."

By 10 a.m., the airfields of the Air Forces of Syria, Jordan and Egypt were ablaze with their hundreds of parked planes, one after another destroyed, exploding and collapsing in flames, creating havoc everywhere. Sirens sounded as support crews and fire engines sped across the tarmac. Even as the attacks continued, many service personnel were killed as they sought to save others. Hundreds of men were burned alive or lay either dying or badly injured as everyone reacted to the surprise early morning Israeli attacks. Nearby the capital cities of Damascus, Cairo, and Amman roads were packed with terrorized citizens running every which way, filling the streets, jamming emergency vehicles seeking to respond. No one knew if more attacks would come to the populated centers or nearby villages. Sirens blasted, mosque minarets blared emergency messages in Arabic alerting the people. With so much confusion of overlapping public announcements, prayers and sirens blaring simultaneously, none could be separated nor understood. Total chaos enveloped the cities, their airports, and their streets. No one knew what to do or where to go for safety. The event was unprecedented and caught everyone by surprise. The destruction was total. News media reported that Egypt lost over 137 (some announced 181) parked aircraft, their entire Air Force, and their support facilities, fuel tanks, barracks, and service trucks. Hundreds of people died as Israeli aircraft, without resistance, completely wiped out one of the most armed and most powerful states in the Middle East, Egypt, so that Israel's tanks and armies could, without any resistance, quickly advance into Gaza and the Sinai with impunity and total air and ground superiority.

Syrian spies learned from their informers on the ground that Israel's plans had been extensive. By the time Prime Minister Eshkol reluctantly authorized General Moshe Dayan to attack Egyptian, Syrian and Jordanian air and ground forces, Dayan had already ordered the pre-planned occupation of Gaza and relocation of its people even as his troops poured into Egypt's Sinai Peninsula.

Israel's government-controlled media, broadcasted for twenty-four hours that Israel was under attack, misleading its citizens and the entire world, so to falsely place the war's blame squarely on the backs of the Egyptians, Syrians, and Jordanians. Indeed, it wasn't until 10:30 a.m., the war's third hour that the first gunfire exchanges with Jordan began on the outskirts of Jerusalem. "Make sure the world knows we are the victims," yelled the Israeli radio. "We are the victims! Not the attackers!"

By 12:30 p.m., the Israelis took the first land at the Palestinian village of Jenin, in the West Bank, which Dayan ordered occupied to the chagrin of Rabin, Eshkol, and others who did not want Israel to take Palestinian land. Yet the goal of taking Jerusalem and the West Bank from Jordan had been planned by the IDF for a long time.

By 3 p.m., the BBC Radio announced that Israel Military Radio was reporting it had victoriously destroyed more than 400 enemy aircraft as they sat parked on the tarmac. They added that the Jordanians, who, in support of Egypt, had reluctantly signed a mutual defense pact with Egypt. After the attack on their airfields, Jordan began retaliatory artillery bombardment of Israel's north army base at Ramat David, and the two countries increased their attacks on each other followed by Israel moving into and occupying Jordanian-controlled East Jerusalem and the West Bank.

Within two days of heavy air and ground fighting, Israeli armed forces occupied the entire West Bank, and Gaza. Israel routed Palestinian men, women, and children from their homes, offices, and shops in East Jerusalem, the cities and villages of the West Bank, including Christian Bethlehem, Ramallah, and Nazareth, and facilitated the takeover of all remaining Palestinian lands by Israeli forces.

The Zionist taking of all of Palestine was complete.

Millions of Palestinians, Muslims and Christians suddenly became destitute refugees without civil rights, basic possessions of food, shelter, a decent future, or hope.

As far as the world was concerned, based on the success of the untrue Israeli broadcasts, Israel was seen as simply defending itself. The U.S. media, convinced after twenty years of very effective propaganda, favored "Jewish settlers farming in their God-given homeland" and sided with the Israeli "counter attacks" against the perceived "belligerent, confrontational Soviet-Allied" Egyptian and Syrian governments. Most Americans, following their media reports and their government statements, believed Israel to be enormously outnumbered. These false, yet effective, messages that three million Jews had defeated one hundred million Arabs filled the American media.

And, since the war took only six days, the world hardly took notice.

The "Winds of Fate" were surely on the side of the new State of Israel. And with the Cold War near its height, in America, it was perceived as nothing more than a peripheral Cold War proxy skirmish. Little was known nor appreciated about the unilateral surprise attacks by Israel, of the horrendous treatment of the Palestinian people, nor of the heavy burden of refugees on the neighboring states of Lebanon, Jordan, and Syria.

And, the world did nothing.

*If your enemy is secure at all points, be prepared for him.
If he is in superior strength, evade him.*
Sun Tzu

Chapter 5

*Cabinet Meeting, Beirut, Lebanon
June 5, 1967*

"Lebanon must do something!" shouted the Sunni Muslim Prime Minister, leading the call at the afternoon emergency Cabinet meeting called by President Charles Helou. "We must act against this Zionist monster," added the Shiia Speaker of the Parliament!

Their opening demands set the tone of this most fractious emergency meeting, reflecting the sectarian nature of the Lebanese political landscape. "We demand that Lebanon support our brothers in Jordan, Syria and Egypt!" complained the Sunni Prime Minister, pounding his fist on the table before him. Each hoped to quickly build a solid Muslim position in the meeting, his vociferous statement, loudly reflecting the anger of his sectarian populace, his representatives and their parochial interests. The various ministers angrily used their portfolios in an effort to convince the rest. "Lebanon must not sit idly by while our brothers suffer at the hands of these unilateral, preemptive attacks by Israel. We have to join our Syrian and Egyptian brothers who are, at this very moment, suffering from the attacks on our people," yelled the Shiia Speaker, representing the south Lebanon constituency most vulnerable to Israel's attacks on Lebanon.

"We cannot stand idly by while Israel seeks to dominate the region with western arms."

Lebanon's constitution, requiring that the president be a Maronite Christian, the Prime Minister be a Sunni Muslim, and the Speaker of the Parliament be Shiia Muslim, formed a triumvirate of democratic governing that assures that all three of the most prominent populations be part of the decision-making process, and enabled a means of seeking a semblance of harmony among the various sectarian constituencies. The Druze cabinet member, representing the Druze population, a minority Muslim sect, eagerly spoke his mind to the group.

"But, wait, we cannot stop Israel. Lebanon is weak militarily and cannot do anything to stop them. I fear our people in the Shouf will once again bear the brunt of the Israeli war machine if Lebanon enters into this war."

The Sunni Prime Minister responded to him with anger and, speaking of vengeance, said, "We all agree Lebanon cannot compete with the Israeli power, but we must send a message. And that message to our brothers in Egypt, Syria, Iraq, and Jordan must be that we stand beside them. We must call on all Arabs, our allies, and the entire Muslim World to use whatever we have at our disposal to stop this Israeli assault on our land, our way of life...our religion...our very souls! And we must act now! Now, I say!" he shouted passionately, again pounding the table with his closed fist. "I say we must send an army into northern Israel today! We must show Israel that there are consequences to their monstrous actions. Are we to wait until Israeli troops are on Beirut's Corniche? Now, I say!"

His calls for immediate action generated raucous shouts of both support and opposition, and, from some quarters, shouts calling for more deliberations. The cacophony of angry, incoherent yelling reverberated through the room...all caused by the frustration and sense of personal shame in their own ineffectual, impotent military compared to Israel's sophisticated vaunted war machine, and Israel's eagerness to use it.

As President Helou listened to the debate and watched the faces of each of those voicing their views, he sought a plausible response that would be acceptable to most of the Cabinet members.

He leaned to François, and in a whisper, said, "They want war, François. They want to do something to restore their pride and self-respect. These are all successful businessmen and politicians who sense a deep, visceral threat to their pride, their very heritage, their history. They don't like feeling impotent."

François, as shocked and saddened as everyone else in the room, wasn't as emotional, reflecting his American-French heritage, whispered in reply and responded deliberately, "It is the same in Syria, Jordan, and Egypt, sir. Israel has become the bogeyman, the monster of the Middle East, and the Arabs are feeling deeply and honestly that we cannot respond in kind. The Americans and the French provide everything Israel demands, and the ally of Egypt and Syria, the Soviet Union, stands for everything Islam hates. Muslims look to the one living God, the same God of Abraham as the Jews and Christians. The Soviets are Godless, an anathema to the Muslim world. Yet, Syria and Egypt are forced to rely on the Soviets only. The West will not provide any aid to the Arabs. We all are proud of our long history of achievement, and are emotionally unwilling to accept another invasion from Europe. It manifests itself to the Arab world as a repeat of the horrific invasion the West recalls as the Crusades, when all of Europe invaded the Holy Land to defeat Islam and control Arab lands."

"You are a child of Lebanon and the West, my friend," the president whispered in reply to Francois. "Therefore, I call on you for your very different and rational view on these extraordinarily emotionally charged issues. Now," he added, "where do we go from here? What is your suggestion, François?"

François tried to rationally explain his views which the President almost always welcomed.

"Excellency, my conviction, as you know, is that Lebanon's future is with the West, not the Soviet Union. I believe we must be patient and see what Washington's position is. Nasser is the one who helped create this mess by threatening Israel's existence and closing off Israel's access to Aqaba. I believe the Arab League should be allowed to take the lead, not Lebanon. We are too small and too weak. We must stay above the fray…at least for now. America has millions of citizens of Lebanese and Syrian heritage, and I believe America and the West care about the security and integrity of Lebanon. That is where we, as Christians, should be aligned."

"Perhaps you are correct. You have been reading my mind, François."

Their whispered conversation could not be heard above the raucous noise of debate, with speaker after speaker demanding to be heard while cutting off others' pleas.

The President looked around the room once again, seeking eye contact and tacit acknowledgement of members' positions. He knew most of those in the room since his early days in Lebanon's politics. In 1947, nearly twenty years prior, he was first appointed ambassador to the Vatican. He dealt with the sectarian differences over the years, and today knew there were similar, clear distinctions in the Cabinet members' positions. Two diverse and equally powerful major Muslim coalitions of Sunni and Shiia Muslims, on one side, were demanding retribution emerging quickly in response to Israel's attacks. One of them, pro-Arab Muslim group led by Rashid Karami, a prominent Sunni, wanted Lebanon to create a northern front against Israel in support of their Muslim brothers, reflecting the growing demands in the streets. The other coalition, led by former presidents and Maronite Christian leaders, Camille Chamoun, Pierre Gemayel, and Raymond Edde, joined by the Druze remained solidly pro-Western, and not wanting to fight the Israelis. Both coalitions, neither with a clear mandate, proved to be equally influential, although not completely controlling groups. Each of the three major sectarian groups had won just thirty-three of the ninety-nine seats in Parliament in the most recent election.

President Charles Helou, now facing an angry gathering, clearly and with a steady voice stated his determination to keep Lebanon out of the Arab-Israeli conflict. He pounded his gavel several times for quiet, then spoke, "Gentlemen, let us calm our voices as we deliberate Lebanon's position and respect each other's views."

Then, again surveying the members by looking into each minister's eyes, gauging their positions and levels of distress, anger, and frustration, President Helou took a deep breath and delivered his counsel. He was hoping for some sort of compromise, recognizing that he had to maintain his position of leadership. He knew the future of his beloved nation depended on the Cabinet's cohesion during these uncertain times of implicit Israeli threats and overwhelming sense of urgency.

"We must together come to a consensus to protect the people of Lebanon and provide for their welfare and safety...we must recognize that despite the terrible and threatening morning's events, we are in no position to militarily respond to Israel's war machine and blatant aggression, no matter how frustrating that is." Then after taking another deep breath, he continued, making eye contact with members as his eyes roamed to the attendees' faces. "Lebanon, as of this moment, has not been attacked by the Israelis. But of course, we cannot assume that that will be the case in coming days. We have no Air Force or true Navy; we have a small army, and we do not have the arms or the leverage of the oil-rich Saudis or the Gulf States. We must, and I believe you all can agree for the moment, defer to the Arab League and to world opinion. We still do not know the response of the United States. Therefore, I recommend that we, as the Americans say, 'Keep our powder dry!'

"In other words," he added, seeing the quizzical, blank stares of the ministers at this bit of American vernacular, "we must be patient and wait and see what the world's powers do and say later today. Maybe we'll have to wait even longer, And, of course, time is of the essence. However, I believe we must agree immediately to demand that the United Nations Security Council call on the Israelis to cease their attacks and withdraw from Gaza and the West Bank at once! I urge you to agree we must first seek a political solution. I believe we must do nothing militarily that would provoke the Israelis to do harm to Lebanon.

"I will now call on each of you to clearly and calmly state your views without interruption, and, I hope you will support my recommendation as we go around the table. We must find a consensus, recognizing that while we wish to come to the aid of our brothers, we must not put the people of Lebanon in harm's way at this time."

Francois noticed, with a hope of resolution, a softening of some of the minor Cabinet members, who were leaning away from an armed response by Lebanon, preferring a political solution.

"I ask for your support so that we can proceed as I recommend. We will always have the options to enter the war in the future if we choose to do so."

The Sunnis initially responded quite adamantly that Lebanon should attack Israel from the north to take pressure off the Syrians and Egyptians, to forcefully show their support for their Muslim brothers there. But, as they voiced those sentiments, they lowered their voices as they began to realize that there was a growing lack of support to attack from the Druze representatives and from the Christians who clearly preferred to stay out of the conflagration.

By the time the heated meeting closed at one o'clock, word was received that Jordan had been attacked and was sporadically bombarding the nearest military targets in Israel, namely East Jerusalem and northern Israeli military bases, as their capabilities were short-ranged. By the same time, the entire Air Forces of Syria and Egypt, Israel's principal adversarial confrontation states, had been totally destroyed in just a few hours. With their Air Forces eliminated without even having left the tarmac, Israel took total control of regional air space, as did Japan in the Pacific region on December 7, 1941. As a result of their preemptive and successful attack, and without fear of air attacks, Israel unleashed their tank corps and armies as they raced south across the sands of Gaza toward Egypt, occupying the Gaza and, within hours, simultaneously, Israeli tanks and infantry swarmed over other Arab territory, including Jordanian-controlled East Jerusalem and the West Bank to as far north as Syria's Golan Heights.

It didn't take Israel long to strike southern Lebanon with a barrage of rockets, gunfire and bombs from their domineering Air Force fighters. However, as a result of the Cabinet's decision, Lebanon suffered only minor strikes in the south, essentially "a warning shot" that convinced Lebanon's Cabinet ministers not to enter the conflict. And that became the decision, led by the wise counsel of President Helou and his trusted adviser, Francois Dubois.

Israeli Prime Minister Eshkol, who also had held the position of Minister of Defense, was forced against his better judgment to relinquish his weakening position against war. Reluctantly, he named his adversary, hawkish General Moshe Dayan, the new Minister of Defense, to replace him, angering Golda Meir and Ben-Gurion, both of whom were opposed to Dayan's extremist, harsh warrior tendencies.

"I hate putting that man in charge of our defense forces, the IDF," Eshkol told them.

But now, as a result, the die was cast.

For many Israelis, his bold aggressiveness was exactly what they had demanded of Prime Minister Eshkol, even threatening to force him out of office as he sought a negotiated, peaceful solution. In the end, he had no choice but to relinquish his position to Dayan.

"If we attack immediately and totally," Dayan declared," we will win. But, if we hesitate, we will be forced to fight a defensive ground battle against the Egyptians and the Syrians. If we lose, we lose everything. I insist with my whole being we must strike now to win!"

Others, like Leah, François' love, and those who opposed the unilateral action, asked the question: "Win what?"

Must we always live by the sword?
Leah

CHAPTER 6

Beirut
June 12, 1967

François, torn between attending every meeting President Helou asked him to participate in, and his responsibilities at Credit Suisse, did his best to properly allocate his time during the following days. At his office he responded mostly by telephone to the anxious pleas of concern by the bank's clients, and, at other times, to the concern of government ministries.

For four straight days, he received surprise phone calls from Leah.

"*Allo*, this is François Dubois speaking."

"Oh, good, François. It is me, Leah, again. I'm calling from Tel Aviv. I am so glad your government chose not to respond to Israel's adventures in Egypt, Jordan and Syria." She thought carefully before continuing, "I believe these hotheads would have moved into Lebanon and occupied your country at least as far as the Litani River, which they have wanted for as long just as they have coveted the Golan, where your father's ancestors lived before moving to Mount Lebanon so long ago. The right-wing desires the ice melt the abundant water and fertile farmland of the Golan Heights. They insist that these lands must soon become part of Israel as they intend to annex the Golan, Gaza, and the Sinai Peninsula. They also want the West Bank and East Jerusalem, which they plan to annex immediately. There is a lot of debate now…fierce debate…about these things. I believe it would be a severe error for Israel to hold on to Gaza and the West Bank because for the first time Jews would become the occupiers and, ultimately, oppressors of another people. That is contrary to the civilized world by way of Geneva Accords and United Nations declarations that the lands conquered by war cannot be retained. Oh, François, I am frightened at what my country is doing. I don't like the direction General Dayan, the Likud, and that Irgun gang leader Menachem Begin are taking us. As Jews, our beliefs do not condone oppressing others."

"It is difficult and painful to watch from here, Leah," François replied sadly. "I just don't understand how you can continue to live with those people under that extremist, paranoid government and still insist you love me! Lebanon has never attacked anyone. We learned long ago that our people prosper much better when we are at peace. Israel seems bent on being the military ruler of the Middle East, and the Arab world is not capable of stopping it."

"François, my precious, I really need to see you…to be with you. It's been five years since our last meeting in Venice."

"Too long, Leah. You must get transferred to your embassy in Rome or Paris so we can be together and discuss these issues in person. I need you to get away from there and be with me to believe you truly love me. I think you are trying to have it both ways, and I can no longer accept that."

Francois stopped short of delivering an ultimatum that might completely sever their long relationship. But he had finally reached the point of being willing to lose her. "I've had it with you and your crazy people."

"But you don't understand, Francois. You can't imagine how impossible it is for me to abandon my people! You can't feel as I feel as a Jew under threat of annihilation."

"Stop it, Leah, dammit! Stop that talk. You are not under threat from anyone but your own people. No one else. They won't make peace when it's offered! You must make a choice. Either you are in love with me or not. I need to know right now. I've lost my patience."

Sensing his seriousness by his words and the tone of his voice, Leah began to realize she could actually lose, in the next few minutes, the most important person in her life, her true love. She silently thought about what he said, closing her eyes, her lips quivering, and tears beginning to well up in her eyes. "The situation is so difficult, yet, I need you in my life."

Nervously, Leah went silent. Then, she whispered, "You are correct, my love, but I am so angry with these idiots who only want war, who are willing to drive all Muslims and Christians out of Palestine. I don't think that's right. And there are a lot of Jewish Israelis who feel as I do. I just wish those with whom I agree were more powerful now."

"Leah," François responded anxiously, "you must be careful. You are saying things some of your countrymen would consider heresy and a betrayal of Israel. Do not say these things over the telephone. You don't know who may be listening. Dammit, Leah, you need to make up your mind. We cannot go on like this. It cannot continue.

"Here in Beirut, we had to face down the demands of our predominately Muslim brothers in the Cabinet, especially those from the south, who are very angry. We did not agree with them to attack Israel in a show of support of Syria, Jordan, and Egypt. This is a difficult time, for all of us. But I worry about you. Make a decision, Leah. It's either be with me or stay there. You can longer have it both ways."

"Hush…just a minute," she said quickly, just as she was about to tell him she would immediately request a transfer to Paris…with a gasp of breath, the line went dead.

Out of the corner of her eye, Leah had seen Itzak approach her as she secretly spoke with François. Itzak's face showed his anger as he forcibly reached for the phone, took it from her and slammed the receiver back in its place. Pointing his finger in Leah's face, he sneered, "Who are you speaking with, Leah? Is it the same person you call every day? It's not your girlfriend as you told me yesterday, is it? My," he sneered sarcastically, "you two have a lot to say, don't you? You must think I'm stupid, Leah! You're not speaking with a girlfriend. Quit lying to me!"

Leah, stunned at Itzak's unusually harsh questioning, drew back from him.

"Don't be cute, Itzak. Yes," she lied, "it was my girlfriend. But maybe you can't understand because you've never had a girlfriend," she retorted caustically, knowing she hit him where his macho attitude lived. She wanted to hurt him.

"You were meant to be my girlfriend, Leah. You were the only one I ever wanted, but you never gave me the chance."

"Itzak, you are crude, arrogant, and threatening…and you always have been!" she retorted.

"My people believe you have been speaking with someone in Beirut, Leah. Is that who you call each day from this very phone?" His emotions of being a rejected lover came to the surface in anger. "You should be more careful, Leah. You have been watched every day. We know you are up to something. You and all your Palestinian lovers," he sneered again, emphasizing the last two words.

"That's a hateful, racist statement, Itzak. You are leaving your religious teachings. You shouldn't do that."

"Look, Leah." he quickly responded, "We were forced to take Gaza, East Jerusalem and the West Bank, and destroy the Air Force and armies of Egypt and Syria. It was them or us. And look how brave our men are fighting…how amazing our leaders are governing. General Dayan acted brilliantly. They have saved Israel, and now we are no longer afraid. We were so vulnerable before. But not now! We defeated our enemies so quickly! One day we will rule the entire Middle East, Leah, because that is our God-given destiny. Read the Psalms! Read Psalm 105!"

Then, as he stared directly into her now moistening eyes, he told her sternly, "And you had better change your thinking if you want to be around when that happens!"

"Don't threaten me, Itzak. I'm just as loyal to Israel as you are." Her voice became shriller as she felt a sense of fear she hadn't felt before. "You and I simply have different views on what Israel is to be. Must we always live by the sword? Why can't we all get along? You know, Itzak, if Israel occupies the Gaza, Sinai and the West Bank, to say nothing about Syria's Golan Heights, the Arabs will outnumber us and soon we Jews could find ourselves in the minority. How would you and your warmonger friends like that? Occupying those lands and people would totally destroy our Jewish ethic for one thing, and for another, we could no longer be a Jewish state nor call ourselves a democracy!"

"You forget, Leah, all we have to do is make all the Christians and Muslims leave these lands. There's plenty of room for them in Egypt, Jordan, Syria, and Lebanon! We'll make them get out!"

"But why should these people leave their homes where they have lived for hundreds of years…for many generations?"

"This is our land, Leah. Not theirs. God gave us this land. King David united all the Jewish tribes and built a strong Israel. And we will build it strong again. With God on our side, we cannot lose. Don't you see? Can't you understand? This is our land!"

"Yes, Itzak, it is our land, but we can share it with those who already live here, can't we? Why not? We are supposed to be 'God's 'Light unto the World,' aren't we?" she demanded.

"Leah, see how our people worship God and tend to the land He has given us. We must be strong. We must not be with the Gentiles. Read the Torah, for God's sake. We are not to be among the Gentiles! We cannot allow them, especially the Christians, to stay. Look what they did in the name of Jesus for the past two thousand years! Leah, you have to see it our way, I'm warning you!"

"Their leaders abused their religion, Itzak, just like you are trying to do. If God intends for the Jews…for Israel…to win every battle, then how do you explain the Babylonian victory in 587 B.C.? And how do you explain the decades of horrid Roman occupation and their destruction of the Jerusalem Temple in 70 A.D.? Itzak, you must be careful with what you wish for."

"The Arabs can never defeat us, Leah. Look how easily we defeated them this time. Six days! Just six days! The Lord has seen fit to fight with us. It is His wish. And don't ever think they dare to attack us now as long as we have France and America with us and our nuclear arsenal at Dimona. Not even the Iraqis, Syrian or Iranians will challenge us now."

"Oh, Itzak, this argument makes me sad. I truly believe the people of Israel have a right to a homeland but must somehow find a way to get along with its neighbors. We must be just. Our mothers and children cannot be subjected all their lives to daily gunfire, bombs and enemies all around us. Is that any way to live?"

"You don't get it, Leah. They don't want us here, and we don't want Arabs and Palestinians here with us. It's as simple as that, and if it takes a hundred years of war, so be it!"

"So, Itzak, you and your warmonger friends are bound and determined to take the lands of these people, throw them out, and subject our people…men, women and children…to a hundred years of living under siege. Is that right?"

Itzak, now becoming impatient with Leah, and not believing she was still determined to look on Palestinians as equals, shouted to her, "You are wrong! This is Jewish land for Jews only! Now get off your position. We don't want to live with…or be near these lowlifes."

"Lowlifes? Is that what you think? Itzak, are you aware that even while living under these conditions, the Palestinians, both Christian and Muslim, have more college graduates, more master's degrees, and more Ph.D.'s than any country in the Middle East. Including Israel?"

"Well, Leah, good for them," he grinned menacingly. "In America you'd be called a 'Nigger lover.' We'll have more than they do soon, as soon as they leave and have no schools here. Besides, there is no such thing as a Palestinian state or Palestinians. Even Golda Meir says so."

"Now your prejudice is going beyond racism, Itzak. You're becoming totally irrational! The states in this region were created by England and France after World War I, and for five hundred years before that, this region was part of the Turkish Empire. There were no states all those years." Leah was now drawing on all the arguments her friends had raised. "Statehood is a Western concept. In America, they said two hundred years ago that there were no Apache or Cherokee or Navajo states. That's true. But states and artificial boundaries are European concepts forced on the natives here and there." Then, lowering her head from frustration and exhaustion, she added, smiling as she lifted her head with silent desperation and inner strength, "Itzak, let us now depart as friends. We will speak again."

"Of course, Leah, but if I were you, I wouldn't be making any more phone calls to your friend. You are being watched carefully. Israel is at war, and you could be labeled a *mrgel*, a traitor, a spy."

Leah turned away from Itzak, stunned at his words and sadly remembering when they were close friends in the kibbutz, sharing common idealistic visions of a socialist Israel and its future. But now, she feared, that commonality no longer existed. She began now to better understand Itzak's attitude and decided to take his threats more seriously, realizing he had friends at high levels in the Mossad, and while she had done nothing wrong, and had not shared any state secrets with François, that wouldn't matter to Itzak or any of his right-wing friends. She recalled certain friends, left-wing advocates, suddenly being whisked away in the dead of night to neighboring places like Cyprus, Crete or Italy. For twenty years, many Palestinian leaders and intellectuals were kidnapped never to be seen again.

As she walked along the busy avenue, she thought of solutions, turning them over in her mind. Finally, while she sat on a park bench watching mothers walk by, pushing their children's strollers, an idea came to her. She must seek a transfer from the Foreign Affairs Ministry in Tel Aviv to the embassy in Paris, the largest Israeli embassy in Europe, the place where Israeli diplomats, likely with the assistance of the Rothschild family, obtained the French Mystère jet fighters and rockets. *Perhaps*, she thought with a smile, remembering longingly, *François can meet me in Paris at the Sorbonne this time. Yes, we should meet at the Sorbonne where we first met!*

Now she was beginning to get joyfully excited as she recalled those wonderful moments...those beautiful evenings with François spent strolling along the Seine, sharing concerts, or museum tours. *Oh, how wonderful it will be, living day to day in a peaceful place where people prefer stability and calm and not the oppressive attitudes that produce the siege mentality. That's it!*

Smiling, she decided, *I'll just have to convince François that after this war, it's time for him to take a leave of absence. He must agree that it is time for us to be away from all this terrible fighting. Soon, then, Paris and François! I'll start the process tomorrow.*

Hold Out Baits to Entice The Enemy.
Feign Disorder And Crush Him.
Sun Tzu

CHAPTER 7

June 10, 1967
Attack on the USS Liberty; Beirut

"François, my dear friend, I have to ask for a favor and have you look into an event that apparently took place only a few days ago…June 8th I am told." President Helou's voice was very low, almost a whisper.

As the president's most trusted friend and confidante, François was often asked to attend random ad hoc meetings with Lebanon's president, even though he wasn't a member of the government, but the Regional Manager of Credit Suisse. Most of their luncheon meetings were held in the president's private wood-paneled conference room next door to his office, which also served on occasion as a private dining room for small groups of political leaders.

Today, the two sat near each other at a polished, mahogany table that could accommodate up to sixteen persons. The president was at his customary seat at the head of the table, with François to his right.

"What is it, Mr. President?" François asked in a low voice, leaning toward him.

"Our security sources, who are in contact with our neighbors' counterparts, have informed us in utmost secrecy that on June 8th, the same day Syria and Egypt joined Israel and Jordan in a ceasefire agreement, Israel attacked a United States Navy ship off the coast of Egypt and Gaza in international waters and nearly sank it. I need to find out if that's true and what really happened."

"My God! What kind of ship was it, Mr. President? Why would Israel do such a stupid thing to its major ally?"

"Apparently, it was an unarmed, sophisticated communications observer, a listening post, what they call a converted Liberty-class Merchant Marine ship and the Israelis didn't want anyone to listen to their communications. After all, we know Israel falsely announced to the entire world for hours that they were under attack and only acting to defend themselves. Israel also was planning further attacks on the West Bank and Syria's Golan Heights, and did not want the Americans to listen to their plans.

"In fact, they never were under attack, but preemptively and simultaneously attacked four Arab countries, including us, with more than four hundred heavily armed jet fighters supplied by France — Lebanon's supposed friend."

Then he added, "You'll recall that after the ceasefire was agreed to, General Dayan ordered his Air Force and armies to invade and take the Golan Heights.

"A few of those Dassault Mirage jet fighter planes manned by American trained Israelis even attacked South Lebanon while they were at it. Lebanon never posed a threat to Israel, as we all know."

"We were simply a convenient target, Mr. President, a place for their pilots to attack Lebanese civilians with no opposition. There was no reason for them to do that."

"It's amazing how little time it took for their fighters to hit Egypt, Syria, and Jordan. Only fifteen minutes from takeoff to Damascus, twenty to Iraq, four minutes to Amman, and less than five minutes to attack the Sinai bases of Egypt. No one had a chance even to take shelter!" he added.

"But," François interrupted, "how do we know all this information about the American ship?"

"Our radio operators and those of Spain and Germany, and possibly Egypt and Jordan, actually listened to the Israeli pilots reporting to their headquarters that this indeed was an American ship. They attacked anyway. All of these conversations were taped, of course. Also, we understand there were Russian submarines nearby that surfaced and witnessed the attack."

"They attacked knowing for certain that it was an American ship?" François asked incredulously with a pained expression on his face.

"Yes, they did," the President replied. "Can you imagine the boldness of the Israelis? And when they failed to kill the crew and sink the ship, the Israeli government created an elaborate false story to cover the crime."

"Don't they call that chutzpah?" responded François.

"Israel has been concocting false stories and blaming the Arab states for everything since 1946! They make us enemies of America deliberately, without any basis. The Israeli story is that they mistook the identity of the ship, although it was a clear day with calm seas, flying those huge American flags. They said they mistakenly fired a 'few rounds of misdirected fire.' Can you imagine those liars?" The President was growing angrier by the minute. "I'm surprised they haven't blame Egypt or Syria!"

"Give them time. Maybe they soon will."

"The Americans are our friends, and if you asked me, I would tell you that if Israel were somewhere else, like South America or in Europe where all those Israelis came from to begin with, the Americans would find all the Arabs to be their best friends and totally committed allies. We believe the Americans are the finest people in the world. My goodness, so many of our own Lebanese and Syrians, mostly Christians have migrated to America and are very loyal Americans."

"For sure," François added, "the Arab governments would never have done what the Israelis did to those poor sailors. Never!"

"The question now is: What is the United States going to do about it?"

"We shall see," replied François dubiously, "but, Mr. President, I believe the Israelis and their allies in Washington will do their utmost to blame everyone but themselves."

"Do you believe the American government will go along with a cover-up, François?"

"Yes, sadly," François whispered softly, lowering his head in embarrassment, "Mr. President, I do."

"What about the families of those Navy sailors who were killed and wounded? What about them, François?"

"Well, apparently the American administration has shown little regard for the millions of Palestinian refugees for these past twenty years. Why should they care about a few sailors?"

"But this is different, François. We are talking about America standing up for Americans!"

"I understand the difference, Mr. President. We'll just have to wait and see what Washington does, won't we? I suggest we not expect condemnation from America, nor a cut back on military aid to Israel, I am sad to say."

"President Lyndon Johnson believes he is politically quite dependent on the support of the American Jewish community and supporters of Israel, doesn't he?"

"Yes, sir, he does. But at some point, I would think he would draw the line and say, 'Enough,' wouldn't you? President Eisenhower did just that in 1956! I mean, here is an apparently unjustified attack on an unarmed U.S. ship in international waters and they knew it was an American ship! This isn't the Barbary Coast and this isn't the eighteenth century! Yet, Israel is the only country since Japan to deliberately attack the United States including that ruse Johnson cooked up in the Gulf of Tonkin to justify his invasion of Vietnam. I just don't understand how Israel can get away with this, do you, François? We need to know what's behind it. I am sure we, and the rest of the world, are not being given the true facts.

"But we must be careful, François. This confidential information has not been officially confirmed, yet it appears there was a small Egyptian fishing boat trolling offshore nearby the attack, about ten nautical miles from Al'Aish, an Egyptian coastal village, and the crew saw it all happen. In fact, an imam sent a lookout up into their minaret because several ships, including Soviet submarines, had been sighted offshore for several days. They thought that since Israel attacked Egypt on the fifth of June, three days before, maybe Israel would attack Egypt by sea also. The fishermen in Al'Aish were very nervous. They are poor and, like our own fishermen, only if they can catch fish each day can they feed their families."

François digested the President's thoughts as he sat quietly listening.

The President continued, "So, they were focused on the sea, and wanted to see everything. But they were shocked when they saw the rockets from the Israeli jet fighters explode on the American ship. They said they saw fire, smoke, and the entire top part of the ship, where many antennae were located, blown off. It was frightening for these poor fishermen; for they were scared the jets would attack them too! The man in the minaret saw it all too. You know, François, despite their government's actions, most Egyptians still consider Americans their friends."

"As do most Arabs, I would emphasize, Mr. President. Did anything else happen? Did anyone come to help the Americans?" asked François, bending even closer to the president.

"Well, actually, the attack began at around two o'clock in the afternoon and we've heard that it lasted for four hours. We need to find out how long it was. The fishermen had seen the ship cruising slowly before the attack, they think about only five knots. Then, it speeded up when the jets attacked, but then, after they kept attacking, the ship slowed down, then stopped. So far as we know, no one saw any American planes come to their rescue."

"What did the Americans on the ship do? You said the United States ship was unarmed. How did they shoot back at the Israelis?"

"The fishermen saw two sailors firing machine guns at the planes, but their guns were too small. Remember, this was basically a converted cargo ship with incredible communications capabilities. After the jets attacked many times, firing hundreds of bullets, three Israeli torpedo boats, going very fast, attacked the wounded ship with torpedoes. After it was hit, it began to list to one side, but it didn't sink, despite the continuous attack. Can you imagine what the Americans must have felt when no help came?"

"No, I cannot. The American sailors were sitting ducks. The Israelis used them for target practice."

The president paused for a minute, crossed himself and whispered, "May they rest in peace, allia hummah."

Following suit, François, silently saying the same sacred prayer in Arabic, crossed himself and whispered, looking to the heavens, "May those poor Americans rest in peace. And all our Arab brothers and sisters who were also attacked."

"The fishermen said they were shocked no one came to the Americans' rescue. Surely there were American jet fighters close enough to protect them and chase away the Israeli attackers."

"You can bet they were, Mr. President. They are all over the Med," François replied. "If any Arab nation did that, the United States would retaliate forcefully and immediately."

The President smiled, "We Lebanese and the Saudis continue to believe the United States is our friend. There are more than three million Americans of Lebanese or Syrian heritage. But it is very clear that the West is very much in bed with Israel, if you will pardon the expression."

"And," François added, smiling, "that includes my father and half-sister. Also, there are many millions more in Central and South America who proudly claim their Syrian and Lebanese heritage."

"Thirty million, indeed, to be exact," retorted the President. "And in Central and South America they actually call themselves Syrian because when their families emigrated, Lebanon was a province of Syria, and they all carried Syrian passports. But in America, since Israel became a state and U.S politics and media so favor Israel and became, in many ways, anti-Arab, thus anti-Syrian, being labeled a Syrian-American is not accepted favorably as being a Lebanese-American. Strange, isn't it?"

"Bizarre. It's hard to understand people sometimes, Mr. President." François rubbed his hand on the polished tabletop, as was his habit when he wished to get to the point in a conversation. "Now, what can I do for you, sir?"

"François, your position as a representative of Credit Suisse and your multiple citizenships from Lebanon, France and the U.S. will allow you to travel just about anywhere without question. I need you to follow up on this Israeli attack. When in Arab countries, of course, use your Lebanese passport, and in the Mediterranean use whichever will work the best."

Then, pausing, he looked directly into François' eyes, and, speaking in a low, forceful voice, said, "I need you to find this ship. If it is still afloat, find out its status. Confirm the damage done, its identifying numbers, name and location. Our allies would like this information, and we are being called on to assist. We want to know all we can find out from the crew, if possible. We do not want to wait for the 'official' statement from the U.S. or Israel. We need to know the truth of this. It doesn't make sense."

"I agree there will be a big difference between their public statements and the truth, Mr. President."

Hearing his assignment, François, hardly an investigator or spy, was surprised at his President's request. "Are you sure you want this of me? I mean, there is a very effective Syrian secret police that could do this better than I, your Excellency. Why choose me?"

"François, listen carefully," the President spoke, sitting back in his chair. "We need someone who is as well-known as you. Your position with Credit Suisse will open doors where a member of the secret police can't get. You can travel on business and it will be perfectly normal. That ship, I am certain, is still in the Mediterranean. They would not have been able to take it very far without it making the news. No one will think twice about your presence. I know you have connections all over the area and maybe they can help you find the ship. If possible, I'd like you to interview the crew members, get the facts and their perspective, and then return only to me."

"Yes, sir, I'll begin at once."

"François", the President gestured as he concluded, "I'm counting on you. We need to understand this situation. It doesn't make sense and that could mean we're in for more surprises. This is critical and I don't have anyone I trust more."

Your friend is your needs answered...
Kahlil Gibran

CHAPTER 8

Malta
June 11, 1967

"Hanna," François called to his assistant, "I have been given an assignment by the President and I need your assistance. Didn't you tell me you had a cousin in the U.S. Navy?"

"Yes, sir, my cousin in Washington, D.C. has a son, Anthony, who is in the Navy."

"Can you locate your cousin? I have to find someone who can help us."

"Certainly, sir, right away."

After an hour of transatlantic phone calls, Hanna returned to François. "My cousin told me his son is indeed in the Navy."

"Can we speak with him, do you think?"

"Unfortunately, Monsieur DuBois, Anthony is now at sea, somewhere in the Mediterranean Sea, and it will be very difficult, if not impossible, to reach him by telephone."

"Can your cousin find out what ship he is on?"

"I'll do my best, sir."

"Do it as quickly as you can! Time is of the essence."

"It's still early in America. I'll stay on the telephone as long as it takes, sir."

"Fine, Hanna, as soon as possible."

Two hours later, Hanna returned with a smile on his face, "I found out, sir, but it will be very difficult to contact him."

"Why is that, Hanna? America is not at war. What ship is he on?"

"Monsieur DuBois, he is on a ship in the Mediterranean. His ship is the USS Liberty."

"Well, Hanna, how would you like to see your cousin's son? I will need you to accompany me on a business trip," François said barely able to stifle his excitement. "Hopefully, we can combine it with a visit with your relative."

It took François just two days to determine there were only a limited number of shipyards in the Mediterranean Sea with a dry dock large enough to accommodate the American ship. A few phone calls to his colleagues in Credit Suisse in Spain, Italy, Greece, and Cyprus convinced him his bank's country managers were as adept and politically imbedded in the commerce and politics of their respective regions, as was François. And like François, they were directed to be well-connected with the local leaders in politics, intelligence, and defense departments. As a result, he quickly learned that the wounded ship, the USS Liberty, was in dry dock in Malta.

That second afternoon, he and Hanna boarded a Middle East Airlines flight from Beirut to the island of Malta. He stared out his window at the sparkling blue waters of the sea, marveling at the beauty of the Mediterranean, especially from 30,000 feet above the cool, cobalt blue waters.

"Here we are," he smiled, whispering to Hanna beside him, "bound on a very important trip."

François was determined to learn as quickly as possible all he could about the attack by Israel, gather all the eye-witness accounts he could, and find out what it meant to the region while the facts were still clear and not jaundiced by political considerations.

But François and Hanna were not the only ones on such a mission.

Two Mossad agents were en route to Malta from the Israeli Embassy in Paris, which was second only in size and activity to the Israeli Embassy in Washington, D.C.

During their flight, François and Hanna listed all facts they knew, names, and prospective questions to which they would like answers.

"We'll be landing shortly, gentlemen. Please secure your seat belts."

"Of course," he replied, smiling at the pretty stewardess as she glanced out the window, leaning slightly toward him.

"Beautiful, isn't it, sir?"

"Yes it is, mademoiselle. Surrounded by the deep blue sea, Malta's beauty makes me forget how important the island is because of its strategic location."

As their plane taxied to the gate, François noticed to his right another flight arriving at an adjacent gate. It was an Air France flight, he would soon learn, that had just arrived from Paris.

"Taxi!" he called to the taxicab slowly cruising toward him as he waved his outstretched arm. After it stopped, he grabbed the rear door handle and glided onto the rear bench seat, followed by Hanna, each clutching his single carry-on bag.

"Excelsior Hotel, please," François stated in his slightly affected British accent that he had acquired at London's prestigious School of Economics.

"Yes sir, right away," said the driver.

As soon as they were settled in their comfortable hotel two-bedroom suite embellished with appropriate luxury accoutrements, as requested by his colleague in the Malta office of Credit Suisse, François called the office and spoke with the office's manager.

"Robert, it is François…François DuBois."

"How is everything at the hotel? All to your liking, François?"

"Yes, Robert. Perfect as always. Thank you, my friend. Dinner? My assistant accompanied me on this trip."

"Of course. I'll let my wife know. See you at eight o'clock?"

"Perfect again. Let's meet in the hotel lounge."

Both, accustomed to being very busy, spoke in brief, relevant phrases that took little communication time.

François and Hanna spent most of the next day at the bank's offices listening to the advice of Robert's colleague, Ganni Abela, a local native and bank employee. François made calls and then met with corporate and government representatives arranged by Abela.

By the end of his second day in Malta, François had obtained most of the information he needed to confirm where the USS Liberty was located, who was in charge, where the crew and officers were billeted, and the person who could provide all the introductions he would need.

"Lucky that our president's office was able to obtain the necessary U.S. Naval Intelligence officers' documentation and identification papers for us."

After arrangements were made to meet with his cousin's son, Hanna, using his fake identification papers, went to the Liberty, passed through the guards and port security, and met with his cousin's son, Anthony.

On his third day, François was escorted by the public affairs officer to the dry dock just inside the perimeter of U.S. Naval Security to the USS Liberty.

"That's it, Lt. DuBois." He said, gesturing to Francois "That's the ship's ID, CTRS, on the bow on both sides."

"Very large U.S. ID numerals."

"Yessir, the security officer replied, pointing at the large gaping hole in the hull. That's where the Israeli torpedo struck. The Navy security officer asked, "I understand arrangements have been made for you to meet with the quartermaster — he's a relative?"

"Yes, my aide's cousin. That's a huge hole! What kept the ship from sinking?"

"It almost did, sir, but the crew acted fast and closed off those sections," responded a voice from behind him.

François abruptly turned to face a young man in the Navy's blue working uniform. "Were you there?" he asked.

"Yessir, I was on the ship. I saw it all."

"Sir," Hanna spoke, "I want you to meet my cousin, Anthony. He serves as the quartermaster aboard the Liberty and saw it all happen from the bridge. He is going to tell us what he saw and also invite some of his fellow crew members to join us later."

"Anthony, it's a pleasure to meet you." François reached out to shake Anthony's hand noticing the steering wheel insignia on his sleeve. "I'm anxious to see the ship and take a few pictures. Do you think we can go aboard the ship? I'd like to see it up close."

"Let me check with the CO. I'm sure he won't have a problem, given your credentials."

After touring the ship and taking the pictures he wanted, François, Hanna, and Anthony picked up two other crew members and went to a close-by off base restaurant for lunch.

"Tell me about yourself, Chris," Francois politely inquired.

"Sir, I'm the radioman and was monitoring the chatter during the Israeli attacks. We knew they were going to hit us before it happened. I sent out Maydays over and over but we were ignored."

"I heard the attack lasted about an hour?" Francois responded.

"Oh no, sir. It lasted four hours — four long hours. I sent dozens of Maydays during that time. They had to have heard us," Radioman Robert replied. "We know the Israelis heard us calling for help. They tried to jam our communications."

"And what is your rating, Tom," Francois continued, turning to the other crewman.

"I'm a Hull Maintenance Technician, Sir. I was below decks when we were hit. It was my job to secure the valves, doors, and batten hatches. It was absolute pandemonium below decks."

"He and his guys were responsible for keeping the ship from sinking," Anthony inserted. "We've since counted 851 armor piercing bullet holes. 851 holes! You saw the huge opening in our starboard hull caused by that torpedo.

"My God, there were three patrol boats after us, sir, traveling at least 30 knots. We were sitting ducks, sir. It was awful. We had just four .50 caliber guns, two forward and two aft, and maybe half a dozen pistols. And those jets just kept coming…they kept shooting rockets and their .50 caliber machine guns. We all had to take cover. Our signalman was hit. He was standing right next to me."

"We never had a chance," interjected Robert, eagerly. "I'm really pissed at those bastards, sir," he exclaimed angrily. "Those sons of bitches flew around us watching us for nine long hours, Lieutenant DuBois. Nine hours! They circled us at low levels thirteen times before they attacked us! They saw our flag, sir.

Dammit, they even waved at us and we waved at them. It was a clear day, sir, with flat seas. And, our guys never came in spite of the number of Maydays I sent. They never came to help us. We finally got a transmission that help was on the way. But even though we were told our fighters were on the way to chase away the Israelis, they never arrived!"

The conversation was interrupted with the arrival of Lt. James Ennes, Jr.

"Sorry I'm late. I was filling out some paperwork."

François stood and welcomed him with a handshake and indicated an empty chair.

"Your shipmates have been recounting the attack. They told me that even though they pleaded for assistance for four hours and were told help was on the way, but they never arrived," said François incredulously.

"Well now," Lt. Ennes, added angrily, "now I know why! And I am very angry!"

"Tell us, Lieutenant? Why didn't they come? Evidently it was made clear that our guys were being killed. What happened?"

"I just got word from our Yeoman, who is close with the Admiral's radioman. Here's what I was told happened: The Liberty radioed for help. We had two aircraft carriers in the Mediterranean; one, the Saratoga, responded by launching two fighter aircraft. Secretary of Defense Robert McNamara was informed. McNamara contacted the White House. President Johnson himself ordered the Admiral to call the fighters back to their ships! They left us naked! Rear Admiral Geis, then commanding the Sixth Fleet, called Washington back personally to question the order. Secretary McNamara came on the line, and then President Johnson, our Commander in Chief! He told Admiral Geis that the aircraft were to be immediately returned, that he would not have his ally, Israel, embarrassed, and that he didn't care who was killed or what damage was done to the ship. He said he didn't care if the ship sank!

"Can you believe this? Geis, like a good sailor, they told me, got really mad, but, reluctantly followed his orders and recalled the aircraft. Our fate was sealed," he remarked sadly. "Y'know, Lieutenant DuBois, America has always prided itself in never leaving its men and women behind…until now. And for Israel! For the first time in U.S. Naval history! Why would our President do that?"

"Yeah, we were left hanging out there to die by our own friggin' President! How are the Israelis allies and we are not, for Chrissakes! Damn! I want to hit someone. I want to kill someone!"

"All of us do, sailor, but we cannot. And we've been told to shut our mouths on this or we'll be court marshaled. I hate it, but we don't need to be court marshaled too. No one would ever believe us if that happened," Lieutenant Ennes replied with seething anger.

"I guess that means I'd better stop asking you questions, huh?"

"I don't care, Lieutenant DuBois. I'll never forgive the Navy or the President for not sending help. Lieutenant, we were attacked without any cause at all. We were hardly moving and were easily identified because of our naval designation numbers and our American flag! We were on the lookout for Egyptian planes because they are backed by the Soviets. The Israelis are supposed to be our friends, so the Navy keeps telling us. And France, our ally, supplied the jets to Israel."

"Our friends? Bullshit! Why would friends try to take us out?"

"I'll tell you why!" interrupted his cohort. "The Liberty is the most sophisticated ship of its kind in the world. We can hear a pin drop before it hits something!"

"Wait, wait. I thought the Liberty ships were cargo ships," interrupted Francois.

"They were. The USS Liberty was converted to an Auxiliary Technical Research Ship. We have millions of dollars in the latest listening equipment. We heard all the Israeli communiqués, including all their pilots' conversations. On the fifth, sixth, and seventh of June, we were hearing all their messages for hours, until our antennae were destroyed by the jets' rockets. We heard them order the attack on the Golan after they agreed to a United Nations ceasefire! Can you believe that shit? After the ceasefire? They kept saying that they were under attack, but they weren't. We knew before anyone else that they were going to attack Egypt, Syria, and Jordan."

"And they thought we'd pass on the information. That's why!"

"But to kill thirty-four of our buddies and injure one hundred and seventy-one including Captain McGonagle? Commander McGonagle was hit badly. We all were hit in some way, but all us guys took care of each other. I even learned how to stitch up open wounds. There was blood everywhere."

"You are lucky they didn't kill all of you!"

"That was clearly their intention! We are trained to handle radio equipment, not man guns against our so-called friends attacking us with PT boats and jet fighters!"

François asked, "Where do you fellows go from here?"

"We don't know. I just got word from the Captain that the White House has ordered the Navy to place a ten-year silence rule on all of us."

"Ten years? What does that mean, Lieutenant Ennes?"

"It means, sir, we are not allowed to speak to anyone or to each other about the Israeli attack, and we are not to write about it to anyone for ten years!"

"So, I guess this conversation shouldn't go on."

"Hell, no sir, we want you to know our side."

"The Navy let us down and now the White House wants us to fight for them only as long as we shut up!"

"Those damned Israelis! What about the families of our buddies who were killed? What are they supposed to do?"

"They're supposed to believe their fathers, husbands, and sons were killed in enemy action, I guess."

"I hope it helps you to know that in addition to your ability to hear and record all those pilots' discussions with Israeli headquarters, radio operators in Lebanon, Spain and Germany recorded them too. Maybe even the Egyptians. So, if America is never told the truth, at least part of the world now knows."

"I'm glad to hear that, Lieutenant DuBois, because, I gotta tell you, our guys feel awful alone right now. To a man, they're convinced we were sacrificed to protect the Israelis."

"Can you believe U.S. Naval personnel were left to die to protect those bastards? By our own government? We were told that the order to turn back was from the 'highest levels.' What does that mean?"

"It means the order came from the White House! I think I speak for the whole crew," Lieutenant Ennes added, "when I say that we all are in the Navy to protect American lives. We are willing to give our lives for America, but not for Israel, especially when they knew we were Americans and we were defenseless!"

As François left the restaurant, he noticed two well-dressed men following him as he walked back to the Excelsior Hotel. He decided to do a little window shopping and used the shop's windows to get a better look at them and to see if they continued to follow him.

If we are able to attack an inferior force with a superior one,
our opponents will be in dire straits.
The spot where we intend to fight must not be made known,
for then the enemy will have to prepare against
a possible attack at different points.
Sun Tzu

CHAPTER 9

June 14, 1967
Beirut: Attack Follow-up

"There is no question that the Israeli attack on the USS Liberty was deliberate, Mr. President," François told President Helou as they sat in the President's office, immediately upon his return to Beirut.

"You feel absolutely positive do you, after meeting with the American seamen, François?"

"Yes sir, I do. We were able to clear all security and convince the seamen to share their story with us. We got there before they clamped a Top Secret classification on the attack. They were told not to talk, but they thought it safe to talk to us, because they thought we were one of them." Then, he added, smiling, "It also helped that my assistant, Hanna, has a cousin who serves on the USS Liberty."

"What a wonderful coincidence, François! It's nice to have lots of Lebanese in America, isn't it?"

They both chuckled at the thought.

"I have their incredible information on my recorder, which I had in my pocket. It is a terrible tragedy directed from the very highest levels of the Israeli government. And, sir, it also appears that from the highest level of Israel's government, they did not want the United States' ship to hear their conversations while they attacked Egypt, Syria, and Jordan, and invaded the Golan, especially after the declared ceasefire.

"The radioman heard Israeli headquarters tell the pilots to ignore the American flag and continue their attack until they could sink the ship, and kill the entire the crew, hoping no one would ever know. They planned to blame it on the Egyptians, even though their Air Force had already been destroyed. They even bombed the ship's bridge with napalm! They strafed the life rafts as the Americans were trying to get in them to keep from drowning! And then, the Israeli patrol boat crewmen collected the lifeless life boats to clear the area so no trace was left behind. The ship's name is quite visible on those rafts. It had to be horrible for the American sailors! Can you believe it?"

"No, François. It is too difficult to believe such a thing would happen." The President, with tears welling in his eyes, whispered as he prayed, "May God have mercy on their souls. You say thirty-four were killed and one hundred seventy-one injured?"

"Yes, sir. And the survivors are very, very angry. But it appears they were sacrificed for political expediency by the White House. It's so hard to believe. But it's true!

"They told me President Johnson personally ordered the Navy to return their fighters back to their aircraft carriers because President Johnson didn't 'want to embarrass his ally, the Israelis!"

"What?" asked a stunned President Helou. "You are telling me that the U.S. Navy people told you their own President Lyndon Johnson actually told them the fighters sent to scare off the Israeli jets were ordered back, leaving those poor U.S. sailors to die?"

"Yes, sir, that is exactly what I was told. They told me this was the first time in U.S. Naval history that the government had left their own behind without help."

"This is the America the entire world respects because they treasure their individuals so highly. But they were expendable for the sake of Israel's possible embarrassment. It's unbelievable!"

Both the President and François were visibly shaken.

François spent the next morning in his office recapturing and dictating all the information he had gathered the last several days: the meetings with President Helou, his trip to Malta, the secular demands of Lebanon's variety of citizens. And, of course, he thought about Leah.

Then, smiling, he said to himself, "One of these days I've got to devote myself to the business of Credit Suisse."

He welcomed the change of subjects as his pulse slowed down.

As he pondered his workload, gazing out to sea with the sun reflecting on the sea, he glanced back at the stack of phone messages and requests for him to call back and rubbed his neck, hoping to get his mind off the war. While it lasted only six days, it seemed more like a year.

He was overwrought, sad, and, like most people across the Arab world, he felt a sense of frustration, impotence, humiliation, and anger at Israel.

"Hanna, the Palestinian State sponsors of Egypt and Syria have now lost all credibility in this terrible defeat. It would not surprise me if Yasir Arafat's three-year old Fatah, leading the Palestinian Liberation Organization, the PLO, now filled the vacuum and began guerilla warfare against the Israelis. If they do, we are in for some difficult times. I can only pray they stay in Jordan and don't come to Lebanon as a safe haven. I'd better approach this possibility with President Helou.

"That war should never have occurred, dammit!" François suddenly shouted aloud, slapping his desk, venting raw emotions.

Hanna jumped as he heard his superior's hand land on the desk.

François continued, "How do we explain the French and their damned Mirage jet fighters, American arms, Egypt's empty threats and dubious actions, Syria's willingness to align with Egypt. And," he added, "unfortunate King Hussein caught in the middle leading a poor Jordan with all those Palestinian refugees. And now, hundreds of thousands of the poorest of the West Bank and Gaza are seeking refuge across the entire Arab world. How will we absorb so many? Why doesn't the Western World constrain the expansionist, armed Zionists? I think President Helou was correct. If Israel was anywhere else…"

As his voice drifted off, he recalled his meetings and conversations with the crew members of the USS Liberty in Malta.

"How, Hanna, could President Johnson call back the fighters sent to drive off the Israeli attacks? How could he ignore the pain of the thirty-four families whose loved ones were slaughtered on a defenseless ship by their so-called best ally in the Middle East? It breaks my heart."

Hold out baits to entice the enemy
feign disorder and crush him.
Sun Tzu

Chapter 10

Leah
Tel Aviv

Leah warily approached the pay telephone on Allenby Street in Tel Aviv more cautiously than usual. She had always preferred the phone booth on this busy street, hoping the high volume of pedestrian and vehicular traffic would offer her anonymity. She sat nearby for nearly an hour before she dared approach the phone, looking around herself several times, watching for anyone acting suspiciously.

I may have to find another place, maybe on Ben Yehuda Street next time, she thought as she made her call to her beloved François. How is he? Is he hurt?

François heard his private telephone ring.

"*Allo?* François DuBois speaking."

"François...this is Leah, your wayward love, calling," she laughed, hoping he was not still angry with her.

"Leah!" His voice angry and frustrated, he yelled, "Where the hell are you? This relationship cannot survive this Israeli attack with you choosing to remain a part of that country!"

"Oh, darling, please don't be mad at me. I can't bear to have you angry with me," she pleaded. "It has been incredible here in Israel. Most Israelis are euphoric with the sudden victory over Egypt's Nasser, Syria's Al-Atassi and Jordan's Hussein." Catching her breath, she continued, "Everyone feels safe again now that Israel occupies the Sinai, Gaza, Golan, and the West Bank. Israel was so small, so narrow, so vulnerable, and believed to be defenseless before. Now we feel safer and not at all defenseless. Many love the boldness and power of General Moshe Dayan and his forces...the superiority of our military! They can hardly contain themselves. I must admit, I feel somewhat proud of my people today.

But many of us who want and prefer peace are saddened. We don't believe Israel should be an occupier and taker of lands belonging to others. And neither does the U.N. They want us to immediately leave the West Bank and Gaza, the Sinai, Golan, and East Jerusalem and return to pre-war lines."

"Why do you think I care about your government? Security does not come by killing your neighbors and taking their homes, their livelihoods. I don't want to hear any more about your precious Dayan, Leah! I think your love has become too hollow for me. Stay there if you wish. But if you do, you can forget about me and our love." François' sense of impotence, anger and frustrations were driving him to take it all out on his beloved, but he no longer cared.

"Don't say that, Francois, please?"

"Are you saying the views of Israeli Jews are divided, Leah? Israel cannot keep all these lands taken by force. It goes against all civilized behavior. It controverts the Geneva Accords, U.N. Resolutions. Surely the world will not let this stand. And I don't want to be involved with someone who supports such arrogance, Leah. You must soon choose. But, I it appears the people of Israel including you support the government's expansionist aim to take and keep the West Bank, Gaza, Golan, and the Sinai."

"I understand how you must feel, François. We are in the middle of a great debate. My colleagues and I would rather not take those lands. We'd rather have peace, if possible."

"Leah! Listen to me! Nasser has offered Israel a non-belligerency agreement but Dayan and Eshkol rejected it. I am also told King Hussein offered a full peace treaty but your hardline government rejected that too. Also, we have been informed that Syria will sign a peace treaty if Israel returns the Golan Heights. The Arabs have accepted their defeat, but Israel wants to keep these conquered lands and remove the people living there. If you choose to remain in Israel with that kind of existence, then, I think it's time for us to say 'Goodbye.' I'm sorry, Leah. I'm furious with you! It just won't work with you there."

"Oh, François, I don't know what's going to happen. So many Palestinians are clogging the roads out of East Jerusalem, including thousands of Christians, even those with many Jewish friends...attorneys, doctors, teachers, hotel owners. All their properties and homes are being taken over and they are not allowed to stay. Homes are being filled with Jewish opportunists. Thousands of Palestinian children are walking to somewhere...anywhere...to Lebanon, to Syria, and mostly to Jordan. It's so sad. But many are staying too. The West Bank still has hundreds of thousands of Christian and Muslim Arabs. Will they become Israelis eventually?"

"What a mess, Leah. And I don't think you are hearing what I'm saying."

"It's so chaotic here, François. Please give me more time. I so want to be with you like before."

"But something has to change, Leah, and I mean now! Are you aware of all your government's actions these past days?"

"I am only aware, François, of what the government tells us, but I don't trust all that they say anymore." She was feeling a range of emotions: frustration, anger, fear of what might happen, cynicism, and yet, like nearly all Israeli Jews, a strong sense of pride.

"Have they told you they nearly sank the USS Liberty...a defenseless American reconnaissance ship?"

"That was a mistake, François. They said on the radio that they thought it was an Egyptian ship, and when they realized it was American, they returned to their bases."

"They lied, Leah. They lied, just as they lied when your government's military radio broadcast that Israel was being attacked by Syria and Egypt even as Israel's fighters were preemptively attacking them," François' voice started rising.

"Don't say that, François. Surely Dayan wouldn't deliberately attack an American ship...would he? Please don't be angry with me," she pleaded.

"Yes, Leah, he did. I just returned to Beirut from Malta where the USS Liberty, an unarmed reconnaissance ship, the world's most advanced, is in dry dock for major repairs after being assaulted by Israeli jet fighters. They kept firing rockets and bombs for four hours; then, three Israeli speed boats torpedoed the ship. Thirty-four Americans were killed. They knew damned well it was an American ship, Leah. They knew and they lied," he reiterated. "The American officer on the bridge, Lt. James Ennes, personally told me what happened." François briefly told Leah about the attack. "I'll go into more detail at another time. I'm too upset to talk about it now."

"Oh, my God, François! They torpedoed the ship? What has Israel done? We are not at war with America!"

"Leah, I think this would be a good time for you to transfer to Europe."

Suddenly, Leah was alarmed. Her government's duplicity and attack on the U.S. ship caused her to be more frightened than ever. "Oh, François, yes...but you must join me. I...I...cannot bear the thought of losing you. I will immediately ask for a transfer to our embassy in Paris," she said eagerly. "Now, my love, I must go." Her concern of being watched grew urgent. She shivered at the sight of Itzak walking quickly toward her and hurriedly said, "I will call you tomorrow...same time."

"Goodbye, Leah," he started to say as he heard the telephone receiver slam loudly onto its cradle, interrupting his last comment. Then there was only silence as the phone went dead.

"Dammit, Leah. What is the matter with you?" Francois yelled at no one. His frustration grew even greater.

"Leah! Who the hell have you been speaking with?" Itzak yelled at her. "Never mind. We already know. Your calls have been traced now for several days."

"Itzak! Let go of me. Itzak! You're hurting my arm! Release me this instant!" Now she was more frightened than ever.

"No, Leah. You are obviously in contact with Israel's enemies. I heard you!"

he shouted.

Itzak was enraged, his growing jealousy of this mysterious Lebanese man, François DuBois, festered, reminding him of the painful rejection by the only woman he had ever coveted. It couldn't be called love...Itzak lusted after Leah, and for too many years he felt the sting of her indifference. She always loved François so completely there could be no room for him or anyone else, even as they lived side by side in the kibbutz.

"Itzak, your crazy friends, like Dayan, have gone too far. Their attack on the American ship, the USS Liberty, was wrong, reckless, and deliberate. How could you support such a thing?"

"You know about the Liberty?"

"Yes I do, Itzak. It's a lie that our pilots didn't know it was an American ship! A terrible lie! Israelis killed thirty-four Americans, Itzak...thirty-four innocent seamen! Our allies!"

"We have no allies, Leah. Don't you get it? They only help us because they feel so guilty since they didn't stop the holocaust. And they wouldn't let world Zionists send Jewish refugees to America. They are not our friends, Leah. You'll see. We Jews are alone and always will be, and we can only depend on each other."

"What about the French? We used Dassault Mirage fighters to attack Egypt and Syria. What about that, Itzak? President de Gaulle provided us with those jets but he insisted we not fire the first shot. Wasn't that proper advice from our friends, our suppliers? After all, they have other interests in the region, Itzak."

Itzak stood silent and defiant in front of her, fists clenched, as she continued her defensive tirade.

"But we did fire the first shot, Itzak. We fired thousands of first shots, bombs, rockets. Is that why Dayan had the government's military radio station broadcast to the world that Israel was under attack when it wasn't? Was that why he ordered the Liberty sunk because it was listening to our pilots' radio conversations, Itzak? Is that why, Itzak? Tell me!"

"Whose side are you on, Leah, for God's sake?"

Leah saw fire in Itzak's eyes, anger like she'd never before seen and it scared her and made her even angrier, but she continued boldly, "I am an Israeli, Itzak. And I am a Jew. And I am just as committed to Israel as you are. I lost my mother and father to Hitler just as you did! You have no right to doubt my allegiance or my loyalty."

Then, with no remaining control over her emotions, tears filled her eyes as she lowered her head and voice and said evenly, "I don't believe we can fulfill the Law of Moses if we don't have concern for others. We are part of a world community, Itzak."

"Leah, you have such naïve beliefs, but you cannot be allowed to use those views to hurt Israel. I will not let you! I think you somehow went over to the other side...helping the Arabs against Israel! Leah, I think you are a mrgel, a traitor!

A spy! And I'm going to prove it very soon. Your calls to your contact in Beirut are being taped by the Mossad. Leah, you can't be allowed to succeed in trading secrets against us! Both of you are going to be dealt with!"

"How dare you call me a spy, Itzak! How dare you threaten me!" she shouted angrily as she stormed away.

I'll get her. I'll get them both! thought Itzak, glaring at her back as she stormed away. Israel belongs only to the Jews. There is no room for people like her and her Arab friends. Ever! The blood vessels in his temples enlarged as fury contorted his face.

I'll get her, he repeated to himself. I'll get both of them, he nearly screamed aloud in his rage.

Itzak intended to scare Leah.

And he succeeded.

Leah, shivering with fear again, protectively wrapped her arms around her breasts as she quickly walked away from Itzak and blended into the bustling crowds.

Itzak called me a mrgel…a spy! I'd better move fast. I'd better go away as François cautioned…oh, François, I need you so much. She was growing more and more concerned about her personal safety, ironically in the supposed safe haven for all Jews.

"I must get away from Itzak and all these people who are so happy about the war's results."

She immediately went to the Foreign Ministry offices and completed the forms requesting a transfer to a European embassy, preferably in France. Her fluent French helped her as well as her ability to speak English without the Eastern European accent of so many Ashkenazi Israelis.

The aftermath of the Six Day War was far different in the Arab world where men angrily marched in the streets demanding action and criticizing their leaders. Everyone cursed Israel and demanded their removal from Arab lands. This was in stark contrast to the "conquering heroes" mentality of Israel. Israelis, for the most part, significantly reversed their malaise of the 1966 recession and sense of weakness, lack of security and despair. Now they were extraordinarily proud of their ability to defeat a claimed "one hundred millions of Arabs," battle cries of exaggeration including numerous uninvolved, non-confrontation states as far as hundreds of miles away as Morocco to the west and Dubai to the east, surrounding the small, therefore, they claimed, defenseless state of Israel.

Yet, within Israel, there were divisive issues. A large Israeli minority felt that Israel must conform to U.N. directives and immediately withdraw from the conquered lands of the West Bank, East Jerusalem, Golan and Gaza. But the powers in place and most Israelis were determined to keep those lands, occupy them and eventually annex the Golan and East Jerusalem. By insisting on keeping their new possessions under their total control, Israel was rejecting Article 49 of the Fourth Geneva Convention of 1949 and several U.N. Resolutions.

These decisions caused Arabs bitter anger and suffering. And for Israel and its benefactors, extraordinary costs were incurred to militarily occupy foreign lands and to control the lives of hundreds of thousands of Arabs, both Christians and Muslims.

Outside Israel, there were many who, while impressed with Israel's military successes in such a brief period of time, nonetheless questioned the actions of the Israeli government, including Walter Rostow, the son of Russian Jewish immigrants and U.S. National Security Advisor to President Johnson, who said, "This (cover-up report blaming America for the Liberty attack) makes no good sense at all."

The Arabs of Egypt, Syria, and Jordan were humiliated and began harshly questioning the wisdom of their leaders.

France's Charles de Gaulle was infuriated with Israel. "They were not to use our planes except to defend themselves," he announced to the world. "They were not to attack first using our Mirage fighters. But," he said later, "in fact, they used them pre-emptively, and they broke the agreement, placing France in an indefensible position."

As a result of his statement, despite his arming of Israel, he was publicly condemned with a favorite epithet of the Zionists. They branded him an "anti-Semite!"

> *The best thing of all is to take the enemy's country whole and intact.*
>
> Sun Tzu

Chapter 11

Paris

On June 7th, Abba Eban, Israel's foreign minister, reported that McGeorge Bundy in the White House had called him and "hinted" the United States would accept an Israeli attack on the Golan. By then, Israel had already conquered Egypt's Sinai, Gaza, the West Bank, and the Old City of East Jerusalem. Dayan wanted to act quickly to attack Syria's Golan Heights before the world could stop it. Because Dayan learned his government might not officially approve such a move, he decided to beat the government so he could show that "Israel was the Boss."

On Friday, June 9th, General Dayan, in his "snatch and grab" frenzy, reported to Prime Minister Eshkol that Israeli intelligence had intercepted a telegram from Egypt's Gamal Abdel Nasser to the Syrian President, Nur Al-Din Al-Atassi, telling him that Egypt had been defeated, and had stopped fighting. 'Syria is also stopping' was the reply. When he reported this to Eshkol, Dayan insisted, "We must fully exploit this situation."

"What a despicable man. He always wants to attack, attack, attack! His life does not include negotiating or tolerance of others. I think he still, deep down, remains very bitter over the loss of his eye." Eshkol later told others.

At that time, it was clear Syria had agreed to the United Nations' call for a ceasefire. At the Israeli Cabinet meeting held at 9 a.m., Friday, June 9th, cabinet members later recalled that Dayan told them he had ordered the seizure of not just the northern Golan, but all of the Golan Heights, its fertile land and its water.

Syria's willingness to agree to the U.N. call for a ceasefire, Dayan told his Cabinet "had created a new opportunity."

As a result, after Syria agreed to the ceasefire, Israel launched an air and ground assault on the Golan Heights, knowing a ceasefire would occur later that day.

Syrian forces, without air cover, desperately fought back all day, resulting in heavy casualties on both sides.

Yitzhak Rabin wrote in his journal later that Dayan, after learning Egypt had agreed to the ceasefire, ordered Israeli forces to attack and seize the Suez Canal from Egypt although its taking would create major problems with other nations which used the Canal.

In his journal, Rabin added in anger, Dayan, as Minister of Defense, in his "snatch and grab frenzy," intended to take all he could, particularly after Egypt, Jordan, and Syria had ceased operations as the U.N. urged.

Israel's forces finally stopped advancing after they conquered the Golan, Sinai, East Jerusalem, the West Bank and reached the east banks of the Suez Canal.

François heard the phone ring in his office. "*Allo*," François Dubois speaking.

"Ah, François," spoke the President. I'm glad I found you."

"What is it Mr. President?"

I have just received a report from Syria. Their informers have been watching the happenings on the Golan Heights. You know Syria will not stop until they get them back."

"Yes, sir, they treasure the Golan waters. What is in the report?"

"Listen, François. I won't read the entire report, but I want you to know the highlights. It states Israeli supplies and soldiers are being sent to the conquered Golan Heights to build the first Israeli kibbutz in what is still part of Syria. They plan to call it Kibbutz Golan.

"They plan to locate it in the once thriving Syrian farming town of Kuneitra, confiscating the farmers' homes, groves, unharvested crops, sheep, cows, and equipment.

"They plan that within one year, more than one hundred Israelis, subsidized by the Israeli government, will be living at the kibbutz, assuming ownership illegally, and defying all United Nation resolutions and international laws. They are also destroying the nearby pretty little town of Banias. An American embassy official surveying the Golan reported that another hundred or so abandoned villages in the Golan Heights were systematically destroyed by the Israeli army as directed by Dayan, driving out the thousands of Syrian farmers and their families.

"What suggestions do you have, François?"

"That is rotten, Mr. President. It again proves when it comes to Israel, 'Might makes right.' I think there is nothing Lebanon can do at this time, but we'd better watch what else the Israelis do, what other areas they try to take over."

"Remember, Lebanon's Shebaa Farms are very close to the Golan."

"That's right! Perhaps we should send Lebanese Army troops there. I'll contact our Minister of Defense now."

In minutes following her last conversation with François, Leah, recognizing Itzak was going to continue to relentlessly harass her, briskly walked, nearly ran to the Foreign Ministry and formally applied for a transfer to Paris. Because of the emergency status in Israel, her transfer met no resistance. She remained in the building processing her transfer request, obtaining several signatures for what seemed like hours. Still, she believed she might not get another chance with Itzak and his friends at the Mossad watching her every movement. Even as she left the building late in the day, she saw out of the corner of her eye someone was spying on her.

"Oh, Lord, will he never leave me alone?" She mumbled to herself. But she had her transfer in her hand. Convinced she had to leave, she decided to leave her meager belongings at the kibbutz and not return. She checked her purse, confirming she had carried her money with her. She waved for a taxi and saw Itzak flag another cab behind her. Anxious and fearful, tears began to flow down her cheeks.

"Driver! Please take me to the airport as quickly as you can."

"I will be safe only when I am with François," she whispered to herself. She knew she could not relax until she was safely in Paris. The tension she felt in the taxi, looking out the rear window at Itzak's taxi did not lessen even as she ran from the taxi into the airport. At the counter, hurriedly, she exclaimed to the agent, while looking up at the schedule of flights above and behind the agent, "One ticket to Paris, please, and hurry. The next flight leaves very soon, I see." She quickly grabbed her ticket, leaving with, "Thank you, Miss." She strode briskly to the gate, looking over her shoulder frequently as she darted into a Ladies Room, hoping to lose Itzak. He didn't see her.

"Hello," she said to the young woman looking into the mirror while freshening her makeup, "will you please do me a favor and swap clothes with me? I'm hoping to surprise my boyfriend when I land in Paris," she smiled genuinely. "I'll pay you well for your trouble."

It took maybe an hour, until she finally convinced the woman to swap her blouse, skirt and scarf, which she wrapped around her head.

"Thank you so very much."

Looking through the slightly opened door, she was relieved that Itzak wasn't waiting for her. She escaped the Ladies Room with the woman and quickly stepped to the gate, staying with her new friend as long as possible.

"I must go now, friend, and good luck to you." She darted to the gate, clamored aboard, took her seat, and shook like leaves on a sycamore in the breeze.

Nervous tears flowed down her cheeks as she sat, frightened more than ever before, impatiently praying for the plane to take off. After several agonizing hours in flight, her plane landed at Paris' Orly International Airport. "Thank you, Lord, for bringing me safely to Paris." Leah was finally relieved to be safe in Paris, assigned to the cultural attaché in Israel's largest embassy in Europe.

After her first full day at the embassy, rested, smiling and energized, she decided to go for a walk alone along the Seine River, breathlessly revisiting the same places where she and her first and only love, François, fell deeply in love, and consummated their love twenty years earlier.

"Oh, I hope François will understand and get over his anger at me when he finds out I left Israel and am now in Paris." She nervously called François' private line in Beirut, this time without the fear of being watched as she had been so many times in Tel Aviv. "François I have left Israel!" she squealed happily. "You frightened me so these past days. I don't want to lose you. I cannot lose you, my greatest love! Please, please come to me…Now! I am in Paris. I rented an apartment near the Sorbonne, near where I lived when I attended school. You must join me, my love. I cannot live without you."

Although she was now forty-two years old, she still reveled in the ambiance of the university, the students, the city, and her memories with François when they first fell in love. And she was still the passionate, beautiful woman she was twenty years earlier, in 1947.

"You are in Paris? Truly, Leah?" Delighted beyond belief that Leah responded as he hoped, hearing his anger, feeling his deep frustration and believing the seriousness of his ultimatum, François nearly shouted with joy into the phone receiver. "You are sure, aren't you, Leah? I mean, absolutely sure? I need to know you have made the decision to be with me, that you are completely certain."

"Oh, yes, François…I am no longer safe in Israel. Not anymore. I know now I cannot live there anymore."

"Well, in that case, I will join you in Paris. But, I cannot leave today. I have important things to complete, but I'll wrap them up by tomorrow morning and catch a flight tomorrow afternoon. I'll have Hanna arrange a room at the Maurice. You still remember where that is. Don't you?" he laughed, recalling that night they shared there so long ago.

"Yes! I remember, darling. I will come to you there tomorrow night."

"Wonderful. I should be checked in by nine o'clock, Leah."

"Oh, François, hurry!"

"Hanna," François called to his assistant, smiling with joy. "I need you."

"Yes, sir, what can I do for you?"

François, happily buoyant and impassioned, gave instructions to his assistant in rapid fire dictation. "I wish to fly to Paris tomorrow after work. I'll need a hotel room."

"At the Maurice as usual, sir?"

"Yes."

"Fine, sir. I'll take care of the arrangements right away. Shall I pack your bags, sir?"

"No, Hanna. I'll take care of that tonight, thank you."

Although it seemed like weeks, within thirty hours, he was in Paris, registering at the hotel by eight o'clock. A quick shower and shave minutes later, he applied his favorite cologne, and unpacked his bags, which included enough clothing for a week. If he decided to stay longer, he knew he could purchase more clothing in Paris. His attire was always continental since his favorite shops in Beirut carried the same suits, shirts, ties, and casual wear as those he frequented in Paris.

By nine o'clock he was slowly nursing his second scotch and water in the hotel lounge when, instinctively, he looked again at the lounge entrance where he saw the familiar form of who, to him, was the most strikingly beautiful and sensual woman in the world...tall and slender, with dark brown, long, wavy hair, wearing a snug fitting blouse, stylish jacket and black slacks. He loved watching her familiar stride...like a model. But what struck his emotions like a magic wand was her smile. It was the same broad, bright and happy smile that she wore the first time they met at the Sorbonne.

"Leah!" he called out as he excitedly stood up, nearly knocking his chair to the floor. "Over here, Leah!" He quickly stepped to her as she approached, arms spread, eager to be in his arms.

"Oh, François, my darling! It is you, isn't it?" she asked rhetorically as her eyes filled with tears of excitement and joy.

"Yes, Leah," he whispered as they embraced tightly, both wanting more, much more, immediately.

"Do you think the hotel would mind if we closed the lounge so we could be alone?" she asked devilishly.

"Who cares?" he replied quickly, laughing.

Although they knew how to behave properly in public, they remained embraced for longer than a moment, François feeling his frustrations and anger dissipate, and permitting himself the release from those emotions to his true feelings of his love for Leah.

Feeling each other's body pressed against the other, hungrily communicating their passionate love with a lingering kiss, conveying their gratitude that even though their separation had been so long, now was the moment of their reunion. This would be their most precious present, a gift from the gods, the culmination of all their frustrations and desires during their long agonizing and conflicting separation.

"How long can you stay in Paris, my love?" she asked, looking directly into his eyes.

"How long are you staying, Leah?" he asked, not yet totally convinced.

They laughed together. His was still a bit of a nervous laugh, hoping.

"As long as you wish," they said in unison, laughing at their intuitive responses.

From that moment, their time together became idyllic. They immediately recaptured their passion for one another as though the past twenty years had not happened. They were in love. They were in their twenties again. And now they were free to believe.

This was a remarkable moment for the two of them. Because of the war, which seemed to conspire with the political barriers they suffered to separate them completely and forever, they had come very close to losing each other and, admittedly with reluctance, nearly ended their love affair.

"When you made your decision twenty years ago, Leah, when you told me in 1948 you had decided to leave me and go to Palestine to help build a homeland for your people, I knew then I would always be in competition for your love, for your devotion. You forced us to endure and separately share a cruelly unsatisfying, constrained love since our time together in Paris. You broke my heart.

"I was so devastated; I just couldn't deal with your decision. For a long time, I tried to forget you, totally. Now, Leah, I do not believe they are your people anymore. You are not like them, and you never will be."

"Oh, François, I know now more than ever my decision caused us so much emotional pain. Although we were separated by just by the few kilometers between you in Beirut and me in Tiberias, there were enormous barriers of political and religious realities since the 1947 war. I never believed things would go so wrong. Believe me, François; I truly thought I could do good things for my fellow Jews. I was idealistic and, it seems, quite naïve. But I never stopped loving you even though we weren't together. But I see now we lost so many years because of my decision."

"I always tried to understand, Leah, but this war has changed my thinking. It should change your thinking too. I wondered during all those years how our love would somehow survive the separation due to our choices to be prisoners devoted to our cultural bonds."

"While I was bound to my commitment to the new state of Israel, and willingly worked each day in the banana fields and gardens on behalf of my kibbutz, I knew deep in my heart I could never stop loving, wanting, or needing you, François. I knew…I believed that we would one day find a way to be together by breaking the tethers that kept us apart. But I was a Jewish refugee whose family and people had suffered so terribly at the hands of the brutal Nazi war machine. Only those who so suffered could possibly understand."

They both believed in their total commitment and passionate love they shared as students at the Sorbonne so long ago and that somehow, someday they would be together, free to share again.

Ironically, the recent Six Day War, which could have made it impossible for them to be together, in fact, made it imperative for them to meet again in Paris.

And here they were...consumed by their reunion in the city where it all began, where their freedom to love, to laugh, to touch, to see, to smell, to embrace, and to speak together could be expressed without hesitation.

This moment for them was theirs alone. The Maurice lounge was now their private world. And while there were others in the lounge, in separate conversations of business associates, tourists, and a scattering of mixed couples, this twosome was oblivious to any sound or activity beyond themselves. Unable to lose eye contact, let go of each other's hand, or even change their smiles of joy, they felt free to dream...to remember.

They lingered in their reverie, connected, tacitly sharing and verbally recalling those memories of their times together as students at the Sorbonne. Finally, she leaned toward her love and whispered coquettishly, "François, let's go to the place where we first met at the Sorbonne. It is not too late for young lovers, is it?"

"No, my love," he replied, smiling broadly, "for us, nothing can ever be too late! After all," he laughed, "now that you are in my arms, I am twenty-seven again!"

"And I am twenty-two again," she giggled. "Then let's go now! I want our first night together again to begin with our first meeting."

"Since I arrived, Leah, I have been remembering every delicious moment we shared. I am helpless in your presence, my darling."

"As am I, my love," she quickly responded.

He thought silently for a moment, and then, looking into her eyes, whispered, "'Re-remembering,' Leah, as defined to me in one of my courses here, means 'creating a reality in the present with memories of the past.'"

"Oh," she said endearingly, "I see what you mean. What a perfect use of the word, especially for us, darling. We can, together, recall all those joyful, lustful moments we shared then and make those memories our reality this very moment," she giggled.

Without hesitation, François signaled the *garçon*, charged their drinks to his room, rose to assist her as she stood from her chair, and led her out of the lounge, striding side by side to the hotel's entrance doors as he gripped her hand. Their bodies leaned against each other willingly as they profoundly began their simultaneous recollection and reunion.

They were oblivious to several people strolling throughout the cavernous, luxurious lobby, some at small tables ordering drinks, others converging at the concierge's desk, creating a busy scene in this large, high-ceilinged opulent entrance area filled with expensive furniture and decorative works of art.

François and Leah, so consumed by each other's presence, took no notice of two men seated to one side of the lobby who had unobstructed views of the lounge and the hotel entrance. After following Leah to the hotel, they remained to furtively watch the couple as described by Itzak and the Mossad intelligence group. As the couple strode by, the two men slowly put down their newspapers that shielded their faces, and unobtrusively followed them out of the hotel.

As Leah and François reached the curb and the hotel doorman, François glanced back for no reason in particular. But as he did, he noticed the two men deliberately turn their heads in unison. He saw them for only a brief moment but something familiar about them registered in his brain.

Who are they? Have I seen them before? He shook his head. *I've visited the Maurice many, many times, to be sure. Maybe they are simply regulars too.*

We'll sure know in a minute.

The Peugeot taxi driver deftly pulled up to the curb. The doorman opened the rear door of the cab, Leah stepped in and François followed. As he settled in beside Leah, the men's faces suddenly flashed before him in recognition.

If your enemy is taking his ease, give him no rest.
Sun Tzu

CHAPTER 12

Paris, Love, Memories and Escape

The two men hailed the next cab and instructed the driver to follow Leah and François in their taxi.

After a few minutes' drive, Moshe commented to his partner, "It appears they are going to the university district."

"Strange, wouldn't you say?" replied Yalon.

"Yes, Itzak claims she's a spy and he is her accomplice. But they look like lovers to me," he sneered maliciously.

"Ah, The allure of Paris."

Turn after turn, the two taxis moved quickly through the crowded, early evening Parisian streets, but the Mossad agents' driver experienced no difficulty keeping the first taxi in sight.

"Stop here, driver," François said as he leaned forward from the back seat. "We'll walk from here."

After they stopped, François noticed a trailing taxi also pull up a short distance behind them. Then, as he reached for Leah's out-stretched hand to help her out of the cab, he noticed the two familiar men from the hotel exit their taxi, turn away and walk behind their car.

Now, sensing they definitely were being followed, François took Leah's arm as they carefully strolled toward the café where they first met. He chose not to say anything to Leah and not let his suspicions detract from their desire that this evening, of all evenings; that it not be anything but a fulfillment of their desire for one another this, of all nights.

"Here we are, my love," he said, smiling, as they approached the café's tables on the sidewalk with the same view of the Seine as when they met.

"Oh, François, this is so amazing. Imagine," she whispered to him, "I am so very happy we came here. All my emotions are high. I love you so much. And this is where it all began. I remember every detail."

"You appeared so sweet and hesitant," he replied with a loving smile as he reached across the table for her soft, supple hand.

"I was very young, alone, and hesitant because I was afraid, François. My family had been killed and I knew I was different. I am a Jew and that caused me to be frightened almost all the time. But you were so cute, funny, and not at all threatening for me."

"You struck me as someone very special, Leah. The war was terrible and so many good people suffered all those years. If there is such a thing as love at first sight, then that is what happened to me. Your gentle demeanor made me more patient, and I very much wanted you to become more relaxed and unafraid."

"Well, you made that happen, François. Thank you for making me feel that I didn't have to protect myself from you and your friends."

"None of us were totally innocent, were we? The war years caused all of us to protect ourselves, until after the Americans arrived, and we all began to feel safe. And," François added, "as we all immersed ourselves in our studies at the Sorbonne, exchanging views in complete freedom, our protective walls slowly came down and we eased into a 'free spirit' syndrome, especially with the university promoting its liberal ambiance here."

"By the time I arrived, François, that evolution must have been complete, because you and your friends were certainly free spirited! You didn't have a care in the world, it seemed. And that was infectious, I must say."

Now holding both hands across the table, they once again gazed into each other's eyes, oblivious to the other diners around them or the myriad couples strolling past. They were in their own world...remembering.

François didn't see the two men again for the several hours he and Leah spent together at the café. And he didn't care. Leah was consuming him with her presence. "Leah, can you believe it has been twenty years since that incredible evening when we first met?"

"Twenty years!" she exclaimed. "Yes, my darling, I know. And you have been deep in my heart and in my mind every day since then."

"You know, tonight it seems those empty years never happened. It's as though we met for the first time tonight, my love."

"It's true," she agreed. "It's so true. The difference is that we know so much more about each other now." She flirted. "Tonight we are remembering every moment we spent here together. And at this very minute I am remembering that night we strolled the walkway along the Seine, your arm was around my shoulders. We saw several couples embracing and kissing each other and you asked me if I had noticed them. Then, just at the right moment, you must have seen the longing in my eyes because that is exactly when you fulfilled my desires, François. You pulled me into your arms and kissed me. You smelled so wonderful! My body went crazy! I loved it! At that moment I knew I had fallen completely in love with you and would never love anyone but you...just from that moment."

"I was going crazy myself, Leah. I wanted you so much...and you smelled so special, the way I remember you. I couldn't stand it, but I still felt your reluctance...

that you weren't quite ready for intimacy."

"I wasn't ready until that precise moment. It's bizarre, isn't it? Had you tried to kiss me as you did…I mean, a full, in love kiss…the night before or even an hour earlier, I'm not sure I would have let you," replied Leah, lovingly.

"Women are so unpredictable, aren't they? You believe you must protect yourselves until you choose the moment. Meanwhile, you drive a man crazy! But when that happens, you become a totally different person. Woe to the man who tries too soon for he runs the risk of inexplicably being turned away. And if he waits too long, that opportunity passes. Maybe there would be another, but that magical moment is gone forever, never to return.

"Leah, I am in heaven here with you remembering our times together, recalling memories of the past and making them realities of the present."

"I must accept, although reluctantly, those years of separation as though they never happened. How can that be?" she asked quizzically. "And yes, they did happen, to be sure, but they have not changed anything between us, have they? You even smell exactly the same, and I love the way you smell."

"No, my love. Not one single thing is more important while we are together again."

She lowered her eyelids demurely, reached for his hand and, with a beckoning, sensual expression asked, "François, let's return to the Maurice. Can we do that?"

"Oh, Leah, my beautiful love. You once again have been reading my mind. I want you now…at this very moment. I need you! Now!" Then, devilishly, he urged, "We could walk into the park where we ran through the hedges and made love for the first time. Remember?" He grinned. "But, then again, I'm not twenty-seven anymore, and I prefer comfort now, so since the Maurice boasts of its luxurious amenities let's let them prove it to us," he laughed out loud.

"Yes," responded Leah, squeezing his hand. "I need you, François. I need you so much. Let's go now."

As the taxi stopped at the sidewalk near the hotel's entrance, they excitedly rushed to the door, giggling, and went straightaway to the elevators and then to his suite.

After opening the door, he picked her up as if she were his bride. "It may be premature to carry you across this threshold, but it seems appropriate to me."

"I love it," she laughed as she wrapped her arms around his neck. He carried her through the living room straight to the bedroom and gingerly placed her on the bed. Immediately, she reached out to him with both arms, pulling him to her. On the bed together, she wrapped her arms around him. François, following suit, embraced her tightly, pressing his body against hers.

"Ohhh, François. I have dreamed of this moment so many times…so many nights alone, wishing, remembering, hoping…"

He felt her firm, full breasts press against his muscular chest as she felt his hips press against her, responding to his urgent desire for her.

"You are driving me crazy, making me grow, my love," he whispered in her ear as she felt him grow larger and harder.

"Are you trying to drive me crazy, François?" she said with a smile as she bit her lip.

"No, I just wanted to reintroduce myself to you," he joked, chuckling. "It may have been twenty years, but nothing has changed when it comes to you, my only, forever love!"

Her senses were on a high, wanting him so much. Her eyelids lowered as did her smile. She began unbuttoning his shirt and whispered to him wantonly, "I want you now."

In moments, they lay together on the bed, touching, caressing, and savoring one another, their clothes recklessly tossed onto the floor.

"Oh, you feel so good, François. And," she giggled, "you are growing so large."

"For you, Leah, only for you," he whispered as he gently touched his lips to her ear, making her shiver.

"Oh, my God," she moaned. "That is so good. Don't stop."

His hands caressed her breasts, reveling in their love, the physical fulfillment of all they admired about each other and the feelings they had stored in their hearts for so long. Her hands moved from his chest downward to his stomach. Then, as she explored his hips with her hands and kissed his chest and abdomen, she saw his eyes close. He groaned as his desire brought him so close to the precipice of lovemaking. He reached for her arms now, pulling her on top of him as they gloriously, hungrily became one.

"Ooohhh, how much I have loved you, François." She was barely gasping the words, almost unable to form them on her lips.

"My God, Leah, I am there. It is time."

"Me too, darling," she said. Then, more loudly, she almost screamed, "Now, François. Now!"

"Oh, Leah. I can't wait any longer!" he exclaimed as they both climaxed, each experiencing their explosion of ecstasy.

"How can I live without you," she whispered, tears of joy flowing down her cheeks.

"We are one, Leah. We have been and will be forever. I love you so much."

"You own me, François. I am yours…totally. But you know that has been so since our first time, don't you?"

Barely able to speak, he nodded and formed a smile, convinced she owned his heart and mind too.

For a long time they lay together, lightly stroking each other's bodies, relishing every sensual moment together.

"Leah, we must find a way to be together…and we must do this soon. This is crazy. Why should we be apart?"

"I don't know anymore," she replied, exhausted and helpless. "There was a time, back then after the war, when I was driven as a Jew and believed deeply in a safe place for all of my people…a homeland we could build without threats from anyone. But that has changed so much more than I ever dreamed possible. Now, I'm not safe there!"

They remained lying in bed side by side, bodies close, feet reaching for each other's, emerging from their sensually charged stupor, her cheek pressed against his muscular shoulder.

"I have some thoughts on that," he replied, "but not now, Leah. Let us enjoy each other tonight. Maybe," he laughed softly, "we should forget the rest of the world for a few days…weeks? Hell," he laughed again, "let's go somewhere so we can be together forever!"

Looking into each other's eyes, she spoke to him lovingly, "François, my love, I am not through with you yet." Then with a knowing smile, she reached for him and gently stroked his thighs, thrilled that her magical touch caused him to grow erect again.

Responding to her stimulation, he whispered, "You asked for it, Leah, so here I come to take you again."

"It's about time." She smiled, "You are becoming a beast! Take me if you dare!"

With that playful challenge, he reached again for her, one hand on her breast, the other on her calf caressing upward onto her supple inner thigh, stimulating her as she once again grew moist. She moaned in response as she stroked him even more urgently, now meeting his eyes with hers, tacitly reaching out to him, urging him on, anxiously anticipating the precise moment.

"Oooh, Leah, I love you so much. My God, how wonderful you feel."

"You are amazing, François," she whispered as she nibbled on his ear, driving him emotionally to the ceiling.

"Not yet," she pleaded, "not quite yet."

"Soon, Leah, soon, sweetheart. I can hardly hold on," he groaned as he slid into her, loving her silently as he drove himself against her abdomen, testing, tempting the precipice, and nearing what would, he knew, be a culmination that would freeze all his muscles and emotions.

"I am there, my love," she screamed softly. "Give me your seed. I am yours. Now…please."

"Hunhh," he exhaled strongly as he exploded in her, releasing all that he had, the heights of lovemaking between a man and a woman totally in love.

"My toes curled, Leah. I can't control anything!"

"I am here with you, François. I am in the same place." she whispered, exhausted.

"What a climax, Leah! And now I am spent. I know now how Samson must have felt when Delilah did to him what you just did to me. No wonder he could, for the first time, not care if anyone cut his hair. He couldn't have stopped her if he tried," he laughed weakly. "I am totally, totally weak. All these years I have treasured the memory of our time in Paris. We have shared more than most people have in a lifetime."

"I feel the same way, darling. Some people live their whole lives treasuring a single weekend," she responded fondly. Then, she whispered, "Now I should let you get some rest or I may wear you out."

"Just give me time and I'll be back, I promise," he replied, grinning slyly.

"I'll be patient, as I have been for twenty years. But only for a short time," she giggled. "This evening is too good to be true," she laughed.

"My prayers have been answered," she said softly as they rolled against each other and happily, drowsily fell into a sweet sleep, entwined, as close together as possible.

Sometime during the night as she lay beside François, who had drifted off into a deep sleep, she quietly pondered her fate. *After Paris? What then?* she thought. *I can serve my people somewhere else. Many Israelis, especially the young, are emigrating to America and Europe, tired of their lives of confrontation with their neighbors. Even the kibbutzim are losing their zeal. The world is changing. I have devoted twenty years of my life to helping build our homeland. And now, because of Itzak and his hardliners, my life has become impossible. My God, he called me a spy!*

For the first time, she began wondering if she should ever return to Israel following her quick getaway.

*All these things shall Love do unto you that
you may know the secrets of your heart.*
Kahlil Gibran

CHAPTER 13

Paris to Beirut

Breakfast arrived in Francois' room at ten o'clock. The room service attendant pushed the cloth covered stainless steel cart bearing a large variety of foods including a pitcher of fresh orange juice, plates of eggs, meats, cheeses, olives, toast, muffins, a large pot of coffee, a bottle of the finest champagne, and a bowl filled with large, bright red strawberries.

"Will there be anything else, Monsieur DuBois?" he asked, while François signed the receipt and slipped the waiter a generous tip.

"*Merci, garçon, merci,*" he replied, wrapped in the luxuriant terrycloth robe supplied by the hotel. "All is perfect. *Merci beaucoup.*"

As they sipped their coffee following their sumptuous breakfast, holding hands across the table, their eyes glued to each other's, not wanting to break the spell. Leah reclined in a silk tufted chaise, also wearing her hotel robe, deliberately keeping it slightly open to allow François a peak at her full breasts as she lasciviously, temptingly, devoured a large succulent strawberry.

François and Leah had enjoyed three glorious days and evenings filled with intimacy, lovemaking and soft conversation, all far away from the realities of their lives.

"I have a toast for you, Leah," François spoke finally, smiling endearingly, savoring her every detail. As he held high his glass filled with a mimosa, she reached for hers, and he said, "Leah, I toast you with all my heart to the most beautiful, most wonderful woman in the world. And as my father taught me, *y'slemley al wish*, 'may God save your face for me.' Some romantics interpret it as 'May the last thing I see on earth be your face.'"

"That's beautiful, François. Isn't that Arabic?"

"Yes, darling, it is. There are many terms of endearment that are a part of the Arab culture. It's a terrible shame that the Western world and Israelis don't learn more about the Arab culture. It's beautiful."

"I do know a lot of Arabic words, but I've never heard that phrase. You are right though, François, it is true that few, if any, Israeli Jews even know an Arab or have even met one. We don't mix and we don't speak with each other. It's dreadful," she added sadly. "We just call each other names…and not very nice names either."

"Both sides are to blame, Leah. But you know, there are many Jews living and working in peace in Lebanon…and Syria too. I have many Jewish friends, and I do business with many all over the Arab world." Then, after a brief second, he added, "I hope the issues are resolved in our lifetime because you and I are going to have to figure out a solution for ourselves, aren't we?"

"The past few days proved to me that it is ridiculous for us to be apart. We must find a way to be together, François."

"Likely, we cannot be together in Israel, especially after this war, and I'll have to find a way for us to be together in Lebanon. In fact," he smiled, "I have a surprise for you." He reached into the pocket of his robe and, clutching a green leather packet, extended his hand to hers.

"What is it, François?"

"It's a Lebanese passport, my love. With this we can be together. As Leah Chalhoub, you can enter Lebanon easily and if you want to travel in the Arab world, you can, by using this."

"What makes you think I want to travel in the Arab world without you?" she giggled at her joke.

"Not without me, you idiot!" he laughed.

Teasingly, she asked, "Where do you want to take me, young man? And what naughty intentions do you have with me? Are you going to seduce me in all twenty-two Arab countries, you fiend?" She laughed the laugh he loved and had missed for so long.

"First, I think you should spend a few days with me in Beirut. You'll love my city. Actually, aside from the beauty of Beirut, its shops, its Corniche, and its mountains, Beirut is a 'state of mind.' It is a place of freedom, of choice, a place where everyone wants the day to be wonderful and full of spirit. Most Beirutis are the happiest people…most of the time. There is a great deal of French influence on the people and their lifestyle. In a way, it's a very large village in its culture. We Lebanese men like to boast: 'We are not fighters! We are lovers!' And life revolves around family, church, and food. Especially food," he chuckled. "The best in the entire Middle East, as you will soon see, my darling."

Feeling mellow and happy, she stepped to the window with her new passport, gazed out over the Seine, and marveled at the views of Paris.

"They say Beirut is the 'Paris of the Middle East.' Is that true, François?"

"Oh yes, Leah. It has the same culture, tastes, and joie d'vivre among its citizens as in Paris. The women excel in their couture as in Paris and are quite continental. You'll enjoy Beirut, I am sure! And we'll be together!"

"I can't wait!" She smiled demurely as she opened her arms, beckoning him, her robe slipping off her lovely shoulders. "Come to me, François."

"Gladly," he smiled, as she led him to their bed.

With their bags packed, they prepared for a new adventure, including Leah's first time in Lebanon. They strode through the hotel lobby, following the bell cap pushing their luggage on the wagon; François searched the area with his eyes, looking for the two unidentified men, hoping they weren't there.

"Stop," he ordered suddenly in a loud whisper, "Dammit!"

"What is it?"

"Follow me into the shop, Leah," he whispered, urgently clutching her elbow.

They blended with other tourists while searching the newspaper racks for a copy of the *International Herald Tribune* and *Le Figaro*, the Parisian newspaper. He pulled her aside while looking at the paper rack and murmured, "I think we are being watched again, Leah. Maybe even followed."

"Who? Where?" she quickly asked, casually looking through the glass window into the lobby.

"There." He gestured toward the two men he had seen earlier as they feigned reading newspapers, trying to be as unobtrusive as possible. "Do you recognize them?"

"Yes, I believe I have seen them before."

"As do I, Leah. As do I. I believe I saw them in Malta. Are they from your embassy?"

"Yes, I think I saw them at the embassy when I reported in and acknowledged I would have a ten-day leave before starting my duties there. Yes, come to think of it, they seemed too interested in me. They are not part of the cultural attaché's section where I will work."

"Hmmm, that's very interesting," he mused. "Perhaps it's nothing," he shrugged his shoulders, ever the optimist.

"Perhaps," she added, wondering. "But it does seem strange they would be here."

"We must be careful from now on."

As they flew on Lebanon's Mideast Airlines from Orly Airport in Paris to Beirut, François used the seven-hour flight time to prepare Leah for her introduction to a nation very different than Israel, a smaller nation by one-half, of just more than three million persons of many religious sects. What was common to the two states was that they were both very complicated politically.

"We have Sunni and Shiite Muslims, Druze, and Christians of various persuasions," he explained in detail. Maronite Christians are one-third of the ruling sector, as the President of Lebanon must always be a Maronite Christian. The Prime Minister must always be a Sunni Muslim, and the Speaker of the Parliament is always a Shiite Muslim. We have Roman Catholic, Antiochan Orthodox, which is my father's church, Melkite, an Eastern Orthodox ritual, yet aligned with Rome, Greek Orthodox, and several Western churches like Methodist, the church that established AUB, the American University of Beirut, where I studied before my mother took me to Paris and the Sorbonne."

"We also have a vibrant nightlife and lots of young people of all persuasions strolling the streets until the early hours of the morning."

"We have that in Tel Aviv too," Leah interjected, "but not in Jerusalem. It's very religious there. The Orthodox influence Jerusalem with stringent rules, especially regarding the Sabbath and social behavior."

François said later, looking at his wristwatch, "Leah, it looks like we are less than an hour from Beirut, and I'd like to bring you up to date on our views of the recent, although very short, war. We in Lebanon have a history of not invading anyone, as you know, but since the Israeli-Palestinian war of the late 1940s, like Syria and Jordan, we have huge numbers of destitute and angry Palestinians in refugee camps, and they still mourn the loss of their lands.

"You know," he added, "eighty percent of all Palestinians living in Palestine were forced to become homeless, jobless refugees living on pennies a day from the United Nations Relief Fund. Eighty percent," he added for emphasis. "It's a tragic and shameful situation, and although twenty percent of Palestine were Christian, the bulk are Muslim. And so, of course, they remain emotionally aligned with the nations of the Arab/Muslim world. As a result, Lebanon is pulled into the Arab-Israeli vice. Think about that, Leah, eighty percent are now refugees!"

"I understand what you are telling me, François, and yet, once I joined a kibbutz after I left Paris, like many Jews, I was committed to building a homeland for us within Palestine. I thought we could all live side by side in peace."

"Yes, Leah, I know. The problem is, the indigenous population viewed the huge influx of Europeans, Jews or not, as another 'Western Invasion,' which the Western world calls the Crusades. During those brutal two hundred years, hundreds of thousands of residents were slaughtered by the invaders, and in that case, some nine hundred years ago, the invaders were Christians. And now, the European invaders and land grabbers are Jews. That is, Zionists. Do you see what I'm trying to tell you? That is why when Israel attacked Egypt, because of Nasser's closing of the Strait which he undertook to take Israel's pressure off Syria, its ally, Muslims throughout the region, including those within Lebanon, insisted loudly and angrily that Lebanon must attack Israel in support of Egypt, Syria, and Jordan. It was only because the Christians, our President Helou, and calm heads prevailed that Lebanon stayed out, just as we did during the 1956 crisis."

"I'm very glad you did, my love, because General Moshe Dayan and his warrior allies needed only the slightest provocation to attack and invade Lebanon just after they invaded the Sinai, Gaza, the Golan and Jordan."

"But there are a few issues I'm still confused about, Leah. Maybe you can explain them to me."

"I will if I can, François, I will try, although I am not in their camp. On the contrary, I am with those who oppose Israel's preemptive attacks. What are your questions?" she asked, concerned, while continuing to look at his face, now wearing a frown. "First," she said, "can we have something to drink? Would you like wine? Or a juice or cola?"

"Of course," he replied, relieved with her request.

"Oh, yes," she exclaimed, "you mentioned Israel's attack on the USS Liberty. We were told surveillance planes circled it and thought it was an Egyptian warship about to attack Israeli forces in Gaza, so they sent for fighter jets to warn it to stay away. But when the fighter pilots saw it was American, they returned to their base. Although, as we were told, they were confused and two fighters did shoot a few rounds at the ship before they left the scene. It was all a mistake with not much harm done. At least that's what Israeli Army Radio announced for several days. Why do you ask?" she questioned, wondering why he even brought up the subject that seemed unimportant.

He sipped from his libation, thinking how he best could inform her of all he knew without upsetting her. He hoped to be totally candid now as he leaned closer toward her, their faces very close now, both leaning back against their headrests.

"Well, Leah," he whispered as he leaned toward her, "what I'm about to describe to you is something I learned firsthand. All of what I am going to tell you is true."

He then proceeded with a detailed description of all he learned from Lebanese intelligence, from President Helou himself, from the Americans aboard the Liberty, and from the tapes of recorded conversations he heard between the Israeli pilots and their headquarters, during which the pilots repeatedly announced that it was indeed an American ship.

She was astounded! "Is this really true, François?" she begged. "There were actually thirty-four Americans killed? And eight hundred and twenty-one bullet holes? All of that is true? My God, François!"

"Yes, my dear, it is all true I am very sad to say. The United States, Spanish, German, Israeli, and Lebanese governments recorded the Israeli conversations and all know these details."

"And the Israeli people do not! I hate that, François! I hate that we are not told the truth! Most Israelis I know would resent this terribly!"

For the remainder of the flight, François changed the tone of their conversation to more pleasant subjects by describing his Beirut, his Lebanon, and his legacy.

"I'm very happy to live in Beirut, the land of my father and his ancestors. My father's ancestors, according to legend, arrived in Mount Lebanon in 350 B.C. Imagine, Leah, twenty-five years before Alexander the Great conquered the city-state of Tyre. The Lebanese way of life is in my blood, and I want you to share it with me. So, prepare yourself for a different kind of society than you've ever experienced. At least," he added with a seductive wink, "at least, since Paris."

"Oh, François, I have waited so long for this day," she whispered as she slipped her arm through his and gripped his hand. He leaned into her and, placing his lips on hers, tenderly kissed her.

And When Love Speaks to you, believe in Him.
    Kahlil Gibran

CHAPTER 14

Leah's Arrival in Beirut

That afternoon, as the flight approached Beirut, descending southeastward over the eastern Mediterranean Sea, François reached across Leah to point out the window. "There," he exclaimed, "is Beirut. On the point of the land. Jounieh is to the north, and with the sun setting behind us, you can see the lights coming on."

"It is a beautiful sight, François," she replied. "I'm anxious to see your city. Beirut has the most wonderful reputation for its cosmopolitan ambience. And the women wear such beautiful clothes. Are they as au courant as the media says?"

"Oh, yes! The Beiruti women love to compete with Paris. And their husbands share in their excitement, jealously showing off their wives in the latest fashions. Actually, those who do are mostly wealthy Christians, predominately Maronites. They aligned with France and keep up with the latest fashions from the designers in Paris. You're going to love Beirut, Leah. We're going to have a wonderful time while we're here. Just you wait!" he laughed, flirtatiously. "Everyone will love you, Leah!" His enthusiasm was growing as they approached.

"Love me? Even when they find out I'm Jewish? And an Israeli?"

He laughed, "We all have Jewish friends. It's the Zionists and the Israeli government we have problems with."

Moments after landing, they were quickly processed through customs and immigration at the South Beirut airport, Leah using her new Lebanese passport for the first time. She was clearly anxious as she handed her passport to the immigration officer. But, as François had instructed her, she smiled demurely. And since she could easily pass for a wealthy Lebanese lady, the officer smiled in return and casually waved them through the gate.

As they arrived at the baggage claim, watching the myriad luggage slide down the stainless steel collection belt, Hanna, François' assistant, rushed up, beaming.

"Your car is waiting, Monsieur DuBois. And I'll take care of your bags. Simply point them out to me."

As François listened to his assistant, he noticed two men surreptitiously standing about ten yards away, hugging close to a stucco column, trying to be unobtrusive as they focused on François and Leah. His mind raced with thoughts and image of danger. Who are those men? He was very concerned, but he didn't want her to sense that concern.

At the curb, François spoke hurriedly to Hanna in a whisper. "To the Phoenicia, Hanna, and keep a sharp eye out for anyone who seems to be following us."

"Sir?" Hanna asked incredulously.

"Yes, Hanna. I'll explain in detail later. I'm sure it's nothing, but be aware of the two men quickly stepping into the taxi behind us. They could cause trouble, although I don't think they'll do anything tonight."

"Yes, sir. I see them. I'll be alert."

"What is it, François?" Leah asked anxiously, turning to him.

"Nothing, I suppose." He shrugged his shoulders as eyes turned to the rear, his brow furrowed from concern. "On the other hand, could it be your Mossad keeping an eye on us? Do they think you are a spy, Leah? Or perhaps me?"

After a moment of thought, he continued, insisting, "We are not going to live in fear, Leah. Tonight we will enjoy the fruits of the most exciting city in the Middle East, if not of the world!"

"I can't wait, my darling." She moved toward him lovingly. "Tonight is our night…our first together in Beirut, and I too do not fear those people." Her voice reflected her resolute attitude.

That evening and for several days and evenings, François introduced Leah to his friends, Beirut's milieu and its culture, a joie de vivre unlike anywhere in the Middle East, or even Europe.

Ensconced in the fabulous Phoenicia on their first night, they dined in the five-star hotel's superb restaurant. Later, François had them driven to the Casino du Liban, nestled in the hills overlooking Jounieh and the sea, just north of Beirut. The lights of the city flickered spectacularly below. Amongst the elite of Lebanon, they stood elbow to elbow with many successful Lebanese businessmen and their companions. They spoke with those from oil-rich Nigeria where Lebanese have lived and succeeded, many believe, as long ago as four thousand years when the Phoenicians first settled there. Nigeria's capital, Lagos, is home to a large population of Lebanese businessmen and traders who, with their families, consider themselves Lebanese-Nigerians, as they have lived there for generations. Yet, like many, they never lost their loyalty to Lebanon, and return often to partake of the Lebanese way of life. Similarly, others from Brazil, Chile, the Caribbean, and the Gulf states of Dubai, Abu Dhabi and Kuwait also return as often as possible. Most quickly found their way to Casino du Liban, Beirut's answer to Las Vegas and Monte Carlo.

"There is something very magnetic about Beirut, Leah. Everyone keeps coming back. Most regularly send funds to their families here. And many have built or bought large and gracious summer houses here, especially in the North.

Douma too has had many of its emigrants return to do the same."

"Having spent only hours here, François, I can already understand why they keep coming back. It is a magnet!" Leah exclaimed with enthusiasm she hadn't felt in months. "The people here are so hospitable, so friendly…everyone has been gracious. And the shows here are fabulous! In Paris, they say your casino compares easily with Paris' Crazy Horse Saloon! I love it and I love you so much for bringing me here. After learning only a bit of Lebanon's way of life from Israeli media, I see a dramatic contrast. I mean, you have to come here to actually understand Lebanon and Beirut."

"That is why, Leah, we Lebanese must maintain stability despite Israel's wars with the Arab world. Lebanon is a unique microcosm of the Middle East in that it seeks to maintain a Western culture and alliance with the West, balancing the sectarian alliances emanating from the various religious factions who too often devote their allegiances to their religious constituencies rather than to Lebanon as a state. Some say it's a continuation of the tribal histories of the region. Tribes have been the basic governing forms here for centuries and centuries, from the Canaanites, Phoenicians, Bedouin Arabs, and the Israelites. Even Israel today is essentially a tribal nation. It was only after World War I that these artificial states' boundaries were even formed created by England and France, employing a European concept.

"But enough of this, my love, let's try the tables in the casino and have ome fun!"

"Let's, François! I feel lucky, very lucky!" She grabbed his hand as he led her through the crowded rooms. Many along the way acknowledged François. "Good evening, Monsieur DuBois…*Ahlen*, François." "*Mahrharbah*," responded the man at the end of her other arm. Proudly, she let go of his hand and slipped her arm through his as they regally moved toward the gaming tables. Leah was still a statuesque beauty, her walk more like a glide; her long, dark flowing hair tumbled onto her bare, muscular sleeveless shoulders. She resembled many of the elegant Lebanese women nearby.

She noticed that the casino was full of Lebanese men in tuxedo with beautiful Lebanese women on their arms, women dressed in the latest Paris fashions and dripping with fabulous jewelry, their hair and nails reflecting immaculate care.

"My, François, you could have your pick of so many beautiful women here. Why do you continue wanting me?"

"Leah, that's a question you, of all people, should never have to ask. It's because I love you. And I take loving you very seriously." He smiled tenderly at her.

"Even if I'm an Israeli?"

"Yes, Leah," he smiled, and then added with enthusiasm, "There's so much I want to show you. In a few days, we will drive south, near Israel, to Sidon and Tyre, those ancient city-states that still have remnants of Alexander's adventures there. And later, we'll visit the remaining cedar tree forests in the north near Douma,

Ehden, and Bsharre. It's very mountainous there with fabulous views." Pausing, he added, "I want you to see…to feel Lebanon. All of it! Maybe I can convince you to want to become a Lebanese!"

"Maybe," she teased, "I do want to see and feel the land of your father."

"If we have time, maybe we'll even venture into Syria. How would you like to shop in the three thousand year old *souk* in Damascus? And maybe visit the ancient Roman oasis city of Palmyra in the eastern Syrian Desert?"

"Really? Can we do that, François? Syria? Even after Israel invaded the Golan?"

"Why not, Leah?" he asked with his hands open, smiling. "You are with me, and you have a valid Lebanese passport. And everyone defers to a beautiful woman," he laughed, trying to lighten her concerns. "But for now, let's have some fun before we return to the Phoenicia. Then we can be alone!"

"Yes, that's what I'm looking forward to tonight, François…when you win your first million," she giggled playfully. They stepped to the craps table and began to play.

Without cares, the two wondrously enjoyed their evening in the casino and, later, in other ways, in their suite.

The next morning, François left Leah at the hotel and went to his office. For four hours, he focused on the needs of his clients, Credit Suisse communiqués, and phone calls from around the Middle East.

Hanna welcomed his employer as he arrived at the offices with a list of demands on his time that would keep François busy for most of the day.

"The President would like you to attend a symposium in Tyre, called by the provincial representatives, to address the current crisis. He would like you to go there today, meet with the attendees, and report to him your summary and recommendations. There, also, is a list of your clients who have been eager to speak with you."

François, smiling, replied, "It never slows down, does it, Hanna?"

"No, sir." Then, Hanna's voice and focus changed as he asked, "Are you sure it's safe to drive to Soor…Tyre?"

"*Shookrun.* Thank you, Hanna," François replied, without lifting his eyes from the paperwork on his desk that he was reading. "Tell the President I'm on my way. I assume it will be at the AUB branch there in Tyre, and that I'll try to return by late tomorrow or the following day at the latest."

Then, after a moment, "Hanna, with regard to my father's project, I've compiled a list of individuals. I need you to arrange a first, exploratory meeting here next week. Set it up. Midweek. On second thought, make it at 10 a.m. on Thursday. Thursdays are the least booked days. Moslems take off Friday and ten o'clock allows us to flow into a luncheon meeting here if necessary."

"Yes, sir. I'll take care of it. Would you like me to drive you to Tyre, sir?"

François had a problem believing he could actually be in danger. *I've been a banker for eighteen years without any danger, so I'll be fine.* He replied aloud, "Actually, I need you here. I'll drive myself this time, Hanna."

"Are you certain, sir? After those two men followed us to the Phoenicia Hotel on your arrival, aren't you taking a risk without a bodyguard?"

Hanna's question reminded François that, indeed, he was involved in two risky ventures: his furtive trip to Malta to question the American sailors, and his relationship with Leah, especially so soon after Israel's invasion.

"Hmmm, perhaps you are right, Hanna. Get me my pistol, and have a loaded shotgun placed in my car. I'll be very careful. I'll call you from Saida (Sidon). We still don't know who those two men are, do we?"

Hanna faced François with a worried look on his face. "Please, sir. Please reconsider, and be careful." Hanna was quite concerned for his employer's safety. "The south is not a safe place these days since Israel declared war on the Arab world. They might even yet attack south Lebanon!"

"I can't disagree with you, Hanna, but the President directs and I must be in Soor as soon as possible. I will be among allies there. They know I'm seeking funds to improve the lives of those in the south. Stay here. However, do those things I ask and have listed, including the cedar project, and be available for my calls. I'll see you tomorrow afternoon."

And off he went to the Phoenicia to pick up Leah and drive her to visit Sidon and Tyre, just a few miles from the Israeli border and an hour's drive south along the coast.

As they pulled out of the parking area, François could not help but notice the black Mercedes-Benz sedan pull out after them. He didn't want to alert Leah just yet because he wanted her to enjoy the trip. Besides, he still didn't know who the occupants were in this mysterious car, but he had to be very alert and aware of their actions.

As they drove south on the coastal highway, past Beirut's international airport, François kept watching for the Mercedes. Sometimes it stealthily dropped back, allowing another automobile to get between them, and sometimes they stayed close.

As they drove beyond the city, they saw miles and miles of banana farms along the east side and later also on the west side of the main highway. To the right they could enjoy viewing the beautiful waters of the Mediterranean Sea.

"Oh look, François!" Leah exclaimed as she pointed. "You Lebanese grow bananas too! Isn't that something?!"

"Yes, Leah, bananas are among our largest exports…mainly to the Gulf States. Now look there," he pointed." See all the greenhouses? That's where they grow tomatoes, parsley, and onions for our national dish, *tabouleh*!"

"And I thought we were the ones who turned the desert green!" she replied with her unique sense of humor.

"Not quite, Leah," he grinned knowingly. "The Fertile Crescent has been the breadbasket of the Mediterranean since Alexander. Lebanon's Bekaa Valley was a major food producer for the entire eastern Roman Empire. I'll take you there. Also, unlike Israel, we have all the water we need. We receive so much snow, and the rivers of snowmelt are absorbed by our uniquely porous mountains. We don't..." François stopped speaking, interrupted by something he saw in the rearview mirror.

They had become too relaxed and distracted as they drove for about forty miles.

Neither had noticed the rapid movement of the black Mercedes as it quickly accelerated toward the rear end of their car.

"We have company, Leah!" François said abruptly, then quickly shifted gears as he sped up.

Suddenly, both felt their bodies jerk as the Mercedes struck their rear bumper too hard to be accidental.

"Damn! Who are those guys?" François blurted as his eyes went to the rear view mirror. "Get down, Leah, get down. They're going to hit us again. Dammit!" He gripped the steering wheel tightly with both hands as he prepared for more jolts.

He looked at both sides of the road for a safe pullover if it came to that.

"They're pulling alongside! Leah, grab the shotgun and be ready to use it."

"My God, François! Who are they?" She was stunned and frightened.

"I'm not sure, but certainly they are not our friends! I'm already going twenty miles over the speed limit. They must be those strangers who have been following us! Quickly, Leah! Show the shotgun...they're pulling alongside. Hurry!"

"Here, François..." she blurted out nervously, "take the shotgun and stick it out the window...I'll take the wheel. Maybe that will scare them off."

"If so, it will only be temporary. But we'll be entering Sidon in less than three minutes. We can get help there."

"But we don't have three minutes! Here they come!" she screamed, now terrified, as the speedometer edged toward eighty miles per hour.

"I see their faces," he said as he quickly looked to his left. "They are not Lebanese. And they are not Arabs." Now he was angry and frightened.

She focused on the car's occupants. "They must be the Mossad, François. They are so sinister! Oh, I am so, so sorry! Itzak is crazier than I thought! And so damned paranoid!" Leah grew more nervous, and screamed, "I hate him! I hate them!"

"They are almost alongside of us!"

"So very close!"

Seconds seemed like long minutes. They were becoming easy targets.

Beads of sweat formed on François' forehead.

"Too close. I could touch their car!"

Closer and closer they came to the driver's side. As they pulled up nearly even with François' car, the passenger in the front raised a gun and aimed at François. He heard two shots…Pop! Pop!…and felt both bullets scream by his head as he ducked. Instinctively, François abruptly hit his brakes, sending the other car far ahead and out of range of the pistol.

Bang! Bang! They heard more shots.

"Idiots! Bastards!" Leah yelled, shaking her fist at the car ahead.

"*Y'uhdadeen*! Curse your country!" François yelled, his lips tightened.

But the second shots weren't from the car just ahead of them.

François quickly shifted his eyes to the rear view mirror and saw another black Mercedes speeding very close behind them. He was astonished to see his assistant, Hanna, driving the car with Mohammed, François' bodyguard, in the passenger seat holding a large pistol out the window and firing shots at the first Mercedes.

Because François was slowing down rapidly, Hanna pulled alongside. He and Mohammed smiled and nodded as they quickly accelerated in pursuit of the two agents ahead.

By now, the cars were approaching Sidon, having left the relatively remote seaside farming district where the passengers in the first car had hoped to finish their attack, turn around to return Beirut, and then disappear. Now, they were forced to continue to Sidon. While it is a fair-sized city, its streets were not as easy to hide within as the complex labyrinth of Beirut's south side.

They were all still driving very fast, heading south. François, remembering he needed to be alert in Tyre for meetings, briefly pulled off the seaside highway, leaving Hanna to pursue the other car. He had to catch his breath, and they both needed to calm down.

But the attackers were clever and turned off to the east, away from the highway and the sea. They drove into the nearby banana farm, bumping too fast along the dirt farm road, their heads jerking around as they bounced along trying to escape from Hanna.

As Hanna turned left into the banana farm, he was greeted by two farmers pointing to the trees on the left. Just then, the first Mercedes emerged from the trees, driving directly toward Hanna's car.

"Lookout, Mohammed! They're going to ram us! Get the shotgun!"

"I'll do my best, Hanna," Mohammed quickly responded as he reached for the loaded twelve gauge shotgun and aimed it out the window directly at the driver's head. He pulled the trigger.

Boom! The shotgun's retort was as loud as its powerful recoil. But his aim was not accurate because the car hit a deep pothole in the dirt road just as he shot the gun. Pellets struck the windshield, but missed the occupants.

"Dammit!" Hanna yelled as he swerved to avoid the oncoming Mercedes that sped by. Hanna hit the brakes and, with a great deal of effort and too much time, turned his car completely around. When he did, he looked ahead and watched the Mercedes disappear to the south toward Tyre.

François went directly into the offices of the Provincial Director in Sidon and described what had happened. Without being aware of Hanna's chase into the banana farm, he told him he was continuing to Tyre for the conference and to be on the lookout for the Mercedes that was chasing them.

Most of southern Lebanon was now home predominately to Palestinian refugees and Shiite Muslims, and while already overburdened by abject poverty in the refugee camps, they were currently being overwhelmed by even more refugees escaping from Palestine's West Bank region and Gaza, now occupied by Israeli forces. Angry at Israel, the people wanted to know: "What did we do to the Israelis to deserve their invasion and taking of our land?" Now, even prosperous doctors, teachers, businessmen and engineers from these areas faced poverty and received little assistance from anyone. The more successful businessmen and their families left for Cyprus or Athens as soon as possible to work and live until conditions improved so they could return to their homes. They all believed that soon the world would require the Israelis to withdraw from their homes and lands and they would return. The poor settled in the shanties of the nearby refugee camps. Fielding those valid and urgent questions was the purpose of the conference, and no one, including François, had satisfactory answers. Among the purposes of François' visit to Tyre was to evaluate the situation and depth of anger of the region for his president with his recommendations.

They enjoyed a delicious fresh fish lunch at François' favorite seaside restaurant in Sidon, overlooking the ancient stone fortress just offshore built in 325 BCE by Alexander the Great. Concern about their attackers slowly ebbed from their thoughts as they became more relaxed while dining.

"Leah," François laughed, with a cynical smile," isn't it amazing that you and I are dining in Alexander's headquarters built so long ago." He laughed out loud with a bit of angst in his voice. "Today it is where the local chapter of Rotary International meets for lunch every Wednesday at noon. What irony." Then he added, "And look at the peaceful people fishing along the shore over there. Sidon lives on fish, you know. It has since this city was a city-state under the Phoenicians. I always find incredible contradictions that amaze me. So much has happened to this region over so many millennia!"

"You are right, darling," Leah responded. "If you read about the Crusades…"

"Western Invasion," François interjected.

"...you find that tens of thousands died here in Sidon, Tyre, and Acre in northern Israel! So much history common to all of us."

"Leah, these countries of Palestine, Gaza, and Lebanon are so small that if one was attacked and occupied, then all of them were, whether by the Egyptians, Persians, Greeks, Assyrians, or the Romans. What an abundantly rich history! And still, these lands continued to rebuild and thrive after the occupiers left. When they were under the Ottomans, these provinces of Lebanon, Palestine, Jordan and Gaza were all part of Greater Syria.

"Now, Leah, we must resume our drive south and refocus on our arrival in Tyre."

"Do you think we'll be safe in Tyre?"

"We'll see. We'll see."

He will win who knows when to fight and when not to fight.
Sun Tzu

Chapter 15

Tyre

As François guided his car into the city of Tyre, he began describing to Leah the remarkable Roman ruins still obvious throughout the ancient city. His pride in his heritage, and awareness of the history and character of Tyre, inspired him to think back to the Phoenician city-state some 4,000 years earlier.

"Tyre was the capital of Phoenicia, and is attributed with discovery of the color purple, Leah, which became a valuable product the early Phoenicians marketed throughout the world as it was known at the time. Actually, early Phoenicians not only traveled throughout the Mediterranean out from Tyre, but from Sidon and Byblos as well. In Africa they created the settlement of Carthage, now called Tunis. They traded with the Etruscans in Italy and the early French in Marseille. Historians even found abundant evidence of their reaching and trading in Britain, which they called the 'Land of Tin,' and even as far as the Baltics. Quite an amazing fact since that took place before the time Moses and the Israelite tribes left Egypt and first arrived in Canaan! At the time, all of Phoenicia was covered in forests of ancient cedar trees that still live today, more than 4000 thousands of years old."

Continuing his story as he pulled the car to the side of the road, he proudly told her about the plausible legend that the Phoenicians of Tyre, commissioned by Egypt's Pharaoh in 2,650 B.C., circumvented the Egyptian empire, which they came to believe was all of Africa, and returned from the west through Gibraltar, having begun at the Red Sea on Africa's eastern seaboard.

"Leah, we are taught that they felt it necessary to find friendly lands for future Phoenicians to migrate to and establish trade settlements in the event that Phoenicia became invaded and occupied, or suffer famine or some other disaster. They traveled with seeds and grapevine plant cuttings, which they would plant when they landed at attractive locations, that is, locations with good soil and water. Only after they could harvest the food would they move on, repeating the same process time and again. That is why they didn't succumb to our latter day illnesses, like scurvy and beriberi. And that's why they would be at sea for years and years.

"Their ships, carefully built with their own workable cedar wood, actually carried as much cargo as the Spanish and Portuguese galleons of the sixteenth century, four thousand years later. It's an amazing legacy, one that transcends the sectarian differences within Lebanon. It is a history that binds us all together. Extraordinary, don't you think?"

François pulled back onto the road and drove slowly down the highway. He focused on the Palestinian refugee camps on his left with their meager shelters; sewage stained alleys, trash-filled fields, sheet metal roofs, block and stone walls of horribly poor housing and pointed to them. "There, Leah, there you can see these trapped Palestinian refugees whose lands, homes, and businesses were taken during *Al Nakbah*, the catastrophe of the Zionist takeover of Palestine. Poor souls, they have so little, yet they were not poor before. They prospered…until Israel. The young ones feel very angry, desperate, and are easy targets for the radicals and extremists wanting revenge, demanding rights to their homeland. Lebanon has absorbed hundreds of thousands of them. But we are not able to feed and house so many. They now account for nearly twenty percent of our population, with so many more pouring in since the takeover of Golan, Gaza and the West Bank. Our government is deeply concerned and is caught in the middle. It's the same with Syria, Jordan, and Iraq. We all are bearing the burden of the creation and expansion of Israel."

François wanted Leah to understand Lebanon's dilemma since most of the refugees were Muslim, and while many Christians were also fleeing, the refugees were establishing and expanding villages in southern Lebanon. Clearly, the dominant population was Muslim, mostly Shiia. François felt his discourse prepared Leah for what she would hear later at the conference.

"Lebanon is a fascinating, amazing place, isn't it, François?" Leah asked. "During the 1940s, just twenty years ago, Christians were the predominant citizens of Lebanon…"

"That's true, Leah, but two factors reversed that situation. First, as a result of *Al Nakbah*, hundreds of thousands of Muslims stormed into Jordan and Lebanon. Many also went to Syria. Our open culture, much like the West, accepted them freely. Lebanon does not have a large army or border police, and while the officers have been mostly Christian, most of the soldiers are Muslim and would not attack fellow Muslims. So, the army, small as it is, is even less effective.

On top of that, the Shiia Muslims propagate at a much faster rate than do Christians or Jews for that matter. So, during the past twenty plus years, most newborns in Lebanon are Muslim, predominately Shiia. Yet, we do have, and have had for many years, a significant population of Jews in Lebanon, mostly in West Beirut neighborhoods. It's called 'The Jewish Quarter,' like in Jerusalem and even in Damascus."

"You mean like the Warsaw Ghetto, François?"

"No, not like the Warsaw Ghetto. They choose to live in West Beirut because it's very free there, almost Bohemian, with many Lebanese intellectuals and

Armenians as well. In fact, the Mossad, which infiltrates much of Lebanon seeking intelligence, has a headquarters in West Beirut."

"Do you think those two men who shot at us are from the Jewish Quarter?"

"I would say they are. Perhaps your friend, Itzak, contacted several Mossad stations, including Paris and Beirut. Maybe even Rome and Damascus too! Who knows?"

"You think so?" she asked incredulously.

"Very likely, Leah," he shrugged.

"Where can we go that is free of them, François?" she asked with a worried frown growing across her face.

"We'll have to be more careful, I think, and will have to maintain our protection and vigilance. Those guys mean serious business, and the Mossad usually has large numbers on each team. What did you do to Itzak to make him want to kill us? Or at least scare us?"

"I did nothing, François," she cried. "We've known each other in the kibbutz for years. I knew he liked me very much, but he grew angry with me when I would not yield to his advances. Then, as we grew apart and he became enamored of the anti-Arab hardliners, while I sought a peaceful life side by side with Arabs, especially the Christians, he accused me of not being Jewish enough. He even called me anti-Zionist! A *freier*! A bastard!"

"So he thinks you and I may be conspiring against Israel?"

"It seems so. And, I guess he has become convinced he can never have me. His jealousy has consumed him."

"That is a very dangerous combination." François frowned, firming his lips, better understanding that they were up against a man whose mind had become irrational and gone to the extreme. The worst state of mind; vengeful, jealous, and threatened.

François, now very concerned, suggested, "Maybe he wants me dead because you love me, not him. And he has become paranoid, believing that you and I and the non-Jewish world are anti-Zionist and anti-Jewish."

"It seems so, François."

"Maybe we have to send him a message. To most in the Arab world, extreme Zionists are the problem, not Jewish people."

"What? How?"

"We'll see what we can do. Those two tried to kill us, Leah!" he almost shouted, angrily. "If it hadn't been for my colleague, Hanna, following us with my bodyguard, I fear they may have succeeded."

"Succeeded in killing us? You and me?"

"I'm convinced now, more than ever, Leah."

"So what shall we do? My love, what can we do?" she pleaded, worriedly.

He became silent, thinking, then pulled their car back on the main road and drove into Tyre. They both remained quiet, lost in their thoughts, not knowing what to say as they tried to understand their predicament, potential consequences and plans of action.

As he pulled into the parking area where the conference was being convened, Leah said suddenly, "Look! There are the two black Mercedes parked there on the side of the street in front of the cultural center."

"That's where we're going, Leah."

She realized, now that they had arrived, she would certainly be the only Jew at the conference, and likely the only woman. Nervously, she moved closer to François and clung to his arm.

He pulled the car to the side and parked opposite the center. In just a moment, he recognized Hanna and Mohammed standing by their car. They aimed their pistols at the two men who shot at François and Leah. There was a crowd of men surrounding the two cars and the four men. The growing crowd appeared to be anxiously moving around, talking with each other, occasionally gesturing at the two men who were the only ones with fair skin and not wearing facial hair. It was much like a group of people gaping for better looks at an accident. These sorts of exciting, unusual events always draw crowds. In this case, especially, because many men were momentarily attending the conference to vent their anger at Israel.

Hanna watched as François and Leah stepped away from their car. "Monsieur DuBois, over here!" he gestured, then stepped to the side while keeping his pistol aimed at the two men. He signaled a second security guard to take his place.

"Monsieur DuBois, these two men are the ones Mohammed and I followed… the ones who were tailing you. Even as you left our building, they were right behind you. I hope you don't mind my deciding to follow you and them, sir."

"No, Hanna, of course not. On the contrary, I am very grateful to you. Perhaps I was too confident that I was not that important for assassins to follow me. But they did shoot at me and the mademoiselle did they not?"

"Yes, sir, and how sad it would be, if I say so with your permission, that they might injure or kill such a beautiful woman."

"And what about me, Hanna?" he laughed. "What about your employer?"

"I'm glad to have you confirm your eyesight and your excellent taste in beauty." François smiled warmly, then leaned to Hanna and whispered, "She truly is beautiful, is she not?"

"Let us go to her now, Hanna. I think she's a bit nervous. We'll both stay close by so she'll feel safe."

They stepped toward François' car where Leah was nervously waiting. "Are those the men who tried to kill us, François?" He nodded yes in response.

"Mamzers! Suckers!" she swore angrily. "And Itzak is a mamzer!" she repeated in Hebrew.

"Sir, we are certain these are the two men because we verified their car's tag number, and it's from the Jewish Quarter," explained Hanna. "We are convinced they are Mossad agents. They each carried four passports: Lebanese, Israeli, USA, and France, and Desert Eagle pistols with silencers, exactly what the Mossad uses. Then, as we questioned them further, they even proudly admitted they were Mossad agents! They sneered, challenging us to do something. They believe they cannot be arrested or jailed. They say they are properly part of the Israeli diplomatic delegation."

"Everyone is aware the Mossad has a headquarter in Beirut, Hanna, but these people in Tyre, mostly displaced from their homes and not permitted to return, are not as genial toward Israel as Beirutis, are they?" asked François.

"No, sir, they are different here in the south. They are very upset with these two. And they want vengeance."

"Give me a few minutes while I speak to the imam and Sheikh Abouzi. They may have some thoughts."

The crowds of young men wearing mustaches grew in numbers and became louder and angrier after word leaked out these were Mossad agents who tried to kill François DuBois, the South's best friend in the Beirut government.

Hanna saw that things could get out of hand if the crowd were left to have its way.

"Mohammed, stay here while I go get Monsieur DuBois. He will know what to do with these two." He sneered as he waved the pistol toward the agents who were still leaning against their car with their hands on the roof of the car, legs spread wide.

Hanna looked to the front door of the cultural center as François emerged with the turbaned, robed imam and the sheikh. François gestured for Hanna to come to them for a small conference.

"You are absolutely sure, Hanna, that these are the two who sought to kill our dear friend, François DuBois, and his companion?"

"Yes, I am, imam."

"And," Sheikh Abouzi asked," you are certain they are agents of the Mossad?"

"Yes, sir, I am."

The sheikh motioned toward a large mustached man standing near the crowd and called out to him," Die La hawn. Come here, Ibrahim."

"Yes, sir?"

"You already know from Hanna and Mohammed who these intruders are and that they attempted to murder Monsieur DuBois and his companion outside Saida?"

"Yes, sir. Hanna and I spoke of this matter."

"Then, Ibrahim," the sheikh said with a slight gesture of his right hand, "take care of them so no one will know."

With a nod of respect, Mohammed replied firmly, "Yes, sir. *B'amrak*, as you command."

Mohammed gave a slight nod to his superior, turned, and went back to the two agents, knowing exactly what had to be done.

"Now, Monsieur DuBois, I believe it is time to begin our conference inside. Please come with us, dear friend. Your problems are now ours. Your trip should be more pleasant from this moment," he whispered with a knowing smile. "Let us now have tea while we discuss the recent events by our cousins to the south. *Y'hara deen bladuk*! Curse their country!"

François, touching the sheikh's arm, spoke, "My companion may also have been the target of the Mossad agents. She too was nearly shot and killed in my automobile. With your permission, I would like to invite her to join us."

"Very well, dear friend. As you wish. The imam and I will wait for you both. Please bring her inside."

*You can be sure of succeeding in your attacks if
you only hold positions that cannot be attacked.*
Sun Tzu

Chapter 16

Tyre Emergency Conference

The conference, attended by over eighty men, mostly residents of South Lebanon, included municipal leaders, imams of the local mosques, and several local businessmen. François DuBois, acting on his president's request, would listen rather than speak. He wanted to hear what local leaders and residents were feeling, what they expected of the government, and what their views were on the Israeli attacks and the responses of the Arab world, the U.N., and the West.

Leah was understandably anxious about being at this conference. The almost palpable presence of deep anger filled the room. She sensed this rage at the people of Israel, and it made her very nervous. But she was with François, and while his presence was comforting, she was still afraid of being the only Israeli…the only Jew in the room. By itself, that fact was unsettling.

Leah glanced around the room, not making any eye contact, stood next to François who was to be seated to the right side of the sheikh; the imam was on the sheikh's left side.

"Francois," Leah nervously commented, "I feel like an outsider. Do you really want me to be part of this? I have no idea what we're getting into. Will I be safe here?"

"We are here only to listen, Leah. I will not be speaking, and you will not be asked to speak. These people are very respectful and while they'll welcome us, they are frightened, nervous and feel humiliated. Just stay close to me. We'll be fine."

"Oh, I won't be leaving your side. Not an inch," she smiled nervously, "I'm frightened too. Don't you dare leave me."

Leah looked around the room at the attendees' faces, avoiding eye contact, with her arm tightening through Francois' arm.

"Francois, look at their eyes. There is a lot of anger and frustration all over their faces."

Francois leaned to one and asked, "Please tell me your feelings, sir, your opinion and what you think Lebanon should do?"

"Monsieur Dubois, you are a friend, but I must tell you, I am completely embarrassed at such a sudden defeat of the Arab armies! I feel deep humiliation. I have never been so angry at the Arab leaders! I cannot believe the Israelis will ever stop taking our lands. But what can we do? We are at war against America. And France and Israel. We are so weak. I do not know of anything tiny Lebanon can do. Our army is so small. Lebanon therefore must stay out of this war. We would be destroyed by the Israelis. I cannot even look my children in the eye, Monsieur Dubois. I am so depressed!"

François asked a few other of the attendees how they felt and was told in no uncertain terms how they had lost faith in the leaders of Syria, Jordan, and Egypt.

"Mohamed!" Francois called to a familiar face. "Tell me what you are feeling and what, if anything you think Lebanon should do now."

"The Arab leaders are so stupid! They make so many mistakes! How can they say they represent us? I don't want them to represent us in Palestine. Egypt and Syria keep getting airplanes arms and tanks from the Soviets, but they are powerless against the Americans' planes and rockets."

Some described their leaders as despots and not very bright.

"I have mixed emotions about Lebanon's non-action, although I recognize Lebanon's weak and vulnerable position," one told Francois. "I just want to do something. Anything! I feel so bad!"

Most attendees desperately needed to speak their minds to someone on the current issues and vent these gnawing emotions that stripped them of their pride and created an overwhelming sense of impotence. One attendee, clearly successful by his attire, in his dishdasheh, gown, iqal, headdress and abayeh, his cloak over his shoulders stepped to Francois, nodded respect to Leah and angrily asked, "Monsieur, I understand you are here for the President. What is Lebanon going to do? Are the politicians going to attack Israel in support of our brothers? Surely we aren't going to put our tails between our legs like beaten dogs and hide, are we? I am so angry at those Israelis and the Americans, who supply them, but I feel sour in my stomach, like I've been punched by criminals. These feelings of pain from humiliation are an insult to our sense of goodwill and justice. Where is God in all this?"

Turning to his companion, he whispered with a gesture, "Leah, we had better get ready for the meeting. I have gotten an earful from these people, but there will be more of the same. Let's be ready to sit and listen. It's not going to be pleasant, I must warn you."

The conference was held in a large, square room, about one hundred feet on a side with a high ceiling, the cement floor customarily completely covered in myriad oriental carpets. Because the cultural center was in Tyre and not in Beirut, the high walls were plain, painted white and barren save for the large framed photograph of President Helou hanging high over the head of the sheikh. Behind the Sheikh were two draped flags: the larger, unfurled one was the distinctive flag of Lebanon with its prominent, iconic cedar tree; the second flag represented the American University in Beirut, under whose auspices the conference was being held.

As is custom in the Arab world, all individuals sat in chairs backed up against all four walls so that all were equals, and each could see other's faces and expressions. None sat behind anyone. Seat locations were always based on the attendee's importance, with the most coveted seats next to the sheikh and imam, descending in importance as chairs stretched farther away to the end of each row. Other leaders sat against the center of the other three walls.

They awaited the sheikh's opening statement that would bring order and silence to officially begin the conference. While waiting, the attendees held private, agitated conversations with their neighbors. As their passions grew, so did their voices as they gesticulated with their hands for emphasis. Some were almost shouting at each other.

As it began to get nearly raucous, the sheikh, an extraordinarily respected leader of the Tyre community, looked around the room, listening and seeking eye contact with each attendee. He introduced Francois and his companion with deference, reflecting his importance to the meeting representing President Helou. He used his capable calculation of finding just the right moment to acknowledge that it was time for the conversations to quiet down.

He leaned to François and whispered, "We will begin now, dear friend. I hope you will receive a clear message from Tyre's citizens about what they are feeling Remember, Tyre is the nearest large city to Israel. These people are worried about Israel's next attack."

"I am certain of that, sir. My friend and I are here to listen and learn. As a wise man once said, 'In his infinite wisdom, God gave us two ears and one mouth.'"

Leah leaned slightly toward François having heard the whispered conversation and nodded her head in support of him, grateful she would not be expected to speak.

"I am nervous, François. Please be my guide."

The sheikh sensed the effect of his eye-contact with the attendees as he noticed the room had grown quiet, but he could feel the anger and tension in the air.

Choosing the right moment to begin, he arose from his chair and announced, "*Ahlen*! *Ahlen*! Welcome and thank you for coming. We will begin our conference momentarily, after a word from our imam and his plea to *Allah* for guidance and truth."

After the imam's invocation, the sheikh spoke again. "We will, as is our culture, allow time for everyone here to speak his mind. Be respectful of the others, no personal attacks, and please restrain yourselves and keep the shouting to a minimum so all can be heard. You all know Monsieur François DuBois who is here at the request of President Helou, together with his lovely colleague. Be courteous. There are over eighty of us here and everyone must have the opportunity to speak if that is what they wish."

Then, the sheikh described the recent events and their impact on the people of South Lebanon and, of course, the Palestinian homelands of the West Bank and Gaza and, the Palestinians in the refugee camps near Tyre.

Continuing, he added, "While we in Lebanon have been relatively safe from the onslaught of the Western-armed Israeli forces, we all have families who are now refugees, repeating the Diaspora of our Palestinian brothers that occurred during *Al Nakbah*, the great disaster of 1947 and 1948. Lebanon, Syria, Iraq, and Jordan are now temporary homes of most of nearly eighty percent, eighty percent, Monsieur Dubois!" he repeated for emphasis, "of the 1945 Palestinian population, a terrible impact on all our lives. Israel is heavily armed, apparently intends to take even more land from the Arabs, and, it seems, has the full support of the West, especially our friends in France and America, which of course is very difficult for us to understand."

After a few minutes, he concluded by saying, "What are we to do? And now, let us allow each to be heard, beginning with Adeeb Bustani seated to the left of the imam."

Adeeb stood and quickly nodded his head to the sheikh, grateful for the opportunity to speak his mind.

"You all know me as a modest man. I am a farmer with olive trees, a few date palms, and a beautiful family of two sons, one daughter and my wife Amal. I do not want war. I want peace. I love my family, my neighbors, and my country. But I am so angry at the Israelis! I do not want them here. They are different. They are pushing, pushing, pushing. They want everything their way. I have cousins in Nablus. I fear that the Israelis will take their olive groves and their homes. They never stop! But what can we do? We have no arms to stop them! But they must be stopped. "

The next man, a Palestinian refugee, sitting to his left, stood, nodded in respect to the sheikh, and began. "Thanks be to God and the Lebanese for their welcome and accepting us. However, my family has been here in South Lebanon living in horrible conditions for too many years. We have been refugees for twenty years! Before then, we were prosperous, never hungry, and never begged for help… even for food for our children. Like you, we are proud people. All my children are educated. For generations, my family had wonderful homes in Jaffa. For four hundred years we lived in peace with the Jews and the Christians. We had very large orange groves. Our Jaffa oranges have been the sweetest in all the world for generations. And now, the Israeli squatters…not settlers…took our homes, our groves, our offices, and our shops. All those Europeans! My family waits for the day we can return. We hate living like this."

Then, catching his breath as he looked around the room at faces he did not recognize, he continued, "When the United Nations speaks of us leaving so the Jews can have all of Palestine, they blame our Arab cousins for not taking us in.

But we want to return to our own homes.

"Can't they understand? We want our family homes back! Our ancestors are buried there. Our hearts are still there. Why can the Jews have a 'right to return' but we cannot? Why can't the world see how we are so badly treated? What did we do to deserve this? We did not cause the Holocaust in Europe! The Europeans did! The West did nothing to save the Jews. Now they do nothing to save us. Why? How, I ask, can we stop this injustice? We need help desperately." Then he broached the subject many wished to support: "Maybe we need to form our own militia here in the South Lebanon."

His face contorted from the deep pain he felt, tears overflowing onto his cheeks, as he asked, "How can we believe Israel won't come and take the Litani River with its vast supply of water? We must be prepared!" He had unknowingly planted a seed, an acorn, which would grow into a mighty oak.

As the opportunity to speak continued, voices grew louder with anxiety and anger blended with the disgusting sense of impotence which raised the level of bile in their stomachs.

Another angry young man stood and began his statement: "My cousin Abdullah lives in Cairo. He works at the Egyptian Air Force base that was attacked by surprise that first morning. He called and told me it was a grim reminder of the premeditated surprise attack by the Japanese on Pearl Harbor on Sunday, December 7, 1941 when the Japanese pre-emptively sought to wipe out the United States Pacific Navy. They, too, destroyed America's aircraft on the runways. Thousands of young men and women were killed. Defenseless, they never had a chance. President Roosevelt himself called it 'A date which will live in infamy.'"

Then stopping to settle himself, he wiped his face with his handkerchief, then spoke again even louder. "This too is a day of infamy. *Al Nakbah*: a new catastrophe for our people. It is not over either. The Israelis want our land…all of it. They now occupy Gaza, the West Bank, East Jerusalem, our quarter! and have even begun sending 'squatters' to the Golan! Beautiful Kineitra, a lovely Syrian farming village, has been attacked and brutalized. Its citizens have fled, and, already, Israelis are taking over the vineyards, the olive groves, and the farms."

"Just as they took over our orange groves in Jaffa," interrupted the man who had spoken earlier, shaking his fist.

"Surely, America will not stand for Israel to break every international law, every Geneva Convention. Surely the international governments won't stand for this!" he cried out with great passion.

"I wish you were correct, but, *Y'eini*," replied another, "I fear no one will make Israel abide by the same rules the rest of the world lives by. They already have atomic bombs, don't they? They have never signed the Nuclear Non-proliferation Agreement. Obviously they have their own set of rules."

"And so must we," yelled another. "We must create our own militia. Palestinians in the West Bank and Gaza need our support and the support of the entire Arab world! They are the best educated people in the Middle East...they have so many intellectuals! They have more college degrees, more masters degrees, and more Ph.D.'s than even those in Israel. The Palestinians provide all the technocrats throughout the Arab world. They will not be able to sit still. Some will leave to avoid Israeli jails, others will work elsewhere, and, I fear, many, especially the angry young men, will stay and fight the Israelis."

"With what? Slingshots?" asked another, sarcastically.

"All will be lost unless the world does something."

"We need action!" yelled several others.

"They have taken the West Bank and Gaza when unarmed Palestinians did nothing. Now, we only seek to return to our homes. I ask you, why would the Israelis stop there?"

"They even attacked Syrian forces on the Golan after Israel and Syria accepted the United Nations ceasefire! Why not just come and take South Lebanon!"

"That one-eyed Moshe Dayan is a butcher! He wants the entire Arab world only for Zionists! They are not 'God's Chosen People' as they claim. They are greedy, arrogant and demanding. For centuries we all lived side by side in peace. There were Christian villages, Jewish villages, and Muslim villages. We all got along fine. We were friends. The Sephardic Jews were kind and wonderful. We all did business together and helped each other during the harvest season. We were happy. But then hundreds of thousands Ashkenazi from Europe came in with different languages, different cultures, and different attitudes. They hated us immediately because we lived where they wanted to be...as if they had a right to whatever they wanted."

"How can those people from Poland, Romania, Russia, Germany, and Hungary have more rights to our homes and farmlands than we do?" asked another.

"We must join together before they take everything!"

Shouts of agreement rung out, while others shouted against the idea of Lebanon fighting Israel.

"We are not strong!"

"We are weak, and it hurts so bad!"

"But we must then become strong!"

"Maybe we should seek help from Syria!"

"Maybe we should support the new Fatah-led Palestinian Liberation Organization, the PLO. Although it is just three years old, Yasir Arafat wants to liberate Palestine for the Palestinians."

"I agree," shouted another. "I am Christian. My family still lives in Ramallah, a beautiful city. Like Bethlehem and Nazareth, it was a total Christian city. We got along fine with the nearby Jewish people, just as we did with the Muslims."

"But they were Jews, peaceful people, not Zionists. Zionists want all of Palestine! No matter if someone has roots and rights."

"And their gangs will kill anyone in their way."

"This truly is not a centuries-old problem. This conflict is only seventy years old. It is a twentieth century conflict," interjected a young university student.

"The Phoenicians, our ancestors, sailed from Byblos, Tyre and Sidon long before Moses crossed the Red Sea."

"And Damascus was a thriving city at the same time!"

"They may take our lands, our homes, and our groves, but they cannot take our history!"

After two hours of continuous demands and grievances passionately voiced by all attendees, the sheikh arose from his chair. His eyes slowly circled the room as he gathered his thoughts.

"I will say a few words before closing this meeting, but before I do, I will ask the imam to share his thoughts with us." The imam nodded then leaned forward.

"Here is my view," the imam said in his soft, strong voice after he stood before the gathering, his arms outstretched. "Have you wondered what would be happening if, as we believe, the West also believed it was Ishmael, Abraham's eldest son, not Isaac, that our ancestor Abraham was to sacrifice? Things today would be very different. What the Israelis, I mean the Zionists, have done reflects badly on them. They have ignored the Laws of God. They have done this many, many times ever since they left Egypt with Moses. How many times have they broken their covenants with God? As Muslims and Christians, we have all studied the Jewish Scriptures. God did indeed choose the Israelites with His love and His laws. Because they followed Him above all other gods. *Allah*, God wanted them to be a light unto all nations by showing that the one living God loves us unconditionally and will never leave us. However, we are all made in His image, not only Jews. All of us are His people, children of Abraham, Jews, Christians, and Muslims. We are all equal in his eyes."

The imam paused, then continued in an even voice, "*Allah* insisted that the Israelites and all people must live under His laws of justice, love and kindness. We must also care for the needy, the less fortunate. The prophets Mohammed and Jesus proved that when you love God with all your heart and soul, you will always live with God. But the actions of the Zionists these days are not following God's insistence on love and justice. What is just in their wanton killings? Yet," he added as he looked again at the faces of the attendees, making eye contact with Francois and Leah, reflecting his warmth and friendship, "I must add that as your imam of our Muslim faith of peace, and as we are all servants of God, we must seek peace if we can. Here is my proposal: If the Israelis will immediately withdraw from our lands that they have now conquered, then we must extend our open hands to negotiate a peace. But," he firmly enunciated, "if they do not, then the infidels must be driven from our lands, our farms, our orchards, our groves, and our homes. And they must recompense those who have been injured or displaced or whose family members have been killed."

After a moment of silence, waiting for his words to be digested, he added, "That is all I have to say at this time. We cannot sit still. We must do something!"

The attendees stood as one, and raising their arms voiced their agreement. "If they leave, we seek peace. If they do not, we must support our Palestinian brothers in their fight to regain their lands. *Inshallah*! Be it the will of God!"

After they all took their seats, the sheikh rose again and nodded to the imam. Then, acknowledging François and Leah, spoke to the group. He stood and cleared his throat as the group gave him their full attention.

"We must be clear and we must understand the Israelis as best we can. We all know the Jewish people have suffered terribly over the centuries…not here, but in Europe and in Russia. In fact, we all know that during the two hundred years of what the West calls the Crusades, and what we call the Western Invasion, it was the Muslims who protected and defended our Jewish cousins from the invading European Christians. From those days, even until the Zionists began arriving in the early years of this century, just under seventy years ago, we lived side by side in peace, as was noted earlier by our young university student. We had our own villages and we traded with each other."

He stopped for his next statement to be absorbed, and then added, "I have studied this human calamity, and as difficult as it may be to understand, strangely, there is a strong similarity of the Israelis to the Chinese. Both have been severely beaten, defeated and abused by the Western powers for hundreds of years. As a people, each has been deeply humiliated. They appeared weak to all the world. And whether they speak of this or not, they use their past suffering for political gain so that they may attain a moral authority. As distinct people, they have been insulted, segregated, and, as we know, were almost totally eliminated by the Nazis in what they call the Holocaust. The Chinese were soundly defeated by the English, and then by the Japanese. The Chinese have not defeated anyone during the past 400 years."

As he looked around at the somber faces, his eyes fell on Leah. She was nodding in agreement. François noticed her eyes well up with tears and felt her arm slip through his for comfort.

"We know the Ottomans tried to eliminate the Armenian people in 1915. They too had their Holocaust. Nearly a million were killed. But what the Israelis and the Chinese have done is to exploit their suffering to achieve that so-called moral superiority, thereby creating a guilt complex in the West, especially in that kind and uniquely generous United States. Both also, and in my opinion, are mining their people's past sufferings to serve their political goals. This is wrong! Yet, they have been very successful. Both of those nations are very strong today as a result.

The Palestinian people surely can and should qualify for a moral authority and seek worldwide redress, sympathy and assistance. Perhaps we should learn from the Israelis. For now, the Palestinians appear weak. Islam appears weak as the

European Zionists aggressively take our lands, remove our culture, and destroy our religion. It is not right. It is not God's will. We must find the ways to stop this aggression. We must be strong," he nearly shouted in conclusion.

Turning to François, he said, "We know, dear friend, that Lebanon is a very small country and cannot do much. But it must support the Palestinians. Lebanon's government needs to pay more attention to us here in the south. Our conditions worsen every day as we absorb more and more refugees. We need so much aid! We need jobs for our young people. Help us. Lebanon must seek worldwide support for a Palestinian homeland. Surely they deserve a homeland if the Jewish people deserve one. Even if the Palestinians get only the West Bank, only one-fifth of what was Palestine in 1946! It is time. Now I must ask: What if Israel is not stopped now?"

Then he turned and addressed the attendees again. "I am certain our friend Monsieur DuBois will leave here with his ears full and will convey our anger and frustration to President Helou."

The sheikh stood for a moment, raised his hands, and beckoned to the imam for a closing prayer.

"*Shookrun*, dear friend. Thank you."

Leah loved François as he loved her and what she had experienced with him in Lebanon. And he knew she loved Israel. She had devoted twenty years of her life to building a homeland for herself and for the Jewish people. She believed it could be a Jewish homeland that would indeed be "a light unto the nations," fulfilling God's wish, and a homeland for the Palestinian people. But as she listened to the terrible stories of what her nation was doing to these simple, poor people who happened not to be Jewish, she became angry as well, for her goals were no longer consistent with the goals of most of Israel's Jews, especially her government.

She asked herself, Why did we allow those Zionist right-wingers, those anti-Arab extremists to do this?

Her uneasiness and guilt grew to the point where she desperately wanted to leave the room. But she knew that was impossible. She understood though that something needed to be done in the days to come to bring both of these peoples together.

As Leah, a dedicated Israeli Jew, listened to this venting of pain, helplessness and anger toward Israel and its aggressive displacement of so many, she became surprisingly empathetic. "Those damn Arabs and Palestinians," as degradingly labeled by Itzak, had suddenly become human beings, people with families and children, people who only wanted the right to live in freedom and peace.

"Francois," she whispered, "I feel terrible. I am feeling great sympathy and love for these people who speak of justice and peace. Deep in my heart that is all I seek for the Jewish people and the Palestinian people. I have an overwhelming urge to speak, from my heart. Do you think that they would listen to me? Would I be in danger if I did? I want them to know there are many Israelis, Jews like me, who wish to live side by side in peace with Muslims, Christians, all people of God."

"Leah, I know who you are, and how you feel. These people are outraged, but they need some sense that someone outside their tribes empathizes with them. They feel so isolated, so alone and helpless. If you speak to their feelings, then I think you ought to say what is in your heart. You'll be well received by most, although some may not want to hear from an Israeli. I'll ask the Sheikh first."

With the Sheikh's approval, Francois nodded to Leah and squeezed her hand.

With a grateful, but very nervous nod to Francois, then to the Imam and to the sheikh, Leah, standing tall and beautiful, spoke in her soft voice, so soft, everyone went silent and bent toward her, not wanting to miss her comments, wondering "who is this woman?"

As she stood, she reached her hand back to Francois. He lovingly grasped her hand, and to show his support, stood next to her, lending credence to her presence for which she was very grateful, smiling to him as she took a deep breath.

"Gentlemen of Lebanon and Palestine," she began, "I am grateful to be here with you and to hear your voices. I am convinced of your pleas for justice and peace, which is my cause, and I wish to speak to you from my heart." Then, after an anxious moment, gathering her thoughts while seeking eye contact around the room, she continued, "I am a guest. And I am a Jew living in a kibbutz. I am NOT a Zionist, and with many others, I oppose their policies. Palestine belongs to all Palestinians, Muslims, Christians and Jews.

"Dear cousins and friends, although I am an Israeli, and one whose family suffered terribly in Europe at the hands of the Germans who killed both my parents, I too feel your frustration. There are many in Israel who desire peace with our neighbors. We are not yet many, but we are growing. Please try to understand that most Jews are kind and generous. We seek security and safety to live our lives in our ancient homeland with our children. May I say how sorry I am you justifiably feel so abused? None of us should be abused nor stereotyped. Not Jews and not Arabs.

"I wish to somehow use this opportunity to establish a dialogue with you. I pray I can somehow play a role in the future with François to promote a positive dialogue of peace. There is so much more I wish to say, but you have been kind to me, and I promise to double my efforts toward coexistence, justice and peace throughout Palestine."

The entire gathering stood as one when she finished, and rushed to her to shake her hand, one by one warmly kissed both her cheeks.

"Leah, my darling. That was the bravest sight I ever witnessed. You were wonderful! I am so proud of you, and I am certain your words will remain in all their minds each day as we go forward."

She knew François was a man of peace. But what could she and he do to make a difference? How could she do anything without returning to Israel?

> *She could feel herself changing as a result of this extraordinary experience.*
> *And let today embrace the past with remembrance and the future with longing.*
> Kahlil Gibran

Chapter 17

Leaving Tyre

After the conference, François arranged for Hanna to follow him with his armed guard, Mohammed, when they headed north to Beirut. Although François realized the dangers confronting him and Leah, he first wanted to stop and take some time to show her the remarkable Roman ruins, especially those of the Hippodrome of Tyre, which is larger than the Circus Maximus in Rome.

François suggested, as they arrived "Let's not discuss the conference for a while, Leah. I want to give us time together to relax."

Describing the Roman ruins, he began, "The stone grandstand surrounding the oval-shaped track originally had a capacity of fifty thousand, Leah! Imagine! Those Romans were excellent builders and administrators, weren't they?"

"And brutal too, François," replied Leah quickly. "They treated the locals badly and, as you know, they destroyed the temple in Jerusalem."

"That was in the year 70, wasn't it?"

"Yes. That's a date all Jews remember. And as you know as well, remembering is what we Jews do all the time."

François smiled as he responded, "Indeed you do. Maybe we Lebanese should do more of that, but we seem to have a free spirit and focus more on today and tomorrow than we do on yesterday."

"I wish we were more like you Lebanese," Leah replied, now laughing out loud, her tension from the meeting now dissipating. "Do your people ever worry?"

"But yes, most of us worry about a lot of things, but we try not to dwell on our problems. We let our political leaders do all the worrying," he laughed.

While walking through the amazing Hippodrome, Leah was surprised to see two thousand year old relics and pottery shards scattered on the ground.

"How is it these ancient examples of the Roman era remain on these grounds, François? In Israel we devote substantial funds for archeological searches and research. We are very interested in our past. Our museums are full of these kinds of relics. Don't the Lebanese treasure these things?"

"Leah," he replied, "it is true the Israeli government allocates substantial capital to forensic archeological research. And that is good. We do also. The people in this region are so accustomed to these sites and their uncovered examples of Rome and Moslem era specimens. Most here have been so poor for so long that they focus on their survival, their poor excuses for houses, the lack of jobs, and effort to get food. This area has very little tourism because of the constant shelling by the Israeli army. Your country is fortunate that it receives so much wealth from the West to afford those efforts. Soon, we hope, there will be a Palestinian state so most of these refugees can relocate, go back to their homes, and not be such a costly burden for Lebanon. But you are correct. Even in Lebanon, many artifacts are researched and preserved in the museums. These relics you see on top of the ground are simply examples left here for locals to enjoy and sell to a few visitors who rarely just take them as souvenirs."

"It's fascinating," she commented, "that there are so many artifacts all over the place that wouldn't even require any digging. I mean, look here. What are those over there?" she asked as she gestured toward rows of rectangular, stone, open tub-like relics.

He smiled, "Those are Roman sarcophagus. Perhaps I should say sarcophagi, the plural form, since there are so many of them. They remain intact, and I'd guess they've been in those exact places for 2000 years!"

Leah pointed, "There are so many! And over there, look at those fabulous mosaic floors. Some are more than ten feet beneath our feet. Some deeper. How do you explain that? I mean, here they are right out in the open during all kinds of weather. Don't they deteriorate?"

"I suppose they could, surely, from wind, rain, and sunshine, but not much. The Roman ruins have been exactly as you see them since they were first excavated after World War II. The people here are very much aware of their historic value. The children are taught in school about these ruins and are brought here on field trips. They are left open for all to enjoy, to look, and to touch. The local ranger keeps theft to a minimum."

Then, gesturing, he directed her attention to the deepest excavation, a magnificent, colorful mosaic floor. "As you can see, the deeper floors were built here first. We believe those are of a Roman villa or perhaps Greek. Our archeologists believe these you see were built nearly a hundred years before Christ. Beautiful, aren't they? The Romans...especially the wealthy and powerful ones lived very well. They had fountains, beautiful décor, and, as you will see over there, the long rows of Roman colonnades and stone-paved streets. The Romans were amazing builders. Magnificent, isn't it?"

"Yes," she nodded, "the Romans were excellent builders and administrators, but they could be very cruel too. Punishment by crucifixion, for example."

"Yes, Leah, and we are taught how they flogged our savior Jesus Christ before they tortured him on the cross."

"Now look there, François." She pointed to another open pit. "There is another fabulous mosaic floor. But it is just half as deep in the ground as the Roman mosaic. What is that from? It's even more magnificent than the first, deeper mosaic."

"That is from the eighth century, during the Islamic Period. The ceramic tile work is exquisite. They loved art, didn't they?"

"Sadly," Leah replied, "with all the anti-Arab attitude in Israel, it is too bad the art and architecture of the Islamic people is so little known or appreciated."

"It's true, Leah. Someday we should travel to Granada, Spain and tour Alhambra. It's a magnificent example of the engineering, architecture and artwork of the Moors who were of Arab descent. It is said today that nearly half the people of southern Spain have Arabic blood racing through their veins. The Moors occupied Spain from 711 until the Spanish Christians Isabella and Ferdinand of Aragon drove them out in 1492…over seven hundred years!"

As Leah strolled through the ruins, she found her thoughts returning to the commentaries she witnessed at the conference.

"Take me into a nearby refugee camp, François, so I may see for myself the conditions of the Palestinian refugees," she asked in her soft voice. "It makes me so sad even to think my people could be responsible for their suffering."

A few minutes later, they drove through the nearest camp and observed the crowded shanties, sewage-stained dirt roads, metal corrugated sheds and crude cement blocks for walls, and sheet metal roofs.

They saw no flowers growing.

"It's so sad," she moaned. "It is so awful. What can we do for them?"

"What can we do?" François responded with a touch of anger in his voice. "What can we do, Leah? I'll tell you what you and your fellow Israelis can do! You can stop taking other people's lands, their homes, and their groves. You can stop taking their livelihoods…their self-esteem! If this is Israel's idea of being 'a light unto the nations,' they've got it all wrong!"

François suddenly realized he was yelling at his love, the person dearest to him. He lowered his voice and continued, "I'm sorry, Leah, but if your people truly believe they are following God's will, they've missed the boat. Even we Lebanese Christians study the Torah. God wants us all…Jews, Gentiles, Christians, Muslims, Palestinians…to do two simple things: 'Love Him with all our heart, and love our neighbor as ourselves.' He wants us, as His representatives on Earth, to love, be just, be kind, and help the poor. What's so difficult about that? The Israelites were chosen to carry the good news, to exemplify His love…His unconditional love. But that didn't define being 'chosen' over all other people. And guess what, Leah? When the Israelites didn't obey the covenant, they found themselves in exile…in

Babylon…for more than fifty years. It was Cyrus, a Persian, who freed your people. He was not a Jew, to be sure, but then Israel under Ezra and Nehemiah decided to 'ethnically cleanse' Judah and Israel by breaking up families and exiling all non-Jews…by separating parents from their children, and husbands from wives. And now, the Israeli government is doing the same thing."

François stopped for a moment to calm himself, then concluded by saying, "Leah, isn't that what your government is doing now, yet again? Taking all the land from its neighbors? Expelling non-Jews, Christians and Muslims? Isn't that injustice? Hatred of your neighbor? Is this God's will? No, I don't believe that. Yes, Leah, there is much we can do to help these poor lost souls. We can give them their homes and their land back. That's what we can do. They won't leave here because they insist they will return to their homes one day. That's what keeps them alive, that dream.

"Lebanon is a small country, so we can only do so much. But I do believe we can do more for the refugees, and I will continue to impress that upon President Helou."

"Oh, darling, I feel so badly. I am not proud of what my country has done. I can't stand it!" she cried. He had brought her to tears. She was sobbing now, her shoulders shaking not only from the harsh words François had spoken, words she knew were true, from the pitiful conditions she had just witnessed. Yet she felt helpless as an individual in a nation that was bent on removing all Arabs, and taking the West Bank, Gaza, and the Golan. She felt guilt and sadness and a nurturing sense that she had to do something to help these poor people who had been driven into the slums of refugee camps so that there could be a Jewish state, a place for Jews only, no matter who it hurt.

"I fear what is going to happen, François. If the world turns against Israel, Jews across the world could suffer. And that would be just as wrong."

"I agree, Leah. That would be very wrong. But Israeli forces are acting brutally. They are taking their deep anger and centuries of abuse at the hands of Europe out on the Palestinians, the Arabs. Remember that a large portion of them are indeed Christians."

"Well, François, it was mostly Christians in the name of Jesus Christ who tortured and killed Jews for centuries!"

"Those were not followers of Christ, Leah. They abused Christianity just as Israel today abuses Judaism. It doesn't make Israel's actions acceptable, does it? I don't believe that."

"No. I agree that it doesn't. But to many Israelis, our success this summer has lifted us from a huge burden of fear, humiliation, and a sense of insecurity. Remember, Israel is a tiny country surrounded by Arabs who hate us."

"Yes, Israel is a small country, but still twice the size of Lebanon. And it appears Israeli leaders believe the more land they steal, the safer they will be. It doesn't work that way. Has anyone in Israel ever asked why the Arabs hate them? Well,

I can tell you that this Six Day War...the brutal Israeli version of Pearl Harbor... the taking of more Palestinian land, the last twenty percent of original Palestine... has fomented a lot...and I mean a lot...of hatred. If your extremists, like Moshe Dayan, believe they have won security and peace, they either are very wrong or very stupid! There will never be a peace in this region without a Palestinian homeland, Leah. Never! Jewish children will be taught to hate all Arabs. And Arab children will be taught to hate all Jews. That's a terrible legacy!"

A bit contrite, he reached out to Leah whom he began to realize had become his representative of the Israeli government, which was surely unfair. He wrapped his arm around her shoulder and turned her unhappy face toward his.

"Leah, I am so sorry you have borne the brunt of my anger, my frustrations. But I will tell you this; Lebanon does not want to be a part of Israel's wars. We want to be left alone in peace. But all these refugees in southern Lebanon are a melting pot of anger, helplessness, and empathy for their fellow Arabs. They will rise up to fight Israel with sticks if they must. They know that they cannot win a war with Israel, but they are left with few options now. Syria, Jordan and Egypt offered treaties for peace with Israel within four days of Israel's attacks. But Israel rejected their offers. Syria agreed to the United Nations ceasefire as did Israel, before Moshe Dayan invaded the Golan. How can you have peace with people like him and his cohorts?"

After they left the refugee camp, François decided to completely change the atmosphere between the two of them. He drove Leah into Tyre, then up in the hills just outside the city.

"Where are we now, François?" Leah asked, still sad and wiping tears from her cheeks. She had been hurt deeply by François' words. She had never seen this side of him. But she also realized that passions of everyone ran deep in the Middle East, especially since the war of 1947-48, *Al Nakbah*.

"I'm taking you to a holy place, Leah. We're going to Cana."

"Cana is in Lebanon?" she asked, surprised.

François smiled. "Leah, we Lebanese, like your people, believe everything of importance is in our country. Actually, Cana, where Jesus performed his first miracle, is indeed here near Tyre. After all, we are in northern Galilee." François showed her the spot where legend says the wedding reception of Jesus' mother Mary's cousin was married, where Jesus performed his first miracle, changing water into wine."

"This is exciting," Leah exclaimed, feeling better now that the political discourse had ended...at least for now.

"Jesus actually came to Tyre more than once, didn't he, François?"

"I believe that is true." Then, pointing, he said, "Look there at that cave in the side of the mountain, Leah. They say that Jesus and his apostles slept there. And over there, carved into the stone of the mountain, are the faces of all the apostles. This is also near where Jesus later met the Syro-Phoenician woman, a non-Jew, who told Jesus that even the dogs got to eat the crumbs beneath the table! Then Jesus blessed her. Christians believe that was among the first times Jesus began including Gentiles in his work."

"That is amazing, François. Well, Jesus was a Jew," she added, laughing, as if saying "gotcha."

"So were all twelve of the apostles," He laughed too, and countered, "If Jesus had been born here in Cana he would have been a Lebanese Jew!"

She laughed and replied, "There you go again, Mr. Lebanese. We'd better head back to Beirut. We're both getting ridiculous!"

As they passed the Roman ruins on their right, Leah turned to François and asked, "What if you and I lived here two thousand years ago as Romans. Would we have been lovers then, do you think?"

"Of course," he quickly replied. "It doesn't matter where we might have lived, my darling, or when. We certainly would have been lovers. Actually, maybe we were lovers thousands of years ago. And I think I'll prove that to you when we get back to Beirut."

"You are a beast, but I do love you, François."

After they returned to the conference center to collect Hanna and Mohammed, who would trail them back to Beirut, they began the drive north with the magnificent blue waters of the Mediterranean Sea to their left, sparkling like millions of diamonds, reflecting the bright sun in the clear sky beginning its descent for the day.

Leah was more relaxed now than she had been since she woke up that morning. "Isn't the sea beautiful?"

"Yes, Leah, and see the beautiful date palm grove to your right? That means we are very close to the Litani River. Lebanon has so much water, Leah. My European clients are surprised when I tell them we even go duck hunting in the Bekaa Valley. The lakes are beautiful there. The Litani water comes from the valley and flows into the Mediterranean near here. The Zionists covet the water of the Litani. Back when European powers established the boundaries in 1929, the Zionists lobbied hard that the Palestine-Lebanon border actually be the Litani River. It was France's influence that kept the river wholly in Lebanon."

"Lebanon truly is blessed, isn't it, François? I believe even Moses coveted Phoenicia. I mean, he and his people were supposedly delivered to this land of milk and honey."

"And that's when all the fighting began. Luckily for us, all the Phoenicians were out at sea," he laughed.

"And, it seems, today is no different, is it?"

Any man who ignores his heritage has no heritage.
Danny Thomas

Chapter 18

Baalbek

François glanced in his rear view mirror and relaxed as he verified Hanna and Mohammed were close behind. They drove the thirty minutes north to Sidon without any concern, then on to Beirut. As they approached the city, François asked Leah, "How would you like to see the Bekaa Valley? We can spend the night in Zahle. It's a lovely city. You will like it."

He signaled Hanna and, at the turnoff near the Beirut airport, turned east and drove up the mountain, part of the Mount Lebanon mountain range that separates the coastal plateau from the lush Bekaa Valley. At the crest, he pulled over and stopped so Leah could view the valley below.

"Oh look, François," she exclaimed, "look how green the valley is! It's beautiful!"

"Leah, you are looking at Lebanon's central valley that eventually connects to the south with the Jordan Valley in Palestine."

"The Jordan Valley is now in Israel," she softly corrected with a proud smile. "It is where I lived for the past twenty years. We grow bananas, mangoes, and citrus there. It is so prolific there now."

"That's right, you've been a real farmer there near the Sea of Galilee, haven't you, Leah? Quite a change from a city girl in Warsaw and Paris," he quipped in good humor.

She smiled and answered, "Well, as much a farmer as a city girl from Warsaw, Poland can be, my dear!"

"Speaking of that, can you still be safe in Israel? I mean, will Itzak and his Mossad friends leave you alone?"

"Well, I really hope so, but I'm not sure anymore. That's why I relocated to Paris ... at least for the time being." After a moment, she added, "I really don't know what the future holds for me...for us."

"We can discuss the future later, Leah. For now, I think we will be safe in Zahle. Also, Hanna and Mohammed followed us, so we should be fine."

"I don't like the feeling we are going to be under surveillance all the time. That's no way for us to live, is it?"

After they checked into the Araby Hotel in Zahle near the Baroudi River, they ventured out on foot, safely followed by Hanna and Mohammed. They finally chose a delightful outdoor restaurant at the same hotel at the foot of the mountain where snowmelt water flows freely, rushing down a small man made channel that actually runs through the restaurant alongside the table where they were seated.

"I love this place!" she exclaimed. "Look at the crystal clear water going right by our table! I can actually touch the water. It's very cold!"

"That's snowmelt from the mountain top. Enjoy it, Leah, enjoy my country. Zahle is the major marketplace for Bekaa Valley products. In this part of the valley, they have enormous vineyards, vegetables, lettuce, and warmer weather foods. To the north they grow wheat, walnuts, and cooler weather fruits, like apples and cherries. It's a miracle valley. To the south are the lakes where we fish. Our large man-made Lake Qaraaoun was built in 1959. We dammed the Litani River, and, now, it is a resort and bird sanctuary that especially attracts migratory birds flying from Africa to Europe. We go duck hunting there sometimes," he boasted with a smile.

"Duck hunting in Lebanon? That's something!"

"And over there," he gestured to the east, "are the Syrian mountains. The crest of the Syrian mountains is the meandering Syrian border with Lebanon. Lebanon is only about thirty miles wide in some places. The two mountain ranges protect the valley and, at the same time, create the perfect conditions that hold the moisture from the sea and provide the best farming temperatures, rain, and sunshine. We believe it's God's way of making Phoenicia, and now Lebanon, so bountiful and pleasant at the same time."

Then, gesturing toward the nearby vineyards, he added, "Legend tells us we have been producing marketable wines here since 1,850 years before Jesus. Imagine!"

"Well, it all looks beautiful to me, François. I'm glad you brought us here. I love to watch nature at work."

After dinner, they strolled along the quite safe streets of Zahle. Later, as they both grew tired, they returned to their hotel room, completely exhausted.

"Ahhh! What a day!" Leah exclaimed, as she flopped onto the bed, smiling.

Lying side by side, very comfortable now, they continued their conversation with enthusiasm.

"We covered a lot of territory in many ways today, Leah. Tomorrow it will be easier. We'll drive north, up the valley, and visit the town of Baalbek and the Roman ruins there. The Roman Theater and the Roman temples of Jupiter and Bacchus are almost intact. They are amazing. You'll love them!"

"Baalbek?" she asked. "Oh yes, the Canaanites lived here and worshipped the god Baal when the Israelites arrived."

"That was about 1,200 years before Christ, right?"

"Yes. And thanks to Moses and the Israelites, soon all people in the region began to worship one living God."

"True, Leah, very true. Over the centuries, even Cyrus of Persia became a monotheist. But it took the arrival of Jesus to convert the Gentiles and Romans to monotheism and, ultimately, to Christianity. Lebanon became the first region outside Palestine to become Christian. It was Peter and Paul who spread the Word to the Gentiles all across the Mediterranean."

"And then Mohammed came forth with Islam and the Koran in the seventh century."

"True," she added. "It's important that everyone remember that both Christians and Muslims believe in the same God of Abraham, Isaac, and Jacob, the living God of love and peace. So, both are successors to Judaism."

"That's not a problem, although in some quarters, biased sectarian attitudes raise their ugly heads, proclaiming their religion is the only correct one over all the others."

"And that's where the problems and arguments begin." They both laughed at the ironies.

"Yet, more Arabs, mostly Muslims and also Christians, especially in Palestine, are convinced all was well between the three monotheistic peoples until the surge of Zionism that began in the late nineteenth century, when thousands of Europeans began to move into Palestine. It got really difficult after the Europeans went to war in the 1930s, and hundreds of thousands came to Palestine from all over Europe after the war."

"You can understand that, can't you, François? After what Hitler and the Russians before him did to the Jews? They, like me, dared not remain in Europe to suffer at the hands of those who, abusing their religion, sought to wipe out all Jews. We had to seek a haven of safety."

"But, Leah, that does not mean everyone but Jews must leave! And now, those very Jews who were run out of their homes in Europe because they were Jews are now forcing Christians and Muslims out of their homes because they are not Jews!

"Isn't it strange, Leah, how you and I can be alone and so close, make love, converse for hours, dine in excellent restaurants, tour a beautiful country, and still, I regret, find ourselves discussing what divides us rather than what unites us? Let's change that."

"You are right, François. Let's make a pact to avoid those issues. Okay?"

"Yes! Let's stay away from those subjects as long as we can."

After that long day almost talked out, they gravitated even closer to each other in the plush bed with beautiful head and foot boards, exhibiting exquisite detail in the heavily embossed hand-tooled and heavily grained wood.

"Leah, these wonderful beds are made in Beirut shops, but the carved end boards come from the north, probably Douma."

"You told me that the woodcraftsmen of Douma were sent to Jerusalem in 930 B.C. to build our first temple with Solomon. Hmmm, I wonder if there are current descendants in Douma from those craftsmen."

"Enough of history, François. Come here and make love with me," she giggled happily.

Afterward, as they silently drifted off to sleep together in their reflections of the day, Leah's head resting on Francois' shoulder, she gently rubbed his chest lightly, and fell asleep, feeling safe with the warmth of her love's body close against her. Both of them were relaxed, at peace, and very happy to be together. Yet, subconsciously, the war had clearly made their lives together more difficult and problematic.

Leah awoke first, slipped into a soft terrycloth hotel robe, and stepped out onto their balcony to view the valley at sunrise. The street was deserted. Leah curled up on a lounge chair and watched the sun rise slowly over the crest of the Syrian mountains. The golden glow and glorious rays caressed her lovely face. That's when she began to hear the morning calls to prayer broadcast from the nearby mosque minarets.

François and Leah spent the next day enjoying the bucolic Bekaa Valley…first walking through rows of vineyards, clutching large bunches of maturing grapes hanging from rich thick green vines, and then driving north to see more of the prolific abundance of the Bekaa.

They stopped along the way and visited with farmers, François translating Leah's questions into Arabic.

"Who lives in those odd dark tents?" Leah asked, pointing across the road.

The grizzled farmer responded, "Those are Bedouin tents. We're able to grow all the vegetables Lebanon's people need, but when we need help for harvesting, the Bedouins somehow appear at exactly the right time every season. When the harvest is over, they move north and work the farmlands there into the last harvest…until the first frost. Then, it's time for them to return to the south for the winter. It's been like that for ages and ages. Thanks be to *Allah* for them. We couldn't do our work without them."

After their visits with villagers, and customary indulgences in offered tea, juice, or coffee, François, Leah, Hanna, and Mohammed, drove into the ancient town of Baalbek to visit the first century Roman ruins of Heliopolis, the "City of the Sun."

"This city, Leah," François announced proudly, "was one of the most ambitious construction projects in the history of architecture and engineering. The city is located at the juncture of two major trading routes of the region: west to the sea, east to Damascus and south to the Jordan River. It took two hundred years under several Roman emperors to build this, the greatest complex in the Roman world. Imagine, darling."

"And here we are, François, walking the paths of so many others so long, long ago. Isn't it amazing? I must take lots of photographs of these incredible Roman ruins. Baalbek is a lovely town. Are the people here doing well?" she asked.

"This is a farming town, so their prosperity or lack of it depends greatly on the success of the farms nearby. The city provides the shops and services for the farming community. Religiously speaking, today almost everyone here is Shiia Muslim. As such, they are solidly connected to the people we visited yesterday at the conference in Tyre where most are Shiia Muslim too, except for the recent influx of Palestinian Sunnis. They've lived in southern Lebanon since the seventh century, so we are told. And now, they are being overcrowded by Palestinian Sunni, Shiia and Christian refugees, some of whom, mostly Christian, will move on in time. Also, families here live in the same family home of their ancestors. Like in Palestine, families occupy their same homes for many centuries."

"The ruins of Baalbek have always been a dramatic and important destination for tourists in Lebanon. Our tour guide will lead the way for us."

Leah and François, holding hands most of the time, spent a fascinating two hours walking around the ruins, touring, taking photographs and listening to the guide.

He told them, "The marble and granite columns were shipped by barge from Egypt across the sea to Tripoli or Byblos. Then, thousands of laborers, slaves, really, rolled each of these ten thousand pound columns up two mountains of four thousand feet in elevation, and then down the mountain to the valley floor."

"Of course," the guide added, "these large fifteen ton foundation stones and columns had to be precisely placed, as well as the enormous six foot crowns sitting atop those fifteen meter columns."

"Remember," François commented, "this was at least two thousand years ago."

"But, isn't it amazing what you can do with one hundred thousand slaves! Ten thousand slaves for each column!" said the guide, with a smile. "And brilliant engineering, too! This Roman city is like a wonder of the world, and it's here in Lebanon."

Following lunch, and a few more hours of viewing the sites, they began the drive from Baalbek to Beirut. They were relaxed, happy, and a bit tired from walking the uneven stone walkways and climbing the uneven stone steps throughout the magnificent Roman ruins.

François proudly explained to Leah, "In 325, Roman Emperor Constantine became a Christian at age forty and converted the entire Roman Empire to Christianity, following his mother who earlier had become a Christian."

François focused on the road ahead, regularly checking his rearview mirror to confirm Hanna's presence, then continued, "Constantine located his new religious center in…guess where?" He laughed, "In Constantinople…now Istanbul, as the American singer Rosemary Clooney warbles! It was at that time that Emperor Constantine ordered all symbols of Baal be removed from Roman structures in Baalbek."

They were having fun now and, gratefully, had enjoyed a completely relaxed, educational, informative, and pleasant day without any incident.

"This has been wonderful, François. Thank you, darling, for a beautiful day." As she snuggled in the front seat beside him, she whispered, "I love you so much. And I'm falling in love with Lebanon."

François turned his head toward her and smiled, "Hold that thought, we'll be back in Beirut very soon." Turning his thoughts to arriving Beirut, he thought out loud, with a look of concern, "I'm sure we'll find out very soon if the Mossad in Beirut is already aware of the disappearance of their people in Tyre."

> *Standing on the defensive indicates insufficient strength;*
> *Attacking, a Superabundance of strength.*
> Sun Tzu

CHAPTER 19

Beirut

Arriving in Beirut, François drove Leah back to the Phoenicia Hotel, but before he came to a complete stop to drop her off, he suddenly veered the car away from the canopied entrance to the hotel.

"What?" Leah asked abruptly.

"Dammit!" François exclaimed as he recognized another Mossad agent, probably assigned on a rotating, twenty-four hour lookout, anticipating the arrival of François and Leah.

"Why did you do that, François? Why didn't you let me out at the Phoenicia?"

"Why, Leah?" He turned his head and motioned toward the lookout. "See him?" François believed he was one of the agents who had followed him in Malta.

Leah looked to where François motioned. They both watched as the lookout signaled with a wave of his arm and a black, four-door Mercedes quickly pulled up to him. He joined the driver and they quickly drove to a position behind Hanna's Mercedes.

"We'll try to lose them and go to the St. George Hotel. The Mossad has apparently assigned a large team to track us."

François and Leah led a speeding three-car caravan from the Phoenicia, and, in an effort to lose the Mossad agents, he drove quickly throughout the labyrinth of old streets and alleys into the Muslim section of south Beirut, away from west Beirut and the Jewish section. They wound their way back to the St. George Hotel, hopefully, free of the Mossad tail.

Hanna blocked the Mossad's car at a strategic intersection so that François could surreptitiously drop off Leah at the St. George, and escape to his office where he quickly called the hotel and pre-registered her there. It took a very deft and complicated effort, and in time, he succeeded so that Leah was safely checked in under the alias of Milhelm Chalhoub.

"Stay with Madame," Hanna told Mohammed. "I'll return to the office and stay with Monsieur DuBois."

François arrived safely at his office, and then called the president to arrange an appointment.

"How did the conference go, François?" asked President Helou. "Was it fruitful for us?"

"There was a strong turnout, Mr. President, and they were an angry group. The population of South Lebanon is not only angry at Israel, but also with the Syrians and with President Nasser, their supposed advocates. They are hoping someone will do something. The people suffer a deep sense of humiliation at the Arab world for being so inept and defeated so quickly by the Israeli surprise attack. They feel a consuming sense of hopelessness. Despair and fear pervade because they feel so vulnerable to Israel's threats. And while they recognize Lebanon cannot wage war successfully against our neighbor to the south, they are overwhelmed and frustrated with the huge influx of Palestinian refugees from now occupied Gaza and the West Bank. They asked me many times, who is going to stop Israel's appetite for the entire region?"

"It appears Israel is willing to go to war against all confrontation states, including Egypt, Syria, Jordan, and perhaps Lebanon," the president replied, sadly. "They will not be afraid of attacking Iraq and, even Saudi Arabia which, while holding its vast reserves of oil, is very weak militarily. In fact, I think the Israelis have already taken a portion of Saudi Arabia. I think they want that oil."

"These are very dangerous times, Mr. President. It is up to the Arab League, the United Nations, and the two world powers, the United States and the Soviet Union, to bring Israel's ambitions to an immediate halt. The Palestinian refugees are so distraught in the south that they loudly demand significant financial and military aid from the Beiruti government to protect them from further Israeli advances."

"To your credit, François, you have been the Palestinians' most loyal advocate for aid, infrastructure improvements, and funding to assist in absorbing so many refugees in south Lebanon. I applaud you and urge you to continue your efforts. It is so difficult for us to effectively reprioritize our government spending so that the south, which has little Shiia leverage in the Parliament, receives its needed share."

"But we must keep trying, Mr. President," François urged. "I'm afraid if we don't, Lebanon will be facing a powder keg of resentment in the south and they will seek localized solutions to their problems, of which they have many. I fear, Mr. President, south Lebanon could become a fertile ground for angry young men who could give up on the central government, its institutions, and its armed forces. They will demand their own militia, mostly to defend themselves against Israel. And with so many Palestinian refugees now locating in that region, there are bound to be conflicts with the indigenous population. In five years, will south Lebanon be Palestinian or Lebanese? Will it be predominantly Sunni or Shiia? It's not the Christians; they are not increasing in numbers in the south. They are moving elsewhere, mostly to the north, to Crete, Greece and Europe."

François was deeply concerned and passionate about the growing threats to the national government, the integrity of his nation, and the fear of an entire region feeling helpless and angry at everyone, while suffering from hunger, abject poverty, dangerously high unemployment, and lack of basic necessities for a decent life.

"This is a prescription for disaster. I fear some may even press for partitioning Lebanon. Mr. President. We must reach out to our people there before a vacuum draws in those whose best interests are served by discord. These good people are attracted to militants, which will cause Lebanon grievous problems. Please, sir, I urge you to call on the Cabinet and Parliament to seriously address the implications of these issues in south Lebanon."

"Yes, François, I agree with you and will indeed present your case to the cabinet. May I have your written observations and recommendations within two days?"

"Yes, sir, you will have them tomorrow. Consider it done. We haven't much time to act.

"Now to another perspective, François," said President Helou, changing the subject. "Have you any indications how your clientele in the Gulf States are reacting? What I mean is: Do you see any change in their desire to continue visiting us, and investing in and trading with our Lebanese companies?"

"If they do reconsider, your Excellency," François quickly responded to his mentor's worried query, "it could be devastating to Lebanon's economy."

"We must continue then to convey the message loudly and clearly that our financial institutions and society remain rock solid, safe and secure. Beirut must remain aloof from this terrible Israeli-Palestinian conflagration for our own very survival. We do not have the population or weaponry to become militarily involved despite our visceral feelings of anger and demands on us to act."

François was convinced that Lebanon should remain as neutral as possible. Yet he felt the same sense of anger and helplessness as those he witnessed in Tyre. "All we can do is hope Israel does not have immediate designs on our rich resources of water, fertile soil, and our coastline."

"And our strong independent and democratic economy which, thanks to the Lebanese sense of free enterprise, has a strong global financial network that is so successful.

"Israel covets our assets and our secular freedom."

"They successfully took the Golan's snowmelt water resources that fill the Sea of Galilee, and they are so eager to control the Litani River that flows temptingly close to Israel.

"Lebanon's water, its financial strength, and its tourist appeal are coveted by everyone, including Syria, Jordan, and Israel. We must keep this in mind and watch with an improved intelligence apparatus any suspicious moves by the Syrian secret police and the Mossad."

"Especially right here in Beirut, Mr. President. I didn't tell you that Mossad agents attacked my car while I drove to Sidon. I believe, with good reason, they are after me since my fact-finding visit to Malta."

"Oh, my God! Really?" The president, blaming himself for putting his friend in the path of danger, became worried for his safety. "I am very sorry, François. I apparently put you in harm's way. God, I hate what this war has done to us. I think you must lower your profile, François. No more espionage or travel for you for a while. I'm going to arrange security for you."

"*Shookrun.* Thank you again, Mr. President. I appreciate your thoughtfulness, and I hasten to accept your security assistance. My two close associates are not really equipped to deal with espionage experts like the Mossad, although they certainly exceeded their duties in that incident and protected me exceptionally."

"Perhaps it is time for us to expel these 'visitors' from our country. While they may claim diplomatic protection, our relationship with Israel is fraught with danger."

"I agree completely with that proposal, Mr. President. It's time now, if ever, for them to leave Beirut…and, to be sure…all of Lebanon!"

"Along with your other recommendations and observations, I will also pose that to the Cabinet immediately, François. Meanwhile, you had better spend your time at your office, and when not there, do not be alone. Your security detail will join you this afternoon."

"*Shookrun*, Mr. President. We are staying at the St. George Hotel for the moment. I don't feel safe at my own residence these days. I'm certain the Mossad knows where I live."

"François, go back to your work and be safe my friend, be safe."

"Hanna! Come in please!" François called to his assistant as he sat at his desk.

"Yes, sir," Hanna quickly replied as he appeared at François' door with pad and pencil in hand, ready for François' needs.

François updated Hanna on President Helou's offer of security, bringing a smile of relief and gratitude on Hanna's face.

"That's very good news, sir. I think you'll feel safer as a result. But may I say, both Mohammed and I considered it our privilege to watch over you these past days. In a way it was our means of doing something in service to Lebanon while our neighbor to the south attacks everyone within reach. We will always be available to you, sir, should you once again need our help."

"And what is Mohammed doing now?"

"Mohammed is stationed outside Madame DuBois' room at the hotel. Tomorrow night I plan to be at the police firing range, refining my capabilities with my pistols and rifles that I have not used in some time. I want to be ready since I believe we will be called on again…perhaps sooner than later."

"Later, I hope," François laughed. "Much later is my desire. President Helou is assigning a security team to protect me and Madame DuBois."

"Tomorrow, sir, you have a group arriving tomorrow morning to hear what you have to say regarding your mother and father's project to plant cedar trees across Lebanon's mountains."

"Yes, that's right. I nearly forgot the meeting. So much has been happening. Tomorrow morning it is. I'd better spend the rest of today preparing and completing my report to the President of the Tyre conference. Have all confirmed their attendance, Hanna?"

"Yes, sir, they have, including the Minister of the Interior. The Minister of Agriculture could not attend because of a scheduling conflict, but his office told me they will provide all the assistance permitted. They have been lobbying the Parliament for more funds to replenish our magnificent cedars, and wholeheartedly welcome this new, privately funded endeavor. They also suggested that they will coordinate through the Minister of the Interior's Office."

"So, all is set for the meeting?"

"Yes, sir," he bowed his head as he backed out of François' office, more relaxed now than he had been in two days.

After dictating his report to the president to Hanna for typing, François suddenly realized how weary he was from his long day and the stress of knowing his every move was being watched. After Hanna announced the bodyguards had arrived, he asked Hanna to bring them in so they could meet.

Hanna introduced François to the two impressive men. One, Antoine Kahlil, a Maronite Christian from Tripoli, was heavy set. The other, Nicola Azar, an Orthodox Christian from the north, was lean and muscular. Both had mustaches, and long, well-trimmed hair. Each was over six feet tall.

"*Ahlen, Ahlen,*" he said as he welcomed them into his office. With a broad smile, he embraced them customarily.

"Are you excellent marksmen?" asked François.

In unison, they smiled confidently and nodded as Antoine affirmed, "We are the best in the agency, sir."

"President Helou asked for the best, so we volunteered," Nicola asserted with a broad smile of pride. "We are prepared to sacrifice ourselves for you, sir."

"Where are you both from?"

I am from Bsharre, replied Nicola proudly."

"And I am from Tripoli" responded Antoine.

"Have many Palestinians settled in Tripoli?" asked François.

"Oh, many, many, sir. There are so many they have nearly taken over the city. So many Shiia. I fear the Christians there, including many of my family, are being overrun and sometimes abused. It concerns me greatly, sir. I wish the government could keep them in the South."

"That is not possible, Antoine! They are refugees, poor, and need our safe haven."

"But, sir, they are changing Lebanon!"

François replied. "It's a difficult situation for all of us, Antoine. But, we cannot deal with that ourselves now. My great concern at this moment is that I need to trust you both completely. I need your total commitment to my safety. We must build a high level of confidence together and you need to know I expect the best. I am certain that you both will want me to send that message to the President."

"Yes, sir, we do," Antoine quickly responded.

"Good. Has Hanna briefed you on my schedule and our recent experiences in Saida (Sidon) and Soor (Tyre)? It may become more dangerous here in Beirut, but I must continue my work and the work of the President. Just keep me safe from those Mossad bastards!"

"Now, we must go to the St. George Hotel. I wish to meet my companion there."

Your children are not your children,
they are sons and daughters of Life's longing for itself.
Kahlil Gibran

Chapter 20

St. George Hotel
Beirut

As François cautiously entered the hotel, he searched the opulent, high-ceilinged main lobby looking for anyone or anything out of place and was relieved at not seeing any suspicious characters. His bodyguards preceded him to search the public areas, including restrooms, before gesturing to François that it was safe for him to step to the elevators. They gave him a key to his room where Leah was waiting. The guards kept a spare room key. After excusing Mohamed, François quietly opened the door so not to disturb Leah who might be resting; he immediately looked to the king-sized, canopied bed almost completely covered with locally handmade slip covered pillows. She was not on the bed. He checked the bathroom and then went to the only spot he hadn't surveyed: the large balcony. Relieved, he saw the back of her head and shoulders as she sat in the chair, looking out.

"Leah?" he asked as he stepped to the balcony.

Leah turned her head toward him, dabbing her eyes.

"Are you alright, my darling?"

She arose and rushed to his outstretched arms, embracing him as she pressed her head into his chest. He could feel her shudder as she held him tightly. After a few moments standing and embracing, he whispered, "What's the matter, Leah? Come inside. Let's talk."

They sat side by side on the elegant damask-covered settee, holding hands.

"Oh, François, I am having a very difficult time. I am terribly conflicted."

"And you are sad, my love. I can see you are very sad. But why?"

"Darling, I am so upset. My emotions range from happiness to sadness, to anger, fear, anticipation…I am so mixed up. I've been sitting on the balcony all day thinking about all that has happened in our lives. I love you so, dearest François, and I am happy that you have shared your beautiful country with me. Everyone here is so nice to me. So friendly! So free in spirit! But, we are faced with danger everywhere. I search all over with my eyes hoping we are not being watched or followed. I am afraid for you, darling…for us. And I am angry that I have brought danger into your life and our lives. I feel a terribly deep sense of guilt about what my country has done to the Palestinian people and to Lebanon.

"Why can't we all get along in peace? Why must there always be fighting and killing? Why? Why must men seek control over others? Why don't I see more clearly that I am happiest when you and I are together?" She paused as she lowered her head, tears streaming down her face as she tightened her grip on his hand with both of her hands. "Why have I wasted so many of the best years of my life? Of our lives? Nearly twenty years ago we fell in love. And, because I believed I could help build a nation for my people, we have been apart for all those years. It was my fault, François."

He was taken by surprise at her outburst of emotions…her questioning their fate.

"Leah, I am sorry you are wrestling with these issues. What is in the past is gone forever. We can do nothing about that. What we must do is look to the future…together. Our love is too great to ignore. We should be thinking and talking about what we do now."

"But our future is a function of our past. Is it our destiny to be apart? Are we to be happy only when we are briefly together? Is that what is happening to us?"

"You cannot return to Israel where you are so unhappy and threatened. We will to be together from now on, Leah.

"Actually, your thoughts sound much like the lives of my mother and father. I've told you their story. They were apart for more than forty years. Forty years, Leah! And now they have found each other again after so many years and are still very much in love.

"I have some good news, Leah. My parents are in Beirut. And while I've wanted to find a way to introduce you to them, it hasn't been right as long as you were still in Israel. Especially, my dear, after Israel started this war. But now, since you are living in Paris, and we've been together, the time may be best now."

"Oh, François, I've wanted to meet your mother and father for a very long time. I think they are both so remarkable to have loved so deeply, so strongly, and to have done so much for those that need help. However, I refuse to think you and I should be apart any longer. And yet, I feel so pulled to the land of my ancestors. We Jewish people have wandered across the world for centuries, never having our own nation. Not since the glory of Israel under King David. You do understand, don't you, François? Tell me you do."

"Of course I understand your deep desire to help build a nation for your people, Leah. I feel much the same toward Lebanon. I believe the difference between us is that I am happy here in Lebanon. I am mostly free here from tensions and religious demands. I love my work and the people I deal with. But it seems to me,

Leah, that you are not happy there. How can you be? Your religious state is always in a state of siege, always angry at your neighbors. It can't be a healthy day to day experience for you or any of your people."

François' exasperation was growing, and he felt a sting of sadness as he listened to her emotional statements. He loosened his hold on Leah, took a deep breath, and walked to the balcony opening and looked out as he pondered his thoughts before he resumed sharing them with Leah. He thrust his hands in his trouser pockets and stared out into the distance as he continued, "You know, Leah, this Israeli attack on Egypt, Syria, and Jordan is devastating to the entire region. It has totally changed the thinking of the entire Arab world, and the Lebanese people."

Then, as he turned to her, he added in stern seriousness, "By invading and occupying Gaza, the West Bank, and the Syrian Golan Heights, the hardliner leaders of Israel have created deep concern across the Arab world that they believe all those lands belong only to the Jews. Some in Syria and Lebanon fear it is a harbinger of new, future attacks, invasions, wars, and occupation of all of Lebanon, Syria, and Iraq to the Euphrates River. None of your neighbors trust the Israeli government and will not cooperate with it as long as Israel threatens them. And why should they? Leah, many fear this is not the end, but only the beginning. Angry Palestinians will take up the sword and deal harshly with Israel. There will be much bloodshed, I fear, and many innocent people on both sides will be killed or badly injured. It is a most terrible time. And it's going to get worse."

"I know, François. That is why I am so sad, so angry."

Perhaps it was because François knew the stories of his mother's father killed by the German invaders into France during World War I, or his mother's mother's death at the hands of the Germans during World War II, and perhaps too it was the unjust Ottoman occupation of Lebanon that drove his father's father out of his homeland, and forced his own father to leave his family home that made François believe so strongly that he must strive for justice, fight the unjust, be kind and loving, and, as his Lord asked, love his neighbor and help the poor that prompted him to speak now with impatience and anger at the actions of the Israeli government.

He felt no prejudices toward any people. He deeply believed in the Lebanese ethics of freedom for all races, and religions and creeds. All Lebanese he knew had close friends and business associates who were Muslims, who were both Sunni and Shiite, and Druze, Christians, and Jews.

"It isn't that the Arab people hate Jews, Leah. Most do not and have been sympathetic to the suffering of the Jewish people over the centuries. But most, if not all Arabs hate Israel…with a passion. Even before this six-day war, millions of Palestinians, over eighty percent, became refugees driven from their homes, their businesses, their farms and orchards, as well as from their churches and mosques. And now, Zionists have taken all of Palestine! And why? Because your fellow Zionists believe that every Jew, no matter where they lived or existed, have the right to be squatters…you call them settlers…and can force these people out without recompense, without any consideration of their rights as human beings. Millions of mothers, children, and the elderly have been ousted from their lands to become refugees, living on pennies from handouts. They are without homes, self-respect, and without hope. Why are Christians and Muslims not allowed? Where is the moral outrage?"

He caught his breath, realizing poor Leah was bearing the brunt of his pent-up anger and sense of helplessness that he vented for the first time. Still, he felt compelled to continue.

"How can a people who claim to be the Chosen People…that is, those chosen by God to teach others how to believe in the one true living God and show others the way of the Lord who demands justice, love of one's neighbor, kindness, and helping the poor…how can those," he gritted his teeth as he said the word, "chosen subvert and poison that mission to one of privilege! Privileged instead of the Chosen. We don't get it. The Arab world and its people did not participate in those inquisitions of Spain and France, or the pogroms of Russia, or the decimation of the Jewish people of Europe under the Nazis. We were not part of that! So, now, why must the Arabs be selected to suffer the loss of their lands, their culture, their religions, their quality of life, and their human rights? Can you or anyone in Israel explain that to the Palestinian people? Or to the Lebanese people?"

Leah's shoulders were shaking and tears were flowing freely down her cheeks. She reached for her handkerchief while quietly uttering short reactive gasps of breath as she buried her face in her hands.

François, stepping aside from his love of Leah for the moment, continued angrily, his voice growing louder, "You left me twenty years ago when you told me you loved me totally. You knew I loved you with all my heart, but you believed you simply had to go to Palestine to build a homeland for you and your people. Is this the land you worked so hard to build? Is this the land that invades and kills its neighbors? Is this the land that replaced our love? Is this worth our not being together? When?" he demanded. "Our love…our destinies…are important too. I do not believe you devoted twenty years of our lives to what it has become. Now, you are not even safe with them. I'm glad you are finally come to your senses now and are here with me!"

Watching François, listening to the man who fills her heart, describe her life and her Jewish homeland in such a way that she had never considered and could hardly believe, caused her to feel a deep sense of despair.

"I…I…don't know what to say, François. I am in great pain, and I cannot continue like this. Please come to me," she pleaded as she stretched out her arms to him. "Help me, François. Hold me, my love, hold me," she sobbed. "I…I am not like those people. And not all Israelis are. We don't believe in taking others' lands. We were told they sold their lands, their businesses, their farms. We did not know they were taken. So, what are you and I to do?" she begged softly.

"Leah, we, in Lebanon, walk a fine line of tolerance and inclusion. By that, I mean we have many religious constituencies which, in many events, regrettably, become more powerful allegiances than to the nation as a whole. It is often very difficult to keep the politics here in balance. Even without outside interference, we have potential crises that could erupt at any time. But," he added quickly, "although we maintain a good working relationship day by day, belligerent activities toward any Arabs, especially the vulnerable Palestinians, affects all Lebanese, all people across the Arab world, like a snake crawling into a crowd. Everyone responds with anger and fear, feeling an impotent capability to deal with life-threatening danger.

Israel, by its punishing treatment of the Palestinians, impacts on every citizen in the Arab world. The fact is, we are all part of extended families in our blood, our behavior, our culture. Sunnis in Saudi Arabia, the Gulf States, and Syria are cousins of the Sunnis in Lebanon and Palestine. This is true as well of Shiia in Lebanon, Iraq, and especially Iran, though Iran is not Arab, and Christians in Palestine, Lebanon and Syria. So, you see, Leah, when Palestinians are beaten over the head by Israeli soldiers, people in Lebanon and the rest of the Arab world get very painful headaches. And, religious groups all over the region rush to aid those of the same religion in Palestine."

Leah, thoughtfully considering François' explanation, softly responded with, "And so it is with the worldwide Jewish community, François. When Israelis feel threatened, so do Jews all over the world. And when they hear the news, the Zionist organizations go to work. And the people, many very wealthy Jews, especially in America, send large amounts of money to us in Israel. Not only that, my love, but they double their efforts to convince America's government to step up their grants to Israel. So, when Nasser threatens Israel with his 'saber-rattling,' or Syrian Baathist strongmen Salah Jadid, Al Atassi, and Assad send a barrage from the Golan Heights into our villages in northern Israel, they do more to help the Israeli government enormously. The money flows in dramatically each time they do it."

"Good point," replied François, "so, from what you are saying, actions by Egypt and Syria are the best friends of Israel's hardliners. Is that correct?"

"Think about it, François. Every Jew in the world remembers...that is what we do best...we remember. We remember how the Egyptian pharaohs held our ancestors as slaves for four hundred years. Then, as you know because you are familiar with the Bible, we remember God's promises to Abraham, Isaac, and Jacob. We remember Moses and his messages from the one God. And we remember the kingdom under our greatest, most powerful king, David."

Taking a breath, she leaned back and continued, "We are all aware of the Babylonian exile, later the European experiences under the Popes, the Christian inquisitions, the forced conversions of Spain and France. And especially, and most recently, we all remember the efforts of the Nazis to exterminate us as a race. It is called the Holocaust for that very good reason."

"But," François interrupted, "that should not justify the Israeli destruction of Palestine, taking all they own, the killings...they are behaving just like the Germans."

"But to many, François, the historical abuse, the forced diaspora, and the Holocaust are used as reasons to do anything to anyone so that we, all Jews worldwide, must have our own state, our 'safe haven,' and our self-esteem. And that place, regrettable to the Arabs, is the state of Israel."

"And, Leah, what about those who are quite safe in America, England, and other places like those? What about them? Do they feel safe where they are?"

"François, I believe it is safe to say that almost every Jew in the world believes in their hearts that they are first Israelis, and then Americans or wherever they live. They believe if Israel were allowed to no longer exist, then they too would no longer be allowed to exist. And I believe most everywhere they do not feel totally safe, and likely never will. That's why we're so paranoid."

"So, if Arab leaders threaten Israel, then Jews everywhere feel threatened?"

"Yes! Exactly!"

"That's quite a statement, Leah. But that certainly explains what actually happens. Maybe you are also saying that if the Arab nations simply stopped threatening Israel, the influences that affect their policies and their financial support would wither? Or at least decrease?"

"It's possible, François. It's very possible. They might change dramatically. But, who really knows? And if that happened, and a 'common enemy' was removed, our politicians would no longer be able to vent their internal obstreperous propensity against the Arabs, but, in fact, they would probably attack each other to the point of self-destruction. After all, if you read Exodus you'll see where God called the Israelites 'stiff-necked' and argumentative to the point of continually breaking their covenants with God time and time again! Many still are that way."

"Happily for them, Leah, that God kept creating new covenants with them, although they endured a great deal of pain in the process."

"Yes, like being driven to Babylonia and the crushing occupation by the Assyrians, the Greeks, and the Romans. But you know something, François? We're still here! No one has exterminated the Jews yet. And I believe no one ever will. We were chosen by God!"

"Yes, Leah, the Israelites were chosen by God to live His laws and show the world the benefits of worshipping the one living God. But, I am sad to say, in the minds of many, the Jewish people have confused the meaning of chosen to become privileged. And what they have done to all of us in this region is to impose themselves on us, taken property, homes, lands, and killed thousands for their own selfish benefit, as though they are privileged, not chosen. They seem to have forgotten to show the way with justice, love, kindness, and helping the poor."

"It would have helped, François, if over the years the Arabs had welcomed the poor souls who sought refuge in Palestine, especially after World War II."

"But they did, Leah. Many did. There was an agreement to absorb up to fifteen thousand immigrants each year. But it didn't take long for over one hundred thousand 'foreigners' to invade Palestine annually. And things got out of hand. Not due to anti-Semitism, but out of fear." Then, after a moment, he added, "They came in huge numbers because other countries, especially the United States, denied their access and kept them out."

"Again I ask. What do you and I do now, François? What do we do now, my love, after we have exhausted our arguments?"

"It's good we can air our opinions, conflicting as they are, and still remain loyal and loving to each other. Now, I have a good idea. Let's go to dinner, Leah," he answered, finally smiling. "I need a drink!" he laughed, a bit anxiously. "In fact, I'm going to call my parents and invite them to join us for dinner tonight."

"But, is tonight a good idea? I mean, if your parents feel as strongly against Israel as you do, and they find out I'm an Israeli, will they accept me?"

"I believe they will love you as I do, Leah. They are not anti-Jewish or prejudiced in any way. They probably have some negative feelings toward Israel's government, but they respect all people and will realize how much and for how long you and I have loved each other."

"Do I look alright? I mean, I've been sad all day. Well, I'll shower and put on new make-up. Yes, François," she smiled hopefully, "please call your parents and ask them to join us tonight."

"They're at the Phoenicia, Leah. How about dining at Café Corniche? There are tables at the water's edge and we can enjoy tonight's full moon in the sky over the Mediterranean. Would you like that?"

Your reason and your passion are your rudder and sails of your seafaring soul, if either your sails or your rudder be broken, you can but toss and drift, or else be held at a standstill in mid-seas.

Kahlil Gibran

Chapter 21

Beirut

As Leah and François left the St. George Hotel with their bodyguards, still wary of being watched by the Mossad agents, Leah, looking at François beside her in the rear seat of the Mercedes taxi, softly asked, "Do you really think your mother and father will like me?"

"Leah, before your move to Paris and your decision to be with me instead of remaining in Israel, I wasn't sure, but now, after our beautiful time in Paris and now here in Lebanon, and your decision to be with me here, I have no doubt about that." He smiled at her, placed his arm across her shoulders and kissed her lightly. "This should be a wonderful evening. My parents are so in love with each other that there is no room for any negative emotions. And they have faith in me."

"But no doubt they would rather you fall in love with a Lebanese woman, isn't that so?"

"I expect they would, but I love you, Leah, and that is what I care about. After they have a chance to meet you and get to know you they too will love you."

The four met at the restaurant at the south end of the Corniche where the boulevard descends to sea level and entered the unique upscale Café Corniche restaurant with outdoor seating under the stars by the water's edge. After François kissed and embraced both his parents, he turned to Leah with a proud smile and said, "Mother, father, it is my great pleasure to introduce to you my *Habibi*, my dear love, Leah."

A nervous Leah smiled warmly and extended her hand to Madeleine, then to Alexander. "I've been looking forward to this moment for a very long time. François has told me so much about you."

Happy to be with their son and whoever his guest was, they responded with smiles, exchanged handshakes followed by warm, welcoming embraces, immediately relaxing Leah who breathed a quick sigh of relief.

"Shall we go to our table now?" asked François, guiding Leah and his parents to follow the maitre d' as he led them to their table located on the outdoor terrace near the water's edge.

The wine steward, in formal attire, approached their table and made a judgment to ask François, "*Pardon*, monsieur, may I interest you in an excellent wine of Lebanon?"

Nodding affirmatively, François smiled and, with pride, ordered a 1956 Cabernet he knew was produced in the southern Bekaa vineyard and winery of a good friend.

In only moments, the steward returned, "Excellent choice, Monsieur DuBois. You always know the best." He expertly poured a taste amount into François' wine glass, stood straight and waited for François to assure him of the wine's quality. Responding to François' nod of approval, he poured the wine in the others' glasses.

"*Merci*, Monsieur DuBois. Your waiter will be with you shortly."

Happy at the way the evening was going, François raised his glass and said, "I propose a toast to the two most beautiful ladies in the world and the best father of all."

Clinking their glasses across the table, the four smiled acknowledging their joy at spending an evening together.

"This is so lovely, François!" Madeleine exclaimed, her feet only three meters from the gently lapping waters of the Mediterranean. "And the full moon above. These are the blessings of Beirut! Are you from Beirut, Leah?"

Glancing to François, caught off guard and hoping for a clue as to how to respond, Leah replied, "No, Mrs. Thomas, I'm not. But I love the city and think the Beiruti people are very sophisticated, energetic, and vibrant."

"Leah," Madeleine replied sweetly as she reached for Leah's hand, "Iskandar, I still call him by his Lebanese name because that was his name when we first met, and I finally found each other after forty-two years of separation at a wonderfully, exciting gala at my friend, the President's estate just five years ago. This is our first return visit to Lebanon and his brother Milhelm in Douma."

"That's amazing, Mrs. Thomas. I hope you'll tell me more."

"I'd love to share that special time with you." Continuing, excitedly recalling their odyssey, she began, "You may already know Iskandar and I met in Marseille when he was eighteen, en route to America, and I was just a young girl of sixteen.

"We've been in love ever since, Leah. I guess you could say we are two people who epitomize living our lives with our hearts, not our heads." She laughed at her own comment, realizing how accurate it was.

Listening, Iskandar interjected, "Leah, are you familiar with Lebanon's most famous philosopher, Kahlil Gibran and his popular book, *The Prophet?*"

"Oh yes, I am. It's my favorite book, Mr. Thomas."

"Well, in *The Prophet*," he looked to Madeleine, reached out and clasped her hand as he continued, "Gibran states: *When love beckons, follow him though his ways are hard and steep.* He goes on to say: *what love can be and how it can be painful.* But believe me, Leah and François, you would be wise to follow him as Madeleine and I have done even though it took forty-two years of shattered dreams as Gibran says, and frustration. But what a thrill when we finally found each other and I met my son François for the first time! Love, like God, is the greatest blessing of life. And I can assure you if it's real, it lasts and endures come what may. And François knows he is loved and has been loved all his life."

"I have been blessed, *Maman*, to have known your love and even though father was in America, and you always told me *Biyee* loved me very much even though he was not with us."

"And," he added as he looked to Leah and reached out to stroke her hand resting on the table, "Leah and I also found love almost immediately when we first met while at the Sorbonne."

"That was twenty years ago, Mrs. Thomas!"

"You have been in love for twenty years?" Iskandar exclaimed, "Are you trying to beat your mother and me?"

Everyone laughed, although Iskandar wondered why his son would be in love so long with this beautiful woman and not marry her. "What's taken you so long, son?"

Carefully glancing over his father's shoulder, François warily focused on his two bodyguards discreetly standing in the background, watching for any suspicious people. Getting an all clear signal, he relaxed and resumed his conversation with his father,

Not yet wanting to fully explain, François smiled and replied, laughing, "Maybe I'm too much like you, father."

Sensing an opportune moment to change the subject, Madeleine suggested, "Has François ever taken you to his father's village of Douma, Leah?"

"No, he hasn't as yet, but he has promised to take me someday. I'd love to see Douma."

Alexander, listening, caught Madeleine's quizzical expression, thinking, throughout twenty years?

"Well," Madeleine replied, "there's no time like the present." She laughed again, then, turning to her husband, added, "Iskandar, why don't we all go to Douma tomorrow. We can visit Milhelm and your friends for a few days. Can you two take off a few days and join us?"

"Well," François replied, "it is Thursday. Yes, let's go tomorrow. I'll call my assistant, Hanna, and he can make the necessary arrangements to leave before noon."

François was feeling much better now, not having to explain to his parents his relationship with Leah at this moment, hoping they would first get to know her before telling them about Leah's insistence on being in Israel those twenty years.

"That's a wonderful idea, Mrs. Thomas," Leah enthusiastically interjected, "I'm really looking forward to spending more time with you. François has told me more than once about your remarkable lives. You are an inspiration. I love your son very much, and now having met you, I better understand why he is so special."

With a toast, touching their glasses of wine, François happily said, "To Douma and my father's ancestral home! I pray the love of Leah and I can approach the deep, enduring love of my mother and father. To tomorrow and Douma!"

Late the next morning as the four rode for nearly an hour north to Douma through Tripoli to visit Alexander's older brother Milhelm, recovering from a severe stroke several years earlier, Alexander commented, "This will be a special visit."

"Madeleine, when we return, I want you to show me a few of your clinics you initiated."

"Yes, we can do that. We have excellent people operating the clinics and schools. I am very proud of your success, as well, Iskandar."

"You deserve to be proud of your clinics, my love. You've helped so many young children. Now, I am looking forward to seeing my brother Milhelm, introducing him to François and Leah, and finding out how he is progressing with his post stroke rehabilitation. I feel badly that we waited so long to return to Douma. I know too that he'll be very happy to see you again, my love."

There are those who give with joy, and that joy is their reward.
Kahlil Gibran

Chapter 22

Douma

"Welcome, Mr. Thomas. Your brother's spirits skyrocketed when I told him you were coming," Ms. Kahlil, Milhelm's therapist, said enthusiastically as Alexander and Madeleine first joyfully entered Milhelm's home. "He seemed to relax his determination last year, but now, I think he'll make good progress. I'm expecting that soon Milhelm will be able to sit at the table and to stand by himself. For a time, he'll need assistance eating and moving around, but if he continues his exercises and responds to his therapies, he'll soon be able to walk around the house unassisted. But I have to tell you, Mr. Thomas, his speech will take a long time to improve. Aphasia requires intensive, long-term therapy. I've instructed him how to exercise his mouth, his muscles in his face and tongue, and how to shape his words, hold his thoughts, and find the correct words…that is, the words he wants to say. It's called 'word search' because his brain damage hinders that.

"It's very frustrating for him, but he is making progress, although slowly. He is tenacious, to be sure, and more determined than ever. Your visit should do wonders for his spirit and lessen his tendency to become depressed. He especially looks forward to seeing Madame Madeleine Moreau again. She is so special!"

"The four of us will stay awhile now and encourage him all we can, Ms. Kahlil. Thank you so much for helping change my brother's life. He's too young to spend the rest of his life in a bed."

"As long as he feels the love, support, and encouragement from his family, and maintains his faith and hope, we can accomplish a great deal. Before you enlisted the help of the hospital, he seemed resigned to his fate. But now, I am encouraged because he now believes he can get better."

"That's the key, Ms. Kahlil. He has to believe. We all do, don't we? I could tell you a beautiful story that has a happy ending and gets happier by the day simply because of faith, hope and believing," he chuckled. "As they say, 'if you believe and conceive, you can achieve'."

"I understand Mr. Thomas." She covered her mouth to suppress a giggle. "I was told the story of you and Madame Moreau. I think all of Douma; even the entire Batroun Province knows your love story."

"I think they know our story all the way to Bsharre and Ehden!" he laughed. "But you know, maybe that's a good thing. There are so few wonderful love stories these days."

The therapist nodded and added, "Love stories inspire hope and faith, Mr. Thomas. And you and Madame Moreau are inspiring a lot of folks all over northern Lebanon. It's a story that strikes the heart strings of everyone…especially women, Mr. Thomas, and I might add, women of all ages, from teenagers to elders. You two have changed the way people think about their futures, sir, their partner, and their loved ones. Maybe their 'hoped for' loved ones too!" she laughed. "I've got a boyfriend myself." Then, after a moment of thought, Ms. Kahlil smiled, and before turning away, said, "I will leave you alone with him now. Please excuse me."

After sharing some time alone with his big brother, Iskandar whispered into Milhelm's ear as they tearfully embraced, "I'm very happy with your progress, brother. You've improved so much! Looks like we located the best therapist for you. Ms. Kahlil says you've gotten over your depression and are now more optimistic."

Struggling to respond, Milhelm sat up and in a whisper replied, "When I heard you were returning to Lebanon, I felt I couldn't let you down. And Ms. Kahlil encouraged me even more."

"Now, Milhelm, I have a beautiful surprise for you. Come in, darling!"

"Oh, Milhelm," Madeleine exclaimed, "how wonderful to see you again. Our son, François, and I owe you and Sara so much. We could never repay you adequately. You saved our lives more than once!"

After visiting with his brother until Milhelm tired, Alexander and Madeleine rejoined François and Leah. Later, the four strolled side by side through the village, met Alexander's many cousins, walked the terraced vineyards, and then went back to the house and simply relaxed under the grape arbor at the house. They were treated like royalty, especially by Milhelm's daughter Katrina, and another beautiful, young cousin, Marina, who overwhelmed them with the customary love and kindness of their gracious family of Douma.

"It's so wonderful to be here with you, Iskandar," Madeline lovingly repeated many times, still using the Arabic version of his name, as they all spent hours walking together viewing the wonders of the valley below with its olive groves and rushing river, the mountain ranges to the east, and the sparkling Mediterranean Sea to the west.

Iskandar and Madeleine watched Leah smile as François pointed to different places he remembered, while his parents recalled their own memories of living in the village; Iskandar in his youth, and Madeleine during the years of World War II when she and François surreptitiously lived with his family after escaping France and the approaching Germans in the darkness of night by fishing trawler from Marseille. They walked hand in hand through Douma, feeling as they did in Marseille as teenagers. It was a conscious recapturing of youthful emotions of their six-week affair in 1920.

When Leah and François moved close by, Madeleine turned to Leah and smiling told here, "Leah, François was just twenty when we arrived in Douma. He and I even learned to milk the family goats...probably the grandparents of those over there," she laughed, gesturing behind *Beit* Chalhoub, the Chalhoub home.

"François," Leah laughed, touching his arm, "tell me, did you enjoy milking the goats?"

"Not at first!" he laughed, remembering. "Uncle Milhelm made me do lots of farm things I never did in Marseille, like harvesting grapes, olives, and climbing those cedar trees."

Leah, holding François' hand as they walked through the olive groves, marveled at the gnarled, ancient olive trees, exclaimed, "I've never been so close to these kinds of old, beautiful trees before, François. Aren't they magnificent?"

"These olives produce the most delicious oil, which is revered in these mountains. It is a fine oil and the crushed seeds are made into a paste which they press into sheets. Then, they roll the sheets into small logs and use them for firewood. Isn't that incredible? They waste nothing in these mountains because there are few trees. Almost all the cedars have been lost to invaders and even the Phoenicians over the centuries."

"Maybe someone or the government should do something about that, François."

"Someday, *Inshallah*."

"As a boy, you climbed the cedar trees in that grove over there, didn't you, Iskandar?" Madeleine asked as she gestured.

"Of course, my love. In my youth, I spent many hours with Milhelm in those trees looking at the sea, imagining all kinds of things. Some days I portrayed Saladin defending the Holy Land from the Crusaders. Sometimes I looked west at the sea, dreaming of America. I spent many days playing among those strong tree limbs. I had quite an active imagination. But," he added with a twinkle in his eyes, "never in my dreams and fantasies could I have imagined you were in Marseille waiting to fulfill my destiny."

Looking at the cedar trees, Leah asked, "How old can those trees get, François?"

"Well, I'm not sure how old they can get, but that grove over there, and those in the distance have trees that I am told are over one thousand years old. There is a grove in Bsharre in the north that has about a hundred trees that are said to be about two thousand years old."

"I've heard they were here when Moses came to Canaan."

"Well," added Alexander, "they say they have many that old, Leah, and there is one magnificent tree in the Bsharre downtown area they say is over six thousand years old. Lebanon was blanketed in these cedar trees long before Moses left Egypt. It's hard to imagine, isn't it?"

"I want to see that tree," Leah exclaimed.

"Then you will," Alexander smiled. "We will all drive to Bsharre tomorrow and see the tree, the forest, and we'll visit Kahlil Gibran's cave. Let's have lunch in Bsharre. There is a nice restaurant under the limbs of that special cedar."

A few days later, as they all visited Milhelm again, young Marina came to them and coquettishly suggested, "Can we make you a picnic basket and have Ibrahim drive you down to the river to Farhilde? There," she gestured, "you can sit by the river on blankets. And, as you know, the olive groves are nearby where Uncle Iskandar worked as a youngster. Some are beautifully gnarled and nearly a thousand years old, they say. Would you like that? You'll be able to be alone for as long as you like." Then, giggling after seeing Alexander's eyes widen with a nod of his head, she excitedly ran to the house and called at the door, "Katrina! Katrina, they do want us to make a picnic basket. Let's add a bottle of our wine from the Bekaa too!"

"Yes, it's so good! Mmm…I think that's better than packing arak," Katrina laughed.

"I agree. Arak is so strong! They'll get silly if they have two glasses of arak. They'll enjoy the wine," replied Marina. "We don't need those four lovers acting any sillier than they already are." Then smiling, she added, "The whole village loves them and their lovebird behavior. They are like teenagers! So adorable! Let's see what they do next."

You talk when you cease to be at peace with your thoughts.
Kahlil Gibran

CHAPTER 23

Figarie

Madeleine convinced Alexander, François and Leah to walk up the steep, winding path to *Figarie*, to the orchards above the village. As they left the house with their picnic basket and blanket, they walked past six family goats in the yard, the family's source of milk for their favorite cheeses.

"I love this place, Madeleine. I have so many wonderful memories as a child here. I guess," he smiled wanly, remembering. "I guess, as boys, Milhelm and I must have milked the great-grandmothers of these family goats. We sure loved eating the cheese my mother made, wrapped in Syrian bread." He smiled as he stopped and patted the nearest female goat. "Much of those years we never thought we were poor. We were like everyone else in the village. But then, when my father left for America, everything changed," he said wistfully.

"Well, Mr. Thomé, it may come as a surprise to you, kind sir," she giggled, seeking to change the subject. "But I believe your son and I milked these goats' grandmothers during those war years."

"Our son, François, the three-piece suit wearing banker, actually milked the goats?" he interjected, laughing, surprised but quite pleased.

"Yes, Iskandar," she said, reflecting on the past, "those years our son and I lived here, we didn't want to tell them our true relationship with you. It was difficult keeping our secret from your loving, trusting family. But we thought that if they knew you had a son out of wedlock, they would ask us to leave the village, so not to humiliate the family. We didn't want that to happen. I felt so close to you here, Iskandar. From when he was a small child, I told François stories about you so that he came to love you, your family, and your heritage.

"Then one day Aunt Sara saw your…my…our cross on François' chest. We suddenly had to face the truth with Milhelm and Sara. As it turned out, they graciously understood. Yet, because they believed we might bring shame to your family, we had to leave the village. That's when Milhelm took us to Beirut and I became employed as Mrs. Kabbani's courtier, dressmaker and companion. We thrived there and came to be friends with so many wonderful people, friends of the Kabbanis and, eventually, President Helou. That's when François began his education at the American University at Beirut. You can be so proud of your family and your son!"

They watched as the nearby goats stretched their necks and reached their mouths down to the green grasses under a clear blue sky. Then they lifted their horned heads as they munched while gazing in the distance, looking indifferent to the world around them.

Madeleine commented, "Yes, Iskandar. Believe it or not, your son François, a 'city boy' from Marseille, milked these goats' grandmothers. And so did I!"

"I don't believe it," Alexander laughed. "My banker son was milking goats here? And you too?"

She watched tears well up in Alexander's eyes, tears of loving pride. "Our son milking the children of the very goats Milhelm and I milked. That's wonderful. What irony, Madeleine," he laughed.

Then he whispered, "Thank you, Madeleine, for François. And yes, I am very proud of you and my family."

As they walked together, her arm in François', Leah whispered to him, "This little, lovely village certainly holds a lot of memories for your family, doesn't it, darling?"

"Oh yes, and it goes far beyond my father's youth. Legend tells us six brothers and their families migrated here to the safety of these rugged mountains. Imagine all of them blanketed with giant cedars, from the Golan in 350 BC, nearly twenty-five hundred years ago."

"That's incredible, François! And these were your own ancestors?"

"Well, the same stories say six families, all named Chalhoub, came here as the village's first settlers."

"Your family has been here all that time? Before Alexander the Great and the Greek invasion?"

"That's the story, Leah, and no one has ever challenged it. See that small stone building over there on the slope? Well, that, we are told was a hospital for wounded Greeks."

"Really!" Leah exclaimed.

"Don't be so surprised by these things, Leah. We have deep roots here. My father's blood runs through my veins, does it not? Aunt Sara taught me these things. And she taught my mother too. We lived here with my father's family for nearly four years during the war until my mother finally told Milhelm the truth of our past. We wanted to participate in all things, so we milked the goats, and tended the vineyards, the fruit trees, and the olive grove. We even walked up the mountain over there to the east and visited the place where my father suffered so badly with severe frostbite in the snowstorm. He would have lost both his feet had my grandmother sitty not massaged his feet with warm olive oil daily for two years."

"That's an amazing story, François. What a family you have."

Then, resuming their walk up the winding, rocky dirt road up the mountain to *Figarie* and the fruit orchards, some three thousand feet above the village, Madeleine said to Iskandar in mock sarcasm, "I'll have you know 'Mr. Mountain Man,' your son and I, these two 'city folk' from Marseille, walked up this very road many times and helped take care of the apple trees, the persimmons, and the plum trees just like you and Milhelm did…let's see…over twenty years earlier."

"Oh, my Lord," Alexander responded looking up the mountain, "Milhelm and I spent most of our young years in *Figarie*. We even built the stone house up there so we could sleep over several days and tend the orchards without having to come back and forth every day. It's a long, hard walk, for sure."

"My father told us…and we later saw for ourselves that, although not often, it snowed up to five meters deep up there.

"That's why Milhelm and I put an opening and a door in the roof. Most of the times the snows are deep, but less than roof height, so we were able to get in and out without having to shovel snow all day." He smiled as his forefinger tapped his temple.

"I am so amazed at how brilliant you are, Mr. Thomé-Chalhoub. So smart," she teased as she lovingly gripped his hand tighter.

It took more than an hour for them to walk up the mountain at a leisurely pace.

Leah and François stepped ahead to the apple orchard, wanting to be alone.

"I am so grateful you brought me here, François, especially with your parents. This is such a special time for me. I feel so free. Look at the Mediterranean! Feel the cool dry breeze! And the sky is so blue!"

Alexander sat down on a large stone next to the apple orchard and tugged Madeleine's hand, pulling her to him. She sat next to him on the stone, wrapped her arms around his inviting shoulders and placed her full lips on his.

"Oh, Iskandar," she smiled, "I do love you so. I have loved you since the first moment we met. And I love you even more now. It's so hard to believe we actually met again. After forty-two years! Your face never left my mind, and my love never left my heart…ever. I am so grateful for you, my love! So grateful," she whispered as she cupped his face in her hands, looking deeply into his eyes as they filled with tears of joy. She loved his moist, brown eyes.

"I could stay here forever, Iskandar! Look! Look at the beautiful blue Mediterranean Sea…the afternoon's sun rays are creating millions of sparkling diamonds on the water!" she gestured, appreciating everything around them, sensing God's blessing of their love.

After a few minutes, Alexander's eyes swept from west to north, seeing all of Mount Lebanon. "See," he said proudly, gesturing to the north, up the Valley of Passion, the deep rift in the land, to the northern Lebanese villages of Bsharre and Ehden, "just look at the beauty of Lebanon's mountains."

Madeleine leaned into him, watching, absorbing the sights, feeling the emotions of love, of hope, of his roots; sharing his very emotions and their destiny together.

"Iskandar," she whispered, her face near his, "how fortunate you are. This land is your land. Your people are here. They've been here for so long on this very land, since before Alexander the Great invaded this region. Imagine! And here we sit, appreciating the same views of the valley, the sea, and the mountains to the east."

"And, Madeleine, don't forget the cedars."

"There aren't so many now, are there, Iskandar?"

"No," he replied. "Sadly, all that we have today are those isolated groves you see to the north. When my ancestors came here from the Golan, there was great turmoil in Palestine and Syria, just before the arrival of the Greeks. At that time, Madeleine, this entire land of Phoenicia that we now call Lebanon, was completely blanketed in those marvelous cedars of Lebanon."

"Everywhere, Iskandar?" she inquired. "Even in the south?"

"All over, Madeleine. All over Lebanon, then known as Phoenicia, and even north into Syria," he answered with visceral pride. "Especially over all the mountains. You see, Madeleine, Lebanon's mountains are very different from other mountains in the Middle East. They were formed in a different tectonic eruption and are porous. That makes them unique in the eastern Mediterranean and beyond. They hold water — lots and lots of water. And with the huge snowfalls across Mount Lebanon…driven by the moisture of the sea…where the snowmelt is absorbed and retained. That same snowmelt eventually finds its way to the Bekaa Valley and finally to Lebanon's two major rivers that feed the farmlands of the Bekaa. The trees love the soil and the waters throughout Lebanon's mountains. My ancestors knew that snowmelt in the Golan is the main source of water for the Sea of Galilee in Palestine."

"So, that's why Lebanon is so prolific and has no problem with water resources," Leah commented to François, "more than Palestine, Israel, Jordan or anywhere. That is something!"

"But," Alexander continued, "you see, Leah, the invaders over the centuries and their demands for pliant, strong wood from the days of the pharaohs consumed most of the trees. And since they need so many years, there has been little priority, incentive or funding to plant seedlings across Lebanon's mountains. People want results in their lifetimes. Until now. There are some, but not enough, who consider replanting important. But today, Lebanon is prospering. So possibly, if peace in the region returns, if tourism remains good and the politicians get along, maybe Lebanon will find the funding and the determination to initiate the replanting of cedar trees."

"Well, Iskandar," she exclaimed cheerfully as she stood very erect, both hands on her hips, smiling happily, "I have an idea! Why don't you and I do something? We'll start planting cedar seedlings here! We could form a new foundation together!

Your foundation in Florida, and mine in Beirut could provide the seed money... pardon the pun," she laughed excitedly, "and we could raise more money for a new, larger program. We'll start small and solicit contributions from others, with just a desk in my Beirut office. Then we can go to America and meet with your friends at St. Jude. Isn't that a good idea, Iskandar? We can do that!" Pleased with her plan, she laughed and clapped her hands together enthusiastically.

"Madeleine, you are again the same audacious delicious, sixteen-year-old I was lucky enough to meet in Marseille." He was excited again, drawn to a purpose which they together could devote themselves.

Alexander called to François and Leah, "Come join us. We have something to discuss with you."

"François," Alexander said, "your mother has a wonderful plan to plant cedar seedlings here in the mountains. What do you think? If your mother and I fund the first phase right here in the Douma area, do you think this plan would work?"

Alexander put his arm across François' shoulders and together they stood, viewing the barren, stone filled mountains with the small groves of cedar trees scattered across the landscape in the distance. François saw her vision and liked it. He could see thousands of new, young cedar trees across the ridges and into the valleys.

"That's a wonderful idea!" François blurted out, smiling, surprised at his own enthusiasm. "We could enlist the young people, the students of Lebanon, as volunteers during the off-school months."

"We should never forget the cedars! Or the young people! Everyone of Lebanese blood cherishes the ancient cedars, and I think with initial funding, it could at least get started. Let's do it!"

"Excellent, François, and, I think your approach, using teenagers, is very powerful. If we can get the young empowered, involved, and take a sense of ownership, the adults will come along."

"I think that's correct. I think this effort would need to involve everyone possible. You know, 'err on the side of inclusion'. Maybe we can even get the government involved."

"Would you be able to get involved personally, François?"

"Let's discuss this further when we return to Beirut, *Baba*. His mind was on Leah. As a matter of fact, there is something else I'd like to discuss with you now."

Meanwhile, Leah and Madeleine stepped to the apple trees and began talking about the seedling project.

"What is it, François?"

"Let's sit over here on this large stone."

When you meet your friend on the roadside or in the marketplace, let the spirit in you move your lips and direct your tongue. Let the voice within your voice speak to the ear of his ear.
Kahlil Gibran

CHAPTER 24

Alexander and François

"Well, son, what's on your mind? By the way, Leah seems like a wonderful woman, and it looks like she loves you very much. Is she Lebanese?"

"She is a beautiful woman, *Biyee*; she's as beautiful inside as she is on the outside."

"So what's the problem? Do you love her? I mean, do you really love her?"

"Yes, *Biyee*. We've been in love almost since the moment we first met when both of us were at the Sorbonne."

"Does she have a good heart? And, I think you haven't answered my earlier question. Is she Lebanese?"

"What is it, Madame Thomas?"

"Leah, are you Lebanese? Or maybe French? I know you and François met at the Sorbonne after the war, in 1947, but that's all we know," asked Madeleine.

Nervous and caught off guard by the direct question, Leah realized the time had come to tell the whole truth to the parents of her lover who, she knew, deserved the truth. "No, I am not Lebanese or French. I met your beautiful, sensitive son as soon as I arrived at the Sorbonne. We became quite attracted to each other and soon fell in love. He was the first man I ever let get close to me. And still is the only man I've known in my life. Ever. I was just twenty-two years old, a refugee who was fortunate to make my way to Paris. Thanks to the Catholic Church, I survived Hitler's onslaught in Poland. My parents, my whole family, were killed by the Germans. I was born in Warsaw and lived my childhood there. I was just nineteen when I escaped in 1944. You see, Mrs. Thomas, my parents were taken to the Nazis camps. I escaped by running to the Catholic Church for safety and the priest hid me."

"So, Leah, you are Jewish?"

"Yes, Madame Thomas, I am."

"And you love my son very much?"

"Oh, yes, with all my heart!"

"Well then, Leah, if you both love each other deeply, and I know how that feels, it's the most beautiful gift of life, don't you think? Can you totally commit to his way of life?"

"Yes I can. I know I can! When we are together, the whole world seems to be separate from us, and I can only see, hear, smell and touch him."

"I believe he feels the same about you, Leah."

"I believe in my heart he does."

"How long do you two plan to wait to get married and have children? What's the problem? I mean, it's been twenty years, Leah!"

"If you both love each other, François, what's taking you so long to marry Leah and have children? Your mother and I would love to have grandchildren."

François kept nervously twisting a twig in his hands, seeking the courage to be completely candid with his father. Even though he was forty-seven years old, a mature, independent man, he still wanted his father's blessing of his chosen companion.

"Well, *Biyee*, there's something you should know."

"And what, my son, should I know," he asked pointedly. "I've guessed Leah isn't Lebanese because you've avoided answering my question. Is she a Christian? Why wait twenty years if you love each other?"

"Leah, I have to know, why wait twenty years?"

"Madame Thomas, in 1948, I had to make the hardest decision of my life. I knew I was deeply in love with François and have been throughout my life ever since. And I believe François felt and still feels the same way."

"But, Leah, I still don't understand what happened. I mean, your being Jewish is not an issue with Mr. Thomas or me. I'm sure he would prefer his only son marry a nice Lebanese Christian woman. But one cannot predict love's choice. We both found that out for ourselves. His father wanted Iskandar to marry a nice Syrian, Christian girl. And he did, although he was still in love with me. But he was in America and I was in France raising François and married already. But that's another story. The point is, parents want their children to carry on their religion, their culture, and pass it on to their grandchildren. But most importantly, parents want their children to live happy, prosperous lives. And," she smiled, speaking for us, "to provide grandchildren."

"Now, Leah, don't tell me François avoided marrying you because you're Jewish? It must be something else. What is it? You know we'll find out eventually, just as Milhelm and Sara found out I was Iskandar's lover and mother of his child. It's just a matter of time. Now, Leah, why have you two spent twenty years avoiding marriage and children? Is he impotent? Are you? Don't make me guess, Leah. Tell me. We need to know. We deserve to know. If you two prefer, tell me and I'll tell Iskandar. He and I can discuss it later."

With tears of anxiety, fear and nervousness overflowing her eyes, Leah asked, "Will you stay here with me on the grass for a few minutes? This is going to be difficult but necessary, Madame Thomas."

"Of course," Madeleine replied, sensitive to this lovely, young woman's plight. She reached out and clasped Leah's hands as they sat side by side. Leah looked over to François sitting on a large stone next to his father, heads lowered.

"Madame Thomas, in 1948, when Israel declared itself a new state in Palestine, a new homeland for Jews, like so many Jews in Europe who had lost everything including parents, siblings, all they owned simply because we were Jewish, like most I couldn't believe I would ever be safe in Europe again and sought to leave. Even in France, under the Vichy government, Jews were taken away, never to be seen again. I was young, idealistic, and naïve. But I too feared for my life in Europe. Can you understand how it must have been, Madame Thomas? I hope so. And even though I loved François with all my heart, I felt compelled to go to Palestine to help build a safe haven for the Jewish people…my people.

"So, I lived in a kibbutz for the past twenty years believing in a homeland within Palestine, co-existing with Muslims, Christians, and Arabs.

"But over the past several years, Israel's hardliners have become too aggressive for many of us and recently attacked and invaded its neighbors Egypt, Syria, and Jordan. Clearly, Israel intends to occupy the West Bank, Gaza, and the Golan Heights. They have even refused to leave those lands. I cannot live there anymore. I have chosen to leave Israel and have taken residence in Paris. I want to be with François the rest of my life."

"Leah is an Israeli you say, François?"

"Yes, *Biyee*, I didn't want to tell you, frankly, because I didn't know how upset you'd be. After all, I know parents want their children to choose someone of a similar religion, culture and heritage. You want your children to be happy and believe that's the best way to achieve that. But I love Leah and she loves me, very deeply. I hope we'll get married"

"And you couldn't find a good Lebanese woman in Beirut?" Alexander asked incredulously.

"Oh yes, *Biyee*, please don't get upset. I have known many beautiful Lebanese women, but it was no use. I have been deeply in love with Leah and, I think you of all people, know how hard it is to love two people at the same time."

"Does she love you enough to be by your side…to care for you? Does she have a good heart?"

"Yes, *Biyee*, yes to all those questions."

"And, she's Jewish. Yet she could easily pass for a Lebanese woman. Does she not want children? What's the problem, son? I mean, twenty years is a long time!"

Still reluctant to tell everything, François finally came to understand it had to be said, and he'd gone too far to turn back.

"*Biyee*, Leah said goodbye to me in 1948 so she could go to Palestine to help build a homeland for the Jewish people. She was a scared young refugee from Poland who had lost her parents to the Nazis, and felt strongly that Jews had to have a homeland to be safe. She's been in a kibbutz now for those twenty years."

"You mean, son," Alexander replied sternly, "you have been in love with a Zionist? With someone whose nation has taken so much from our people? François, she has been part of an enemy state. You are Lebanese and French. You live in Beirut, know all sorts of fine people, and," he added, "you have deprived your mother and me from having grandchildren. Do you realize how stupid that sounds? I don't care if she's Jewish. Yes, I would prefer a Christian for a daughter-in-law. But, I think someone who served in the Israeli army, was part of the Israeli takeover of Palestine, and caused so much pain forthe Palestinians and Lebanese would not be my choice!"

"But, *Biyee*, I agree with you. It's why we've never married. She has now renounced the policies of Israel and moved to Paris. She has always, for twenty years, sought a path to peace, contrary to the Israeli hardliners to the point where the Mossad considers her a spy, an enemy of Israel. She wants to be with me in Lebanon."

"Look, son, you are now, what? Forty-seven years old and you can do what you want, marry who you want. I cannot make that decision for you. She seems like a good person who loves you very much, but there is a lot to think about.

What if you have children? How will they be reared? Will she always align with you and Lebanon? Or will her heritage pull her back to Israel?"

"I think we should discuss this further."

I am willing to do what I can to convince you, *Baba*. Let's finish our visit, enjoy a few hours in Bsharre, and, when we return to Beirut, let us discuss this further."

The day after visiting Bsharre, they completed their goodbyes with customary embraces and cheek kisses, and a few tears, to the villagers with eager promises to return soon, especially to visit with Milhelm.who loved Madeleine, especially since she and her son had lived in the Thomé-Chalhoub family home throughout the war.

Madeleine and Alexander, ebullient with thoughts of their new joint project as they left the village, waved to the villagers and the bald, soon to be cedar-covered mountains.

Still, all four were deep in their own thoughts throughout the drive back to Beirut.

What will become of this relationship between François and Leah? pondered Madeleine and Alexander silently.

You give little when you give of your possessions.
It is when you give of yourself that you truly give.
Kahlil Gibran

Chapter 25

Cedars Foundation Meeting in Beirut

After they arrived in Beirut, Alexander and Madeleine entered The Phoenicia and spent the last hours of the day alone. At dinner in their suite, they shared their thoughts and concerns regarding François' affair with Leah.

"I think Leah is a lovely, sincere and honest person, Iskandar. She must love François a great deal to leave her country after twenty years, don't you think?"

"But she chose Israel over her love for François, Madeleine. Doesn't that seem important to you? I mean, is that going to be her future pattern? Will she claim to love our son, and then decide to return to Israel? Like all young men and women there, she served in their army...the IDF! Doesn't that tell you where her loyalties are?"

"I know, my love, but she shared a lot of her history with me on *Figarie*, and I believe she sincerely loves François with all her heart and will make him a wonderful wife. She was young, alone, a refugee, idealistic and, I suppose, afraid to stay in Europe. The Jews were treated terribly for many years. The Germans and the Vichy gave them every reason to flee."

"Yet, I have trouble, Madeleine, convincing myself that she will devote herself to our son. Their cultures are so different. And what if they have children? What then? We won't be around all the time to lend support. What if Israel and Lebanon go to war again? What will she do?

"And what about her acceptance here in Lebanon? Will his associates, friends and political colleagues accept Leah? Will his future stay as bright?"

"Oh, Iskandar," Madeleine replied, "our son is not a fool. I think our visit with them will prompt them to address these important questions. And when they do, I believe they will come to the correct decisions. We must have faith in François, Iskandar. Let's, together, believe in them to find their way. Let's not attempt to tell him what to do."

"Well, my dear, he sighed, you may be correct. He and I spoke up in *Figarie* and he knows my concerns. I suppose you are correct. You've always been wise and caring. Yes, let's have faith. Leave it to them and God."

"Good, Iskandar. Now, I am tired. And we decided it's time to return to Florida. We leave tomorrow!"

"Yes. You'll have to pack for us in the morning while I have a frank discussion with our son.

"Our flight to New York via Paris leaves in the late afternoon. I'll have my office incorporate the new foundation François agreed to chair so he can begin work on setting up the program to begin planting cedar seedlings across Mount Lebanon so that one day the land can be like Phoenicia was so long ago."

After several hours, Alexander accepted his son's explanations and convinced he and Leah would find their way to the right decisions, he rejoined Madeleine and together, that afternoon, boarded their flight on Mideast Airlines for Paris, then America. Within two weeks, Francois arranged a meeting in his offices to initiate the project.

"*Ahlen*! *Wa Sahlen*! Welcome, my brothers and sisters. We are so grateful you have come to meet with us to explore the proposed restoration of our magnificent cedar trees across the high mountains of Lebanon."

François Dubois stood in his elegant, wood-paneled conference room at the head of the long, mahogany table, and welcomed those he had invited to participate in a project proposed by his mother and father. As he looked around the glistening, well-polished table where his invitees had taken their seat, he smiled and made eye contact.

"You are all my friends and more," he chuckled. "You are all my cousins, as well," he smiled, recognizing the Lebanese extended family culture.

"Aren't we all cousins, *habibi*?" one responded laughingly. "We Lebanese believe each of us is related somehow to every other Lebanese. Our culture fully embraces the extended family syndrome, does it not?"

All exchanged smiles, and nodded their heads, knowingly. Each of the attendees acknowledged they represented most, if not all, of the religious and geographic sectors of Lebanon.

"Even if we don't like someone, we still claim them," said another as everyone joined their laughter with his own.

It was a relaxed, positive meeting with everyone eager to hear what François had to say.

"Yes, indeed," François commented. "What we wish to explore today is the wisdom and possibility of planting cedar seedlings across the higher mountains of Lebanon to begin a very long-term privately financed project to restore our land to what it was when Moses crossed the sea. This will be our gift to the people of

Lebanon."

"Why not go back to when our ancestors, the Phoenicians, sailed the world some two thousand years before Moses left Egypt? That would be before they began cutting the cedars for their ships," quipped one of the attendees.

Why not, indeed," François responded with a smile, agreeing so the meeting wouldn't get caught up in ancillary issues. "As we go around the room, let each of us state who we are, our location, and our religious affiliation. Hanna will record our meeting."

He paused after acknowledging Hanna.

"Of course, you all know me, and you are familiar with Mr. Khalil, Minister of the Interior, who will guide us today in all things related to public lands, government permits and the like. Now, next to me is my true cousin," he smiled broadly, "Marina Chalhoub of Douma, in the Batroun province high in the mountains, just north of Beirut. Marina?" he asked, proudly smiling.

Marina Chalhoub, twenty-five years old, was quite beautiful, endearing, intelligent, with a deep love for Lebanon. At five feet, six inches tall, only slightly shorter than François. She was physically strong, yet agile. As a mountain girl growing up, doing her share of the work, she had developed a firm body, yet maintained an appealingly sensual feminine countenance. Her naturally wavy auburn hair was cut just above her shoulders. With a minimum of make-up, natural beauty was captivating. Her light olive skin was smooth, and her deep green eyes caught the attention of everyone. She loved to wear casual, Western-styled clothing, including jeans, and feminine cotton blouses.

"I am convinced that she is one who will passionately embrace this exciting project of planting cedar seedlings. I know, with her in charge, the Douma region can be the pilot project. I am very happy she is here to initiate this wonderful effort."

Marina, with a lovely, modest smile, stood up and nodded to François. "We in Douma are excited to be part of this fabulous project, and promise to do all we can to make this effort succeed. After all, the initial funding and the idea came from Doumani citizens. And we wish to become among the first to plant these seedlings, to give of ourselves to the future of Lebanon. We have already met with students in our school who are enthusiastic. After all, the children are our future."

Adeeb Tanous, a Maronite from Bsharre, proudly declared, "My village is the true historic land of the cedars. And that's true for the twentieth and the next century," he added with a smile.

"Well," another joked, "at least that's what the folks in Bsharre boast, since most of the trees remaining already grow north in or near Bsharre."

"But many also grow in Jabal Tannourine, in the higher mountains," added Milhelm Chidiac.

"That is true," Adeeb responded. "We do have more of our beloved ancient cedars than any other place, except perhaps near Ehden, north of Bsharre, but of course those trees are much younger perhaps only one to two thousand years," he chuckled.

"The only reason so many cedars live there to this day," joked Abdallah Sheraf from Beirut, "is because the Greeks, Romans, and even the Ottomans couldn't successfully climb those rugged high mountains or traverse Wadi Qadicha, the Valley of Passion. So they've been safe there for centuries," he laughed.

The group then discussed the exciting prospects of this project, getting deeply involved in its details and scope. After all those attending voiced their enthusiastic willingness to do their parts and to lead groups from their respective regions, the Minister of the Interior addressed the group, responding quite favorably to the plan, and answering many questions on the minds of the attendees.

"We in the government feel as you do that our magnificent historical cedars are the symbol of our human aspirations, and our characteristics of tenacity and resilience, and must be restored. We each have drawn the strength and pliancy of our cedar wood into our blood, our sinews, and, I may say, into our very souls. They are us and we are they. These trees bind us together as Lebanese no matter where we may travel or live. Clearly, we in the ministry will do all we can to enable you and your benefactors to succeed. We all know our history and the importance of our majestic cedars that bind us. And, while this moment may not be timely under the circumstances, considering the Israeli attacks that have so terribly disrupted our nation, we all can recall, knowing our heritage, that in the year 965 before Jesus, King Hiram of Phoenicia, having been an ally of Solomon's father, King David, accepted the offer of King Solomon to build the temple in Jerusalem using our cedar wood, craftsmen, and stone masons to. In those days, our ancestors, the Phoenicians, were very close with the Israelites. It is a shame that today's governments do not appreciate the centuries of closeness with their neighbors, isn't it? Be that as it may, in the time of Phoenicia, all of our lands wererе - blanketed with these magnificent, ancient cedar trees. And now, with the support of François' parents, and I hope, many other fellow Lebanese, may we succeed in this significant program to create a cedar tree recovery of our blessed nation."

As he looked around the table to discern the genuineness of the commitment of the group, he continued, "The first of our efforts, we believe, should, of course, be in those locales with the greatest possibility of success. We should target test areas on public land. And, I hasten to add, when I say 'public,' I fully mean on lands owned by all Lebanese citizens. There are several reasons why I say this. This will avoid accusations of favoritism and disputes. Also, unlike on private lands, we can protect the seedlings from animals grazing, like our goat population which," he chuckled, "as we all know, will eat just about anything in sight. Especially young tender plants. Our ministry will be very happy to provide all cedar seedlings and help you determine the best locations for planting beginning this summer before the first snows."

François, grateful for the commitment of the government ministry, asked, "So, we can we assume you will coordinate with the Ministry of Agriculture?"

"Exactly," responded the Interior Minister. "Actually, I've already spoken with the Agriculture Minister. They have a seed and seedling program with plenty of healthy plants, and fertilizers. But they do not have the funds to hire men plant them that your program can provide. Based on their ongoing experimental programs, they can predict a survival rate of over eighty percent if planted and cared for properly for up to six months. They will provide teams to instruct your people on the proper planting procedures, abundant water to meet your water requirements. Protection, planting, and care of the seedlings are your duties."

François, appreciating the Minister's support, replied, "Our responsibilities are to raise funds, assemble villagers, especially the students, to learn from their instructors, plant the seedlings, water them, erect protective fencing, and monitor the seedlings for at least six months. We will coordinate with your staff for any other needs as well. Public awareness is key to this project. We hope to begin this summer with the first plantings."

"We applaud your commitment and your optimism," commented the Minister.

As soon as François finished speaking, hands went up. François nodded to Sharifa Salman, a lovely, blue-eyed, fair-haired woman in her thirties whose smile melted the hearts of the men in the room. She represented the Druze community in the Shouf Mountains east of and near Beirut.

Sharifa spoke enthusiastically, "We can begin by planting a few hectares in Barus, on the higher mountains of the Shouf. And we can do it soon. It won't take long to organize."

"We must be among the first as well," exclaimed Adeeb. "We'll have our students of Tannourine and Jajg ready."

And so it went among the attendees. All were eager to be first, and, happily, it appeared no one wanted to be last. By the time the three-hour meeting ended, all targeted areas were committed, with the initial plantings to occur in the higher mountains. The following summers they would focus on expanding the small initial areas and then begin in new areas.

François ended the meeting with a proud statement. "This project can be a truly monumental gathering of all Lebanese, something all of us can be proud of and involved in. It will be a grand healing effort that all of us will remember, particularly after the Israeli war. We are Lebanese! We are Phoenicians! We are a proud people who will come together as never before! Remember, this will be a volunteer effort of contribution and giving of ourselves."

After all attendees left his offices, François sat back and reflected on the meeting. He felt very good about the initial meeting of the program, yet knew his optimism should be tempered by caution. Surely, there would be a few dropouts, and likely Murphy's Law would raise its ugly head.

"The devil is always in the details, Hanna," he often commented. "And, if anything could go wrong, it will, as Murphy said."

"Always, sir! Always, as you say!" was Hanna's response.

François estimated the costs of fencing, transportation of the planting teams, water tanker trucks, coordinators, and pay for all planters, drivers, etc. and established the program's budget for two years. As he dialed his parents' number in Florida, he knew the message he would convey: "We're moving ahead this summer and will do our best to stay within the initial budget. Clearly, however, we will need to raise more funds to accomplish more than merely a few hundred hectares of saplings. Lebanon, while a small country, has many mountains to consider. This could be a generational program requiring millions of dollars over time. But, I promise, we will have a strong and effective beginning."

François knew his parents would be as pleased with his progress as he was in expecting the first test plantings to begin in a matter of a few weeks.

Hanna commented, "This project which you have carefully crafted to include all sectors of the population, must bring all Lebanese to support this effort, which should help reduce the divisive sectarian character of our people so they will join together. This can be a catalyst for national bonding. Perhaps the people will put aside their tribal, sectarian and religious differences."

"If even for a while, that could be a very good thing, Hanna," François replied with a cautious, yet hopeful, but realistic opinion. "Perhaps, Hanna, let us hope for success. *Inshallah*. God willing."

"I do know this," Hanna replied with a smile, "there should be no downside to your plan. God himself blessed Phoenicia by covering our lands with our magnificent cedars. But man has consumed them over the ages. Now, you are going to show they can be replaced…by the people, so that once again our lands can be blanketed with our unique cedars. The people will be very proud."

"We are His instruments, Hanna. He has now given us the resources, thanks to my parents' love of Lebanon and, it appears, the will of the people to begin to restore what God blessed Lebanon with. Let us pray this project is successful. We are but a beginning. It will take many years and many citizens to make a difference."

"You are correct, Monsieur DuBois, but as it is said, a long journey always begins with the most important first step."

"Hello," Alexander spoke into the telephone after the second ring, "Alex Simon here."

"Hello, *Baba*," replied François, with his broad smile "this is your son calling from Beirut. I have very good news for you."

"Just a moment," Alexander answered, "let me get your mother on the other phone. She has been anxious for your call too."

"Hello, François, my darling!" As Madeleine spoke rapidly in English with her French accent, her smile broadened. "How are you coping with all the terrible events in the region? We worry about you all the time. Are you safe?"

Although François tried to call his parents at least weekly, he had been too involved with his business affairs, necessary travel, and starting the cedar plantings. He waited to call them until he had good news about the cedar seedling planting project. For the next thirty minutes, he happily brought them up to date with the progress he had made.

"We will consume a good portion of your financial commitment during the next several months, but this time next year we may need more funds. I will be happy to send you a status report and budget so you may use it to seek more contributions from your friends and other Lebanese expatriates."

"That's wonderful news, son. Wonderful!" Alexander replied with a strong sense of pride in his newfound son. "It is so wise, actually imperative, to invite and include representatives of all religious persuasions. That was good, son. Always err on the side of inclusion," he advised. "Make sure everyone gets credit."

"Your father is absolutely correct, François. Even as I began building clinics in Beirut, I needed so many others' support and financial contributions. I always made sure everyone got their due credit. You make your father and me very, very proud."

"How else could I be, Mother? With the blessing of your example, and my father's involvement in Florida charities and with St. Jude Hospital in Memphis, you taught me well, both of you. And, Father, you will be pleased to know that cousin Marina Chalhoub in Douma is the director of the project in Batroun Province, and especially in Douma. Hers will be among the first test projects along with Bsharre."

"That's wonderful, son." Alex smiled, his chest filled with pride. "Marina is a beautiful woman and full of energy. She'll make you proud."

Then, he added, "François, we will be attending a fund-raising gala in Memphis for St. Jude, so if you can get your report to us shortly, we can discuss it with our fellow members of the Board of Governors and seek financial support. I'm sure Danny Thomas will support us."

"You will receive my report very soon, Father, including photographs of the first planting, too."

"I have an appointment next week with Anthony Kabbani here in Beirut in hopes his family will contribute significantly as they did with Mother's projects."

"I'm sure they will, my love," responded Madeleine. "Would you like me to call them too?"

"That would help, Mother. Yes, that would be a good idea."

Each of them could feel their combined enthusiasm building.

"With all the bad news and huge influx of refugees resulting from that terrible six-day war, I think most of my friends will want to be part of this wonderful project."

"And be sure to tell them this is a tax-exempt foundation," he noted with a chuckle.

"Oh, yes, that will matter to some, but not to those who would shrug off that tax benefit issue," Madeleine laughed. "But that does help."

After a moment of thoughtful silence, Madeleine spoke again. "Guess what! Your father and I are going to take a trip! He's taking me to Marseille to celebrate the fifth anniversary of our reunion, and the forty-seventh anniversary of our first meeting and the beginning of our love for each other. Isn't that exciting? I can hardly wait!"

"Actually," Alexander added, "we were in love with each other the day we were born. We just didn't know it until Uncle Hanna and your grandmother introduced us that evening at dinner in *Place du Liban*."

"Oh, Iskandar, just your mention of *Place du Liban* excites me. I love you so much."

"We'll be in Marseille for a week, François. Then, we hope to tour the South of France in ways we couldn't afford in 1920."

"Wonderful, *Maman!*" François quickly replied, with a delicious warm feeling as he thought, *Maybe I can bring Leah so they can get to know her better. I sure hope they find a way to accept Leah*, he thought. "What a great idea!"

"We'll send you a copy of our itinerary, son," said Alexander, loving the sensation every time he uttered the word son. "We'll be flying out in a few weeks."

"I'll try to join you, for sure," François was happy to reply. "Leah is in Paris for the time being. We see each other every other weekend. We can join you there."

"Wonderful, François. See you then."

"François," Alexander asked, "have you pondered my concerns and discussed them with Leah?"

"Yes, *Biyee*, I thought seriously about your points. We agree they must be resolved before going further. And we will resolve them to my satisfaction. She wants to be with me and knows my needs." Wanting not to get into a long discussion, Francois decided to end the call.

"*Biyee*, I'll call again soon. Maybe I'll get a chance to speak with Helena. How is she? And how is her love life? Please give her my best."

"I will. She asks about you too. Maybe soon you should come to Florida and visit. She'll give you a run for your money, especially when she's on her horse."

"We'll talk again soon, Dad, I promise. Next week, same day. Gotta run now. Goodbye."

As François gently placed his telephone on its cradle, he became pensive, asking himself, *Are the Israelis after her too intensely, or maybe they are after me. Or maybe they want to kill both of us as long as we are together. Spies? Ridiculous! But they are not convinced. So the danger persists as long as her friend Itzak feels threatened. God, how awful are the deadly sins…paranoia, coveting another's …then there is the question of where we can live. Certainly I cannot relocate to Israel. They don't want Christians there. And I belong in Lebanon.*

François rested his hand on the phone for several minutes after their goodbyes, then lifted it again to call Leah.

"*Allo,*"

"*Allo,* Leah. This is François. And how is your day going?"

"I'm fine, François, but I miss you. Each day is the same as the day before. I'd rather be with you."

"Well, today is Thursday. Can you come to Beirut tonight or tomorrow for the weekend? I miss you too. And we have so much to talk about. I've been doing some thinking, Leah. I want this relationship to grow, to find a way for us to be together all the time."

"I feel the same way, darling. We do need to resolve our issues we both have not fully addressed together."

"Yes, I will leave Paris tomorrow so we can be together and bring what we know we must deal with out in the open. Let's resolve them together so we can live our lives without lingering questions."

"Wonderful, Leah. Call me with your flight number so I can meet you at the Beirut airport."

"I'll see you tomorrow afternoon, my love."

"I can hardly wait, Leah."

Leah's Air France flight 12 arrived on time at 6 p.m. With only a carryon bag, Leah quickly walked from the gate into François' waiting arms.

"I love you, Leah, and welcome to Beirut!"

"Mmmmm, I love being in your arms, François. I've missed you. It's been three weeks!"

Taking her suitcase, bodyguard Antoine commented, "My partner, Nicola, is coming with the car, sir, to accompany you to the hotel. We will stay with you day and night."

"Thank you, Antoine. Leah, let's have dinner at our favorite restaurant."

An hour later, François and Leah sat at a quiet table at Joseph's, a small, elegant restaurant in the Hamra district, near Beirut's most upscale shops featuring ladies apparel and fine jewelry. Antoine and Nicola stood guard unobtrusively watching over the two lovers.

After they enjoyed their first sips of a fine Lebanese white wine, eyes focused on each other, François smiled and reached out across the table, inviting Leah to grasp his hand. "Leah, you know I love you with all my heart."

"And, François, you know I love you with all my heart. I want to be with you always. How can we get there?"

"We both know the issues, the questions, and that we love each other. But, Leah, you know I cannot endure the possibility you would ever leave me again, drawn by the magnet of your heritage. We have to commit to each other forever and resolve questions including: Where do we live together? What about children? I mean we're both still young enough. You know I can't live in Israel. The extremists want to remove Christians, Muslims, and all non-Jews. It's the same as it was after the Babylonian exile when Nehemiah and Ezra, when families were divided. Non-Jews were forcibly removed."

"I know, François, I know Israel is not the home for us. Not just for you, and, I must say, no longer a place where I can live. Not even alone. All they want to do is go to war, take more land, and live under siege. But, can I live with you here in Beirut? I've come to admire the Lebanese, I so love the land, and, for me, even Moses wanted to be among the cedars. But what would that mean for you? I mean would your family accept me? Would your colleagues, friends and business associates pull away from you? These are questions we must answer."

"And what about children, Leah? We both believe in our religions. As the saying goes: 'If your mother speaks Chinese, you will speak Chinese.' I respect Judaism. After all, we moderate Christians believe we are an extension of Judaism, that Jesus, our Lord and son of the living God, the same God, came by God to fulfill the prophecies of the ancient prophets. My preference, Leah, is that we live in Lebanon and, God willing, if we have children they be raised as Christians while being taught the history and the law of Judaism, of Moses. After all, there is and always has been a Jewish community here in Lebanon. It's the state of Israel, not Judaism that is the issue. Can you unequivocally commit to not returning to Israel?"

Leah, listening intently, lowered her head, hoping to do what most Jews have difficulty doing. She knew that to be with her love, and, hopefully have children, she would have to separate her religion from the state of Israel and Zionism.

"It's been very difficult, François, for me to turn away from the state of Israel. You must know that. Yet, I have made this decision. I choose you, darling, forever. I am convinced I can come to love Lebanon as you do. I do so far," she giggled, smiling broadly, grateful the issues had been brought forward and, in her mind, satisfactorily answered.

"And children? We've never spoken about children. How many shall we have, Leah?"

"Well, young man," she laughed, "I'm now forty-two. There's time for two, maybe three. I'm not sure I'm ready to give up my religion, but if we live in

Lebanon the children should know both religions, don't you think?"

"I'll think about that, Leah. Now I think it's time for us to order dinner. We may have to revisit these issues again, but I'm satisfied for now, darling."

"Yes, my love, both of us must ponder these things so we are both absolutely certain."

> *Your soul is oftentimes a battlefield,*
> *upon which your reason and your judgment*
> *wage war against your passion and your appetite.*
> Kahlil Gibran

CHAPTER 26

Damascus, Syria

The next morning, François and Leah, joined by Antoine and Nicola, began their drive to Damascus. It would take more than an hour's drive through the Bekaa Valley to the border checkpoint on top of the next mountain range, the Syrian Mountains. After that stop, it was a fairly short drive down the mountain to the city with magnificent views of that grand, ancient metropolis of Damascus.

As they drove through the Bekaa Valley to connect with the road up the Syrian Mountains, François noticed that Leah was taking a number of photographs as they passed interesting sights, including the tents of the Bedouins, who came to work for the farmers. In the distance, within her viewfinder, she could see Syrian tanks parked and hunkered down several feet into the soil to provide low, reduced profiles from the air and anti-aircraft installations with the tanks and guns pointed south down the valley toward Israel. "Monsieur Dubois," Antoine asked as he looked at Francois, "you see how the Syrians incorrectly assumed Israel would attack from the south, up the Bekaa Valley instead of from the sea? It was Syria's Ministry of Defense, Hafez Al Assad's belief that if Israel were to strike Syria, they likely would attack from the south. This assumption proved to be wrong on June fifth, and, as a result of Israel's devastating, total destruction of Syria's Soviet supplied aircraft, the President and his Minister of Defense, Hafez al-Assad are under intense political pressure. I saw that in this morning's newspaper. Minister al-Assad and President Nur al-Atassi are now at each other's throats. No one knows where this will lead, both are very strong politically. Al-Assad is, after all, an Alawite, a minority Shiia sect who seeks a secular state and Nur al-Atassi is Sunni, Syria's majority by far, and does not want a secular state.

"Al-Assad's allies and supporters are successful minorities who prefer a secular state, including Druze, Christians, and members of his Alawite tribe from northwest Syria. The minorities always band together for their own safety and welfare.

"Atassi is a domineering president, but both men are very demanding and zealously protect their power. As you know, Monsieur DuBois, President al-Atassi came into power in 1966 after a coup d'état by the Baath Party. Al-Atassi is from the dominant radical wing and quickly removed members of other parties from the government. Al-Assad, a pragmatist, is also a Baathist party member. He became Atassi's Minister of Defense but has had many significant differences of views from al-Atassi. They don't like each other, and it's only a matter of time before there might be another coup. This time by al-Assad."

"Sounds pretty tenuous to me. I hope that doesn't cause us problems at the border."

As Leah was taking photos, she caught Antoine's attention, who turned in his seat to speak to her. "Pardon, Mademoiselle, but I must ask why you are taking pictures of the Syrian tanks and anti-aircraft teams over there."

"What are you doing, Leah?" Francois asked, alerted. "You shouldn't be taking pictures of Syria's military emplacements! They might think you are an Israeli spy."

"Oh, my God!" Leah replied, embarrassed. "I didn't realize I was doing that. I wanted to photograph the Bedouins, the farms, and the mountains in the distance."

"Leah, put down your camera," François quickly instructed. "It is not a good idea to be taking pictures here. Especially now. The Syrians are very nervous. If they see your camera, they may stop us and confiscate your camera and film. And they might want to interrogate us. There are thousands of Syrian military and paramilitary personnel in Lebanon these days. Most are on alert here in the Bekaa, prepared for more possible Israeli incursions from the south".

Caught off guard, she nervously shut off her camera and placed it inside her bag.

Francois saw Antoine look sternly at him, shaking his head.

As they continued along the road at the base of the Syrian mountains on the eastern edge of the Bekaa Valley, François told her, "Leah, the border between Lebanon and Syria is usually not a major detail. But with the tensions that have arisen because of the Israeli takeover of the Syrian Golan Heights and the destruction of the Syrian air force on their runways, the Syrian authorities are very angry, very suspicious, very cautious. So, we must be on our best behavior. Mine is a diplomatic passport and I pass through here very often, mostly on business, and many times on behalf of the Lebanese government. So they know me. You are safe, but they may ask you difficult questions. You have a Lebanese passport. Remember, your official name is Leah Chalhoub, a well-known Lebanese name of Douma, a popular, but very small mountain village. You have only recently moved back to Lebanon from France where you have lived for a number of years.

"We will be approaching the border as we ascend the mountain. Don't be nervous, and do not take any more pictures."

"Don't be nervous? How can I not be nervous? I'm a wreck! My country's behavior led by that warmonger Moshe Dayan attacked this country after both Syria and Israel accepted the ceasefire. No wonder they're so angry. Don't let them take me from you, François. I am very nervous. Please stay by me."

"Be calm, Leah, everything will be fine. *Inshallah*, God willing."

As the Mercedes pulled up to the official border at the top of the mountain, Lebanese police and armed soldiers stood on one side, and armed Syrian soldiers on the other side of the horizontal steel bars blocking traffic. Lines of cars awaiting clearance were long. Traffic was heavy in both directions, but it didn't seem enough to cause a serious delay. The lead guard raised his open hand instructing them to stop. Nicola stopped the car, handed the guard his passport, auto ownership papers, and explained his purpose for entering Syria, describing François and his colleague, and his obvious bodyguard, Antoine, in the front passenger seat. After the guard inspected the passports and visas that François provided and looked throughout the interior, he directed Nicola to pull over to the border offices, a one-story stone building where Leah and François were instructed to enter. Francois looked nervously to Nicola and wondered what was to come.

"This is very unusual, Nicola," Francois commented in a whisper, with a worried frown. "We've never had to go inside before. What's going on?"

Nicola shrugged and replied, "They told me the Syrian secret service captured a pair of Israeli Mossad agents two days ago, and they were questioned at length in Damascus. They are being extra diligent now, more than ever." Francois and Leah followed the border patrol officer into the offices. "I have your documents."

After ten minutes of anxiously waiting, a Federal agent entered the large room. François noticed their passports in his hand.

"*Mahrharbahr*, greetings," said the checkpoint officer in charge to François. "Follow me please," he directed as he led the two into his small, austere office where he gestured to two chairs opposite his desk. After he sat down behind his desk, he held their passports in his hands, looked them over, and, as he looked at François and Leah, he tapped the passports on his desk and said slowly, "I am sorry, Monsieur Dubois, but I am going to have to ask you a few questions…alone. And, your companion will also be questioned separately."

As the Federal agent stood up, he asked Leah to join him as he ushered her out of his office and took her into another room. Then, he returned to François. "I am very sorry, Monsieur DuBois, but since the fifth of June, our government has become very cautious and restrictive. The Israeli attack has caused extraordinary intensive political pressure on leaders of our government. I am sure you understand. They are forcing us to take measures out of the ordinary."

"Certainly, sir, I do understand, but I do not understand the problem you have with Mademoiselle Chalhoub and me. What is the issue here?"

"To be very candid with you, sir, the Syrian secret service captured agents of the Israeli Mossad just two days ago. One was based in Beirut, the other, a high-ranking agent from Israel. After several hours of secret service questioning, one of the agents declared he was seeking an Israeli agent in Lebanon, a tall, beautiful dark-haired woman named Leah Wolsinski who has lived in Israel for a number of years. As a result, all border checkpoints have been alerted. We must be very cautious. As we speak, my colleagues are questioning her and taking several photographs of your friend. We must find out if Mademoiselle Chalhoub is this woman."

"But, sir, with all due respect, you have no right to do these things. She has a Lebanese passport, and is my friend. We only have plans to visit the *souk* in Damascus and a day trip to Palmyra. This is a simple overnight tourist visit. I come through this checkpoint all the time."

"I understand," the officer replied diplomatically, "but our people are very nervous these days. As you know, and I believe because of your high position, I can share with you in absolute confidence that as a result of the total destruction of our air force by the Israeli Air Force who now occupy our the Golan Heights. Our secret service, is receiving a lot of blame from the highest levels of our government. Even our Minister of Defense, Hafez al-Assad and our President Nur al-Atassi are under intense pressure. They are now blaming each other for the surprise destruction of our Air Force. Our president is blaming al-Assad and al-Assad is blaming the president. We must stop all Israeli incursions, all Israeli spies before our government is weakened any further. When extraordinary events like this happen, someone must take the blame, and as they say, 'fall on their sword.' No, sir, we do not wish to be among those who will suffer enormous indignities by allowing the wrong people into Syria, especially during these trying times.

"Please express our regrets to your good President Helou, for we know how much he appreciates your work and how difficult are these times. Syria and Lebanon both are accepting hundreds of thousands of pitiful Palestinian refugees. Jordan is receiving even more. We are all in this together at great cost in humanity and capital."

Then, as he stood once again and looked at his watch, he said, "They should be finished shortly. If all is acceptable, I'm certain you will be on your way. If not, I would advise you to return to Lebanon as soon as possible, where your companion will surely be kept under very tight surveillance, I am certain!"

"We are already under surveillance, sir, by the Mossad itself, especially since I returned from Malta on a fact-finding trip, at the direction of our president, to inspect the American ship USS Liberty that the Israelis attacked," François replied nervously.

"Yes, I am aware of that attack. It is difficult to believe the Americans didn't rescue their servicemen, nor make Israel pay. Had Syria done that, we likely would have been attacked by the United States too."

Then, François described, without details, the results of his Malta investigation.

"And you know all the facts? You must be careful, Monsieur DuBois. I am certain the Mossad wishes to silence you and the sooner the better. Perhaps, as a result of your experience, I can find some way to help.

"Well then, Monsieur Dubois, depending on your companion's questioning results, you'll either be wished a pleasant stay in Syria, or you'll find yourselves under surveillance in Lebanon by the Israeli Mossad and the Syrian secret service, both of which operate without constraint in Lebanon. I am sorry to tell you these things, sir."

François felt his hands moisten as he found himself worrying about Leah and her past for the first time. For twenty years his love for Leah occupied his mind. Now, the suspicion by both the Mossad and the Syrian Secret Service that she may be an Israeli spy became an issue of life or death. Hers and his.

As the seconds ticked by, feeling more like hours, François' mind raced with emotional ups and downs, especially regarding Leah. Who is Leah? Marina had asked him. Now he wasn't so sure. He could not believe she was a spy for Israel, serving Israel's interests, pretending to be his love and future bride. Neither he nor she had been prepared for this terrible turn of events. He didn't believe she could be a spy for anyone.

He followed the border official out of his office toward another room where Leah had been taken. As they entered the interrogation room, his eyes went straight to Leah's eyes. He could see her anguish and tension, and he worried even more.

"Please excuse our interruption," the official with François said to the two male interrogators sitting at the same table opposite Leah. "May we come in?"

"Yes, of course," one of the men replied. "We have completed our questioning. *Ahlen*, welcome."

"Can we leave now?" interjected François, asking the official with a mix of anxiety and frustration. "We would like to continue with our visit to Damascus, if all is well."

One of the seated officials nodded his approval to Leah, permitting her to stand and step to François' side. "You may go now. We have all the information we need at this time. And, Monsieur DuBois, recognizing your position in Lebanon, we do not wish to detain you any longer. However, in time we may need to meet with your companion again. I trust she will be made available if that becomes necessary."

The interrogator, while diplomatic in his statement, also included in his voice a tone of warning to Leah and François. "We expect to see you both here again in two days as you depart Syria and return to Lebanon. Those were your plans, weren't they?"

"Yes, of course. In two days we shall be returning to Lebanon through this very checkpoint. *Shookrun.* Thank you, sir."

"I suggest you be absolutely certain of your arrival here in two days," the official emphatically replied briskly.

Together, Leah and François received their stamped passports and quickly exited the checkpoint offices and returned to their Mercedes where their two bodyguards were patiently waiting. As they stepped into the car, Leah's hand nervously and anxiously reached for François' hand and squeezed it tightly. "That was a most unpleasant surprise, Francois. I did not expect to be questioned by the Syrian secret service!"

"Nor did I, my dear. What was the issue?"

"They told me several Mossad agents had been interrogated by Syrian secret service…and their reputation is not unlike that of the Mossad in that they usually obtain answers for every question…they were told by at least one of the agents that a certain 'fortyish woman named Leah Wolsinski was in Lebanon seeking important information in behalf of the Mossad.' In other words, an Israeli spy who may be seeking to enter Syria to determine certain vulnerabilities of the Syrian armed forces."

"Yes, I heard a portion of that. As a result of the complete success of the surprise morning attack by the Israeli air force on June fifth, there appeared not only to be a complete breakdown of information of Israel's intentions by the Syrian spy network in Israel, but also of the absolute vulnerability of the Syrian air force and its lack of preparedness. Actually, they are not certain what new information about Syria the Mossad could obtain that would now be valuable, especially at this moment.

"That may be why we both were not detained much longer, or even put in prison."

Then, thinking for a few moments as they sat in the back seat together, François thought perhaps it would be wise to turn around and return to Beirut immediately. But, thinking that might be a bad sign to the officials who remained at the checkpoint office doorway watching them, François decided to completely change the atmosphere by leaning forward, tapping Nicola's shoulder and saying, "*Yallah*! Let's continue our drive to Damascus. And, best not exceed any speed limits, Nicola," he added with a laugh, more nervous than he wished.

François had driven to Damascus many times each year to visit with his clientele there and, on many occasions, on behalf of his President to deliver messages and retrieve responses. For many political reasons, Syria and Lebanon still hadn't actually exchanged ambassadors since the two countries became independent of the French protectorate edict; Syria in 1941 and Lebanon in 1943. While the two countries had extraordinary family, private business, and social relationships over the years, many in the Syrian government regime still had difficulty accepting the fact that Lebanon was an independent state, and no longer a province of Syria as it had been for centuries.

Most Lebanese emigrants to the Americas were Christians, dating back to the mid-nineteenth century and had Syrian passports that stated they were from the Lebanon province of Syria. Most called themselves Syrians for years as they lived and prospered throughout the Americas. Interestingly, however, those in the United States found themselves having to declare that they were Lebanese, not Syrian, not Arab, particularly after the Arab-Israeli War in 1948, and to avoid political labels since the U.S. media and government heavily favored the new Israeli nation, which painfully created enmity in the United States toward Americans from Syria, and, later, immigrants from the rest of the Arab world. It didn't help that during the current Cold War, the Soviet Union, America's Cold War adversary, was an ally and supplier of arms to Syria and Egypt.

Still, Syrian-Lebanese relations were strained due to the Syrian government interference in Western-oriented Lebanese internal affairs.

As François considered these facts, he found himself baffled by the intrigues and sometimes bizarre actions of nations in the Middle East.

It's all very tribal, and all powerful regimes ensure the people are held back by the lack of individual freedom with multi-cultural democracy, a free market economy and western oriented politics found only in Lebanon. Maybe that is why the Syrians and Israelis covet Lebanon so dearly, he thought as they motored down the mountain highway toward Damascus, the huge, bustling ancient, yet metropolitan, city suddenly appearing beneath them.

Leah turned to François and, with tears in her eyes, pleading, she whispered to him, "Oh, François, I am so nervous. They questioned me in Arabic, but I told them I could not speak fluent Arabic because my family and I had only recently relocated to Douma from France where I had lived since I was a child. So, I spoke to them in French. They were very dour and seemed extremely suspicious of me."

François, noticing that she was speaking to him very fast in fluent French, was sympathetic toward her. And he was pleased with her quick thinking.

"I told them I was born in Lebanon, but my family had moved to Paris in the 1920s. I hope I said the right things. I hope and pray they believed me. I'm no spy for Israel, François! You must believe that. Tell me you believe me, please. I must have your confidence. You know I am not an Israeli spy! It's that damned crazy, jealous Itzak!"

François, torn by his love for Leah, and his growing concern for their safety, put his arm around her shoulders and whispered to her, "I do believe you, Leah. You are no Israeli spy. I love you and we will get past this terrible and dangerous situation. Let's try to enjoy this day. In two days we will return to Beirut and safety. Close your eyes now and rest for a while."

As she put her head on his shoulder, she found it hard to relax. She was very worried.

And even though François heard his own words, he too was deeply concerned. Perhaps they could no longer be safe even in Beirut, especially with the possibility that they would be watched not only by the angry Mossad, but now by the very suspicious Syrian Secret Service.

My God, what have we gotten ourselves into?

Leah finally emerged from a short, restless nap, looked out the car window and exclaimed, "Damascus is huge, isn't it? And so spread out. There don't seem to be many tall buildings like in Tel Aviv, François."

"Leah, almost all buildings in Damascus are six stories or less. And, since the *Hamediyah Souk* and Omayyad Mosque are the central commercial and spiritual anchors of the city, most inhabitants live in or near the old city. They claim Damascus to be the oldest continuously occupied city in the world, more than 3000 years. It is an exciting city, to be sure, filled with contrasting ancient and modern artifacts and cultures.

"But after our detention at the border, I'm not as upbeat as I wanted to be." Leah, avoiding his eyes, responded, "It seems a Mossad agent told them I looked like an Israeli Mossad agent who was in Lebanon and traveling to Syria."

"Why would they say that, Leah? You're not a spy, are you?"

"Of course not! How could you say that?" she said indignantly.

"I try Leah, I guess I'm very upset with all that has happened," he replied softly. "Please forgive me. I believe you love me, I also know you have loved the idea of Israel and have lived in Israel twenty years. He was pained by his mixed feelings and instantly regretted what he was saying, venting his concern.

"It was Itzak, François! I know it! They only told me that a Mossad agent, under questioning, divulged that a woman named Leah Wolsinski was an agent in Lebanon. It was Itzak's doing! He's the only person who knows my name! He has spread that poisonous message to get even with me because I wouldn't agree with him nor become his lover!"

"Itzak wants revenge, Leah. He is so jealous of you and my affections toward you. He'll do anything!"

François' emotions began to swing again, fearing the worst, hoping for the best. He thought, *If she is indeed an Israeli spy, then she's been damned good at it! Even when we make love. Even in Douma. Why? Why would she do these things?*

"Leah, we need to be careful and, now that we are here, we must enjoy ourselves. I promised the border agent we would return to Lebanon in two days, so now we should go to the *souk*, relax and, just be tourists for a few hours. See for yourself how the Syrians live their lives. We'll stay the night in the new Sham Hotel in the city. Then, in the morning, maybe we'll drive east to Palmyra.

"I'm very disturbed, Leah, by the detention at the border, the questioning of you, and the accusations."

"They are all very disturbing to me too, François!"

"I love you, Leah, and I want us to share our lives together, forever. Yet, I must admit, that the border incident has caused me discomfort. This whole Itzak spy thing has me rattled. Now, let's enjoy these two days and I'll deal with this when we return to Beirut.

"Leah, I learned early in life to compartmentalize my life's experiences, helping me survive my many diverse activities. At the same time, while immersed in my banking career, flying all over the Arab world, to Europe and beyond, I became deeply engrossed in the politics of Lebanon, the President's domestic needs, and the regional tensions. If I couldn't compartmentalize, I knew I'd go crazy sometimes. Now, with my personal life on its edge, I am surely being tested as never before."

Listening in silence, Leah was taking everything in, watching out her window at the people, the buildings of the old city, marveling at the growing crowds as they approached the renowned *Hamediyah Souk* and the Omayyad Mosque.

"We are at the *souk* entrance, sir," Nicola announced. "We will park now. Antoine and I will walk just a few steps behind you."

"Excellent, Nicola. We will stroll through the *souk*, and as we approach the other end at the mosque, we will tour it. Let's go now, Leah. You will witness free enterprise at its best. What you will see is exactly how the *souk* has been the center of local commerce, legend tells us, since a thousand years before Christ. Imagine! And most of the small shops…and some are very, very small…have been in the same families for centuries. It is almost impossible to buy or even lease a space here today."

"Why is that, François?"

"The fact is, many shops handed down by generations have had to be split among heirs. As a result, they get smaller and smaller. Most shops are only on the first or second floor, while some operate with a two-story layout. Watch out," he smiled, "as we walk the central mall. Those store owners who need business will almost accost you, a fresh face with a foreigner's look. They will do almost anything to get you to buy from them, whether it is home furnishings, shoes, *ouds* (guitars), brass tables, samovars, gold…oh yes…the *souk* has a special area for gold merchants only! But they say the best prices for gold are in Aleppo."

As they entered the *souk*, a walking tea merchant with an enormous polished, glistening silver samovar strapped to his back yelled to them while bending over, pouring hot tea in two cups and thrusting them toward Leah. "Tea, Madame? It is delicious! You will love it!"

"François, what shall I do? Is it healthy?"

"Yes, it is healthy and tasty. He is inspected by the government each day. We'll each have a cup. It's very tasty."

"He's quite picturesque in his *keffiyeh*, François. And that beautiful, shiny, tapered samovar on his back. It's almost as big as he is!"

"The cups are small, enough for a few sips. We'll drink here by him and return his cups. Here, love, enjoy!"

With the transfer to Syrian pounds that François exchanged at the border, he purchased two cups of fresh sweet, hot tea. So began Leah's initiation to the Damascus *souk*, a two-storied, very long, open air, but barrel-roofed, covered mall, perhaps a thousand feet long, filled with thousands of shoppers, hundreds of shops on either side, young boys venturing out of the stores beckoning shoppers, cajoling them to enter their family's shop or that of their employer. One approaching Leah said, "Please, Madame, you will enjoy our hospitality, our beautiful textiles, carpets, our spices, our brass…come with me!"

The only place Leah had ever experienced such high pressure shopping was in the old city of Jerusalem in the Arab Quarter where the *souk* was much smaller, but generated very much the same activities.

"You can and should bargain for anything you want," François told her.

"You do the bargaining for me," she laughed.

It took them a good hour to window shop and stroll through the *souk*, Leah taking photographs the entire way. "It's so picturesque, François! Is it like this all the time?"

"All the time. This is a huge city of millions of people, and this is where most people sightsee and shop. So it's busy with locals and, it's also a major tourist attraction. You'll see visitors from many nations here. See there at the end? That is the Omayyad Mosque. Legend tells us the head of John the Baptist is in the tabernacle you'll see in its center. It's really a magnificent tribute to him, all white marble. The mosque was built on the site of an early Christian church. Of course, Islam didn't arrive in Damascus until the seventh century, six hundred years after Jesus."

"It's really fascinating, François. I…"

"Stop, Leah," interrupted François. "I just got a signal from Nicola. Two men are following us."

> *Would that I could be the peacemaker in your soul that I might turn the discord and the rivalry of your elements into oneness and melody. But how shall I unless you yourselves be the peacemakers, nay, the lovers of your elements?*
> Kahlil Gibran

Chapter 27

The Souk

After a few hours in the *souk*, having visited with François' favorite merchant whose shop was located at the statue to Jupiter not far from the mosque, where they couldn't resist purchasing several mosaic boxes and two silk prayer rugs, they decided to call it a day and go to the hotel. The Sham Hotel was beautifully decorated with a huge lobby atrium that included, on the periphery of the ground floor, the elegant shops, mostly for tourists, and restaurants that were decorated as though the diners were sitting under Bedouin tents, ceilings draped in cloth with oriental-style, yet, modern lighting. They feasted on fine wines, a *mezza* of numerous delicacies, including hummus, *baba ghanoush*, goat cheeses, *fistok* (pistachios), *tabouleh*, spinach pies, rolled grape leaves, *laban* (yogurt), *lahamishweh* (shish kebob), and seafood from the Mediterranean.

After dining, François asked Leah, "Did you enjoy your *mezza*, darling?" forgetting the doubts that filled his mind following the events at the border checkpoint.

"Oh, yes, I did! All your foods are fabulous. So tasty! The hummus and *baba ghanoush* are wonderful! Although I can't help but still be very bothered by the questioning I had to go through. It was quite unnerving, to say the least. That damned Itzak! How dare he!"

"We are still very much at war, Leah. Even though the parties have all agreed to a ceasefire, Israel still occupies Syria's Golan Heights, all of Palestine, Gaza, and Egypt's Sinai. The people and governments remain at heightened alert. And yes, your friend Itzak," he sneered at the name, "is still at war with you…maybe us."

"What are we going to do? What can we do about him?"

"We'll have to deal with him at the proper time, Leah. My contacts are primarily in Lebanon, so we'll have to wait until we return late tomorrow. You'll be safe there. I'll make certain you will be. And you'll be much safer there than in Israel."

"And likely safer there than here in Syria, too. François, I'm very scared."

~~~

François wasn't feeling all that confident either. While he still believed in her innocence, he wondered if there might be a grain of truth in the suspicions of the Syrians. What if she is involved?

For the first time ever, he felt uneasy being in Syria, even as a tourist. It just seemed so very different this trip.

As they finished their dinner and headed toward the lobby, Nicola signaled François that the area was safe.

François, followed by his two bodyguards, led Leah across the marble floor to the elevators. He could not help but look around the atrium to see if anyone was watching them. He saw two tall men wearing turbans and long, brown gowns walking toward them.

Leah also noticed them and instinctively gripped François' hand tightly as she whispered breathlessly, "Who…who are they, François?"

"Don't worry, Leah. They are probably Iranian Shiia mullahs, and some of them are so somber in appearance that they scare lots of people. But they are just tourists who come to Damascus, and sometimes to Beirut, to breathe the fresh air. Their government is very restrictive under the Shah. He is one tough cookie!"

"I'll feel better when we are in our room with a guard at the door. Let's go straight to the room, François. I'm very nervous. I don't understand this whole situation we have found ourselves in."

Neither slept well that night. It was a fitful time with one or the other rising to pace around the room. Dressing early the next morning to the rhythmic sounds of the morning prayers being broadcast from minarets across the city, not completely rested, they joined their guards for an early breakfast and left the hotel at 7 a.m., hoping to be gone before anyone would expect their departure.

"We are driving east, Leah, to the ancient city of Palmyra, a Roman city that has the most amazing oasis in the entire Middle East. The oasis is at least three miles long, filled with ancient olive trees, date palms, pomegranates, and gardens all fed by a single artesian well that brings forth pure water all the time. During Roman times, they say Palmyra was governed by Queen Zenobia."

"A Roman city governed by a woman? How exciting! Was she a good queen?"

"Well, she was until she challenged Rome by printing her own coins with her sons' pictures on the coins instead of the Emperor's," he chuckled.

"She did that? How courageous of her! How daring!"

François smiled. "Oh, for sure, she was, as you say, daring and courageous. But, as it turned out, she was also quite foolish because Emperor Aurelian came to Palmyra."

"What happened then?"

"The Emperor literally destroyed that desert city, killed her sons, and took her hostage back to Italy."

"My God! I was aware of the Roman destruction of Jerusalem, but I did not know about Queen Zenobia and Palmyra!"

"Palmyra was a fabulous eastern trade center of the Roman Empire. Wait until you see the colonnade of columns, the baths, and the monuments. It's incredible. The archeologists continue to search for other major facilities. They really look forward to finding the theater. That will happen soon, I'm certain. They believe that it is under wind-blown sand now, although most of the land between Damascus and Palmyra is hard desert."

During the four-hour drive east on the Baghdad Highway, they first passed miles and miles of endless wheat fields, then miles of pistachio groves, olive groves, and farming villages.

"See, Leah," he said smiling, "even the Syrians have turned the desert green."

"Oh, François, what are those cute cone-shaped buildings?"

"Those are called beehives, Leah. They are desert family dwellings built of clay, and are extremely strong and efficient. With their conical shape, the hotter air inside rises to the top and keeps the families cool in the lower portion. They can also withstand the strong winds that blow down from the rugged mountains on either side of this vast desert valley. Actually, Leah, Syria is quite self-sufficient in its ability to feed itself, even to the extent that they export oil, wheat, nuts, olive products and fruits as well. Damascus is built atop a huge reservoir of water. Not much oil in the north, but enough to fill their needs."

"What are those, François?" She gestured to the distance on the right.

"Those are the first efforts at planting huge new olive groves and pistachios out here in the desert. They are joint ventures between the government and private enterprise. Despite the presence of the Communist Soviets, Syria has millennia of dedication to free enterprise. You saw that at the *souk*, didn't you? Even with the Cold War, and Soviet military assistance, not one Syrian work at the Soviet Embassy. The Soviets are considered Godless and counter to the religious beliefs of all Syrians, Moslems, Christians, and Jews!"

"There are Jews in Syria?"

"Of course, Leah. Jews have lived well in Syria since the Mesopotamian Diaspora some twenty-five hundred years ago. There are very successful Jewish artisans and businessmen who prosper in Damascus, Homs, and Aleppo. Islam is a late-comer, arriving only recently, in the seventh century."

Both tired, they dozed off and on for part of the last hour of the drive. François awakened as they felt the car slow down and come to a stop.

"We are here, Monsieur DuBois. We are in Palmyra."

"Well done, Nicola. No one followed us?"

"I saw no one, sir. It was very pleasant and quiet, except for all the trucks traveling to and from Baghdad. There is a lot of trade between the two cities, and Baghdad is just 250 miles farther to the east."

François shook Leah's shoulder to wake her. As he did, her camera fell to the floor.

"Wake up, Leah, we are here. I thought you left your camera at the hotel. But since you didn't, you can take many pictures here in Palmyra."

"Oh," she murmured, yawning, "we're in Palmyra?"

"Yes. Look around, Leah. It's an incredible sight! Look at the Roman colonnades. They extend for over a mile. There is so much to see, and yet, they believe there is still so much more to uncover from the sands."

He opened his door, extended his hand to assist her as they both exited the Mercedes. They stretched their arms wide and tested their legs.

"It's a good thing we brought hats and sunglasses. It's very warm here."

"And it's good you wore light clothing. It's hot throughout the day. But when the winds pick up later as the sun begins to go down, it will become very cold. That's why we brought sweaters too. We have a few hours only to tour the city remains and show you one of the largest and most prolific oases in existence. You are going to see a rare sight!"

"Monsieur DuBois, we have been approached by a local man who offered to be our guide. I've checked his credentials. I know him well. His name is Mohammed Nayli, and he would like to meet you."

François looked at the guide and was impressed. He was well-manicured, wearing a conservative dark suit, white shirt, and thin knit tie, and while his suit was well- worn, it was neatly pressed. He was slender, and stood about François' height, nearly six feet tall. Because he was fluent in Arabic, French, and English, he was one of the most favored guides in Palmyra.

François gestured from alongside the car toward the small gathering of children and a few camel owners, all eagerly seeking to provide their services to these tourists who, hopefully, would share some of their wealth for errands, candy, and postcards sold by the children, and camel rides by their fathers.

"They are so modest and, it would appear, very poor people, François. Let's take a camel ride. I've never been on a camel. We never had any in the kibbutz," she whispered to him.

"Why not? Let's do that, and we'll be helping the local economy, as well."

Nicola walked with them over to the camel drivers and made the necessary arrangements. The drivers then, with their sticks, gave commands to the two camels who went down on their front knees, lowering their backs and saddles so François and Leah could climb on, assisted by the owners. Up they went while their two camels yawned and made their obnoxious sounds. Once they settled themselves in the rugged, wooden saddles, the drivers reached with their sticks and touched the legs of the camels to signal them to stand. As they stood up violently, rocking their riders, who, unaccustomed to this motion, swayed backward and forward, gripping onto the saddles so they wouldn't fall off. Their amateurish motions prompted the boys to laugh and the girls giggle at their visitors' clumsiness. They covered their mouths with their hands to try and muffle their sounds of amusement.

Once comfortable in their saddles, the drivers, following the guide, slowly walked the camels and their riders down the hard, stone-covered, crunchy desert surface past each of the two rows of Roman columns. There was little depth in the well-worn sand road as the archeologists, financed by the government and foundations, had provided quite passable and level areas in hopes of promoting comfortable visits by foreign tourists, mainly from Western Europe. Archeologists from universities in Germany, France, and England joint ventured with Syrian museums and universities, searching for important artifacts, evidence of Roman occupation, lifestyle, pre-Roman and early Islamic architecture. The decades-long endeavor included exploring the mounds on the nearby rolling hills that also brought forth magnificent ancient burial tombs, statues, friezes, family portraits carved in stone, and burial slots where family bodies were placed and stacked horizontally, as in private underground mausoleums.

"This is so exciting, François!" Leah laughed, holding onto the saddle with both hands.

"It's very different than riding a horse, that's for sure, Leah. Look at the columns at the baths over to the left. This is amazing!"

"And camels smell much worse than horses, too," she giggled.

After nearly twenty minutes of camel riding, they came to a stop, and took one last visual, lingering sweep of the old city. Leah took some more photos, especially of François' camel, with long, loose tassels hanging from the saddle and blankets. The camels' necks and heads were also colorfully decorated by the owners, expressing the pride they had in their personally trained, treasured animals. They are poor, came from modest one-room stucco homes and diligently tended their treasured camels. They also tend their meager plots within the tall, thin, clay walls that surrounded and subdivided the oasis gardens, the only green area of trees for miles. From the top of the camels, François and Leah could see above the high mud wall surrounding the oasis into the treetops of the lush date trees that flourished alongside the ancient olive trees within the oasis compound that seemed to stretch for miles in an area of bleak, ochre-colored sand and gravel desert, surrounded by high rolling, rounded, brown, barren mountains.

"This is the Syrian desert, Leah. It is very firm, not totally sand. It is very different than in Arabia and the Gulf states. Historians say this entire area was under the seas over a million years ago. They have carbon-tested seashells, and conch shells that the Bedouins have picked up from the desert floor. That too is amazing."

"What intrigues me, François, is that Syria, while so prolific in the north and west with all those farmlands, is so barren at first glance here in the east. So few people here, and not many visitors. Yet, as we were driving here," she added, "I saw small herds of what looked like wild camels walking in the distance. There were those beehive homes clustered into small villages. Then, we saw Bedouin tents with goats, chickens, camels, and children. It's really a different culture and quite picturesque, isn't it?"

They got off their camels once the animals rested again on their front knees, abruptly bringing their riders forward, testing their riding skills, while holding on tightly and laughing at their predicament.

"Now, sir," said Mohammed to François, "we can go into the oasis where, I am convinced, you will enjoy yourselves."

He turned and, gesturing them to follow, led them to an open, shallow pool of crystal clear water. This collection of water serving the stream into the oasis is thirty feet square and about three feet deep.

"This," Mohammed spoke, "is our only source of water. It is *Allah*'s blessing to all of us in Palmyra. There is a spring that feeds this pool. People come here to fill their pots and jugs daily for use in their homes. It also feeds the trees and gardens of the townspeople.

"Although there are not so many people here now, it is said more than 100,000 people lived here during its best years under Queen Zenobia. It was a busy trading city, replacing Petra in the south near Aqaba."

"Now," Mohammed suggested, "let us walk in the oasis. I think you will find it fascinating. What you will see has been the same since Queen Zenobia was overthrown in *272 A.D.* by Emperor Aurelian."

After they stopped by the well-pool where all the clear artesian waters that feed the oasis and the city emerged, they marveled at its clarity and sizable flow.

"The water from here flows down this narrow winding stream," he pointed, "and feeds the entire length of the oasis. It's a veritable forest out here in the desert."

"The stream looks very small," Leah commented. "It's only about a foot deep and four feet across."

"But it flows steady all the time," Mohammed replied. "It does have its limits, of course. Follow me and you will see amazing things."

As they entered the gate through the ten foot high mud-stucco wall, they stepped alongside the stream, keeping their feet on firm soil as they looked around.

"These stucco walls are only about four inches thick, but they don't fall down, do they, Mohammed?" François asked, impressed.

"No, sir, they do not. They are all interconnected, which gives them strength, you see."

"There seem to be sections of land walled off, some small and some larger. Why is that?"

"Each section is owned by family, and as each family grows, portions are given to their sons, so the sections become smaller and smaller."

"Look, François!" Leah exclaimed. "Look at this beautiful olive tree. How old could it be, Mohammed?" she asked, pointing at what she thought was a young tree.

"Madame," Mohamed replied, "that tree is young, probably less than one hundred years old."

"That young? Here?"

"Yes," he answered, "but look at the large stump next to it from where it emerges at the soil. That mother tree is more than a thousand years old."

"And the bigger stump next to it?"

"That's the grandmother tree. I would say it's over two thousand years old."

"The grandmother's and mother's roots feed the young tree then?"

"Yes, that is true, and the roots must be very, very deep. The oasis has many, many very old olive trees, date palms, and pomegranates. Toward the lower end, there are many vegetable gardens. All get plenty of water."

"Really? From that little spring? How do they do that?"

"The water is carefully monitored, Madame. Each family is permitted to remove their wooden gate for one day…a full twenty-four hours…each month as the stream flows by."

"So, their trees get water just one full day each month?"

"See how each tree has small dirt ridges around the tree base with a channel formed from tree to tree? In that way, every family gets an equal share of water, and every tree gets its share as the water flows within the family's portion."

"Incredible! And so simple!" commented François as he watched and listened.

"There is so much food here for the birds, the townspeople have regular hunting seasons within the oasis. We have many, many birds here. God is good."

"Look over there, Mohammed. What's going on?" François saw a group of six men working with axes and shovels with a small child watching. The men were vigorously cutting the roots of a beautiful, tall, and prolific date palm tree with abundant golden dates, one of a cluster of six. "What are they doing?"

"I'll ask, although I have a feeling that I already know," Mohammed replied. After chatting for a few minutes and strolling over to the group, about fifty feet away, still within the same family plot, Mohammed spent a few minutes with the men, gesturing, then returned with a smile on his face.

"The men are in one family; a father and his sons. They are seeking to move a mature date palm to another spot. It is to be the parents' wedding gift to the eldest son who is marrying a young woman in the village. The tree is considered a valuable gift, and since it is rich with plump dates. It is considered a good omen and a blessing to the marrying couple. They are very happy to work so hard with their simple tools. Many men will come to help them when the tree is to be moved so it can be relocated slowly to a hole they have already dug over there," he said as he gestured toward the hole.

"They asked if my visitors, the two of you, would share a cup of sweetened tea with them. They are heating the water over their small fire. The boy is excited to see visitors. They honor you and hope you will honor them by joining them."

After Leah and François joined the group, Leah silently gestured to François, looking at the pot of water and demitasse clear glass cups, tacitly asking if she should drink the tea. Smiling and nodding yes, François extended his hand to the young man squatting by the fire, who was reaching out with a cup of tea to him. Leah, overwhelmed by the kindness and generosity of these poor villagers, accepted, with a smile, her cup and sipped while nodding her head and saying *"Shookrun."*

Leah turned to François and murmured, "Could you please tell them in Arabic that this tea is very tasty, and that I like it very much?"

After a few minutes of exchanging friendly smiles and congenial conversation, the boy brought Leah a freshly cut branch of dates from a palm, as his gift to the beautiful lady, bowing to her, shyly reluctant to speak. Gesturing for her to pull off a date and eat it, he watched her. She pulled off several, and offered them to François, Mohammed, and the boy.

"Yum," she said, biting into the fruit. "It's delicious! I've never eaten a date as fresh as this!"

After visiting a few more minutes with the boy, François, wanting to share, handed the boy a goodly amount of money, equivalent to about twenty U.S. dollars. The boy, not knowing what to do, looked to his father and handed it to him.

"Shookrun," the father responded gratefully, as he bowed in gratitude.

Mohammed, understanding both cultures, said, "The boy is overwhelmed, and while the father did not expect anything in return, he is very grateful. These are very poor people. Their trees and their home are most of their belongings."

For the next hour, Mohammed led the two deeper into the long oasis.

As they reached to touch the red, plump, hard-skinned pomegranates hanging on the trees, stroked the ancient gnarled olive tree trunks, and marveled at the sight of such a large, prolific veritable garden of Eden, Leah commented, "It's so beautiful here, and so quiet, François. And it's so large! I always thought of an oasis as a small pond with a few date palms. But this is an incredibly rich garden and forest fed by this silly running stream. And these kind villagers…they are so benign, so vulnerable, and so gentle. I am impressed and grateful you brought me here. In Israel, the political polemics are so angry. Our images of Syrians are totally opposite of what we've seen here."

"Well, Leah, I think poor farmers are gentle wherever you go. Their expectations are kept in check, and they have little interest in politics."

Following their lengthy walk through the gardens and trees, they returned to the car.

"Thank you, Mohammed, for such a wonderful experience. That was a rare treat."

"I'm glad you enjoyed your visit, mademoiselle. Palmyra is a fabulous city. It is a poor one today, but it has a remarkable history that I am obliged to tell you about.

"Palmyra, known as the 'place of palms,' is the main source of water between the Arabian sea coast and the Euphrates River. It has been settled since the Neolithic Stone Age. It came under Roman rule during Tiberias' reign when it became known as Palmyra. It was allowed to be independent as a buffer between Rome and the eastern rivals of Parthians and Sassanians. With the Roman annexation of the Nabataean city of Petra, and the rise of Antioch, Palmyra became the major caravan trading station of the east-west trade from China to the Mediterranean Sea, replacing Petra because of its shorter travel distance. Palmyra's fortunes soared because of its location and its water resources. Under the Romans the people learned the language and improved their skills, but Palmyrenes kept their own culture as they concentrated on trade.

"In the year 129, Emperor Hadrian visited Palmyra and granted it the right to raise its own taxes. In the third century, Roman power in the east faltered under the Persian Sassanians who advanced as far as Antioch. At that time, a courageous Palmyrene leader, Septimus Odainat, inspired, organized, and armed the citizens that led to a victory over the Sassanians and drove them out of Syria. His wife, Queen Zenobia, then his widow, was a remarkable and beautiful woman who then reigned from 267 to 272. She took on the Roman Empire and actually conquered all of Syria, Egypt, Arabia, and Anatolia, her five years were the height of Palmyra's fortunes. Legend tells us she actually defied Rome by having coins made with her own sons' faces impressed instead of the Roman emperor's. That's what drove Emperor Aurelian to invade Palmyra. He killed Palmyra's sons and supporters, and captured Queen Zenobia and took her back to Rome. He was so impressed by her courage and her beauty that, instead of imprisoning or killing her, he placed her in a villa in Tivoli, near Rome, where she lived out her days as a philanthropist.

"Palmyra had all the luxuries of a prominent Roman city. Excavation efforts are revealing the massive baths, theater, colonnades, and tombs…all of which are very impressive. Even though Palmyra was a large, busy and important city during Queen Zenobia's reign, once land caravan trading ended, Palmyra declined in importance. Today it is really just a poor city, these ruins and water are the major assets. We hope tourism may flourish in the future. There is so much to see and enjoy here."

Thrilled with what they had seen, they walked to their car and drove into the market area of the city, saw the single, modest hotel, and walked around the downtown shopping district.

Soon, as the sun began its descent toward the horizon, the air began to change, convection currents grew in volume and intensity, and the temperature dropped several degrees. Small swirls of sand erupted from the ground, announcing the arrival of cool air from the mountains colliding with the hot air of the desert. The small sand twisters scattered across the area as villagers pulled their kaffiyehs across their faces for protection. François and Leah, following the lead of their bodyguards and Mohammed's instruction, got back in their car avoiding the swirling, biting sand and prepared for their long, desolate drive back to Damascus.

After two hours' drive, Nicola noticed in his rearview mirror a black Mercedes approaching them from the rear.

"We have company," he announced to his fellow guard, Antoine. Turning his head, he informed François to prepare for visitors.

"We are still two hours from Damascus, and these are the most remote miles on this highway. There are no towns nearby, and very little traffic. If they are the Mossad, this is where they will try something," Nicola warned them.

Automatically, Nicola's right foot pressed heavily on the accelerator while he tightly gripped the steering wheel in preparation for maneuvering the Mercedes in a way that would help him elude the approaching car and avoid being an easy target. He had been very well trained in these defensive driving tactics. Antoine, beside him, quickly retrieved his guns, ready for whatever might happen next.

The murderer is not unaccountable for his own murder.
Kahlil Gibran

Chapter 28

Return from Palmyra

"Step on it, Nicola. We have to stay ahead of them," François instructed.

Nicola responded by pressing down on the accelerator, increasing their speed to eighty, then ninety miles per hour.

Driving west toward Damascus, Nicola shifted his eyes from the road ahead to his rearview mirror, keeping the black Mercedes in his sight.

"They are coming closer, Monsieur DuBois. I am certain they intend to overtake us here, in the most desolate part of the drive, before we get close to the city. What would you have me do?"

"What can we do, Nicola?" François shifted his position in the back seat to look back through the rear window. He couldn't believe what he saw. As a second Mercedes quickly drew closer, he saw behind them in the distance the first Mercedes flip and roll over onto the side of the desert road. It rolled twice, almost flying in the air. Then it hit the ground violently and burst into flames with an explosion.

"Did you see that, Nicola?"

"Yes, sir, I did. This is getting too dangerous. Brace yourselves. Here they come!"

Shifting his eyes to the closer Mercedes, he realized it was now closing in on them.

"They must be going over ninety!" exclaimed Nicola.

"They're only a hundred meters behind us now, Nicola. Who are they?" Then, looking at Leah, he ordered her, "Keep down. Lay your head in my lap. The rear seat should protect us. And this car is protected with extra steel plates to deflect any gunfire. At least, it's supposed to."

All of a sudden, the Mercedes following them increased its speed, likely now traveling over one hundred miles per hour began to move to the left lane.

"Not again, François! Dear God, not the Mossad trying to kill us again like they tried to near Tyre! What are we going to do, François? I've never been this frightened. Are we going to die?" She started to cry, her body shaking from her fear.

"Nicola," François shouted nervously, "you're experienced in evasive tactics, aren't you?"

"Yes, sir, I am. And we are about to take measures to avoid them. And we will fire back at the first sign they make to attack us."

Just then, the Mercedes shifted to another high speed gear, veered around their car and pulled alongside. As they did, Antoine focused on the occupants, trying to determine their next move.

"They are Syrians, Monsieur DuBois! They must be Syrian Secret Service. There are four of them."

"Oh, my God, Leah. I am so sorry I brought you to Syria."

"So am I, François! This is horrible!" she cried aloud.

The Mercedes, now alongside, pulled threateningly close to Nicola's door. Both cars were just inches apart at very high speeds. Nicola could have reached out his window and touched the other car. Antoine and François tried to read the faces of the other car's occupants.

Suddenly, Antoine and François, both looking at the passenger in the front seat, realized he was lowering his window. As the window lowered, they fully expected a pistol to be raised and aimed at them. But the window in back was not lowered so those in the rear seat could fire at them.

"What is he doing, Antoine?" François cried out urgently.

Then, very quickly, the passenger in the front seat stuck his head out of the window and yelled at the top of his lungs, "Kiff! Wakiff ala janab halla!"

"They want us to stop and pull over at once. I must do as they say, Monsieur DuBois. We have no choice. It is too dangerous to challenge them, especially this far outside the city."

"Then pull over, Nicola. Do as they say!"

The tension in their car was palpable. Leah screamed, tears flowing with fear. *It's over*, François thought.

Both cars, still side by side, slowed down.

"My God, what is going to happen to us? Are we going to die?" Leah, sobbing, trembled in fear, gripping François' arm so tightly she nearly cut off his circulation.

François, hoping to keep her from screaming, held her other hand, telling her, "It's going to be alright, Leah. If they wanted us dead, we'd be dead already."

In the front seat, Antoine, furtively gripping his automatic machine gun, was ready. Nicola wiped the perspiration from his forehead and face with his sleeve as he allowed the car to slowly coast to a stop off the pavement. The other car pulled up close behind them, and four heavily armed men got out of their car and walked to François' car, two men on each side. As they approached, Nicola and Antoine were ready with their guns, but would only respond to gunfire from the Syrians. If they did shoot, it would be a deadly shootout with at least six dead. The bodyguards knew that, so Antoine and Nicola wisely removed the possibility that they might accidentally fire first by keeping their fingers away from the triggers.

The leader of the Syrians stepped to the rear door, and, signaling to François, shouted, "Get out of the car! Quickly! Now! And lay down your weapons!"

With those orders, François pulled on Leah's hand, and all four nervously exited their car, wondering how long they had to live.

As they stood together, side by side, beside the car, François asked. "What is this all about?"

"You are in grave danger, Monsieur DuBois. We were ordered to follow you from when you entered Syria. It is a good thing for you because the Mossad has been following your every move. As a result, we have been following four Mossad agents who intend to kill you both. They were behind you at the *souk*. They even followed you to Palmyra!"

"They were in Palmyra? We never saw them!"

"Oh, yes, they were there, even in the oasis. We watched them and you while you sipped tea with that family. They were nearby. And so were we. We overheard their plans. They are after you, Monsieur DuBois because you know too much about Israel's attack on the American ship, the Liberty. They want to kill you so you cannot be a prominent witness to their efforts to kill the entire crew and sink the ship. As for your companion, they believe she is a spy in collusion with you, Monsieur DuBois, against the Israelis.

"And that, Monsieur DuBois, makes your companion our friend," he added with the beginning of a smile.

"Thank God, Leah. Suddenly the Syrians are the good guys!" François whispered to her. Then, turning to the Syrian, he asked, "Now what?"

"Without going into details, I can say with total confidence that those four Mossad agents are no longer your concern. They have joined their forefathers back there about two miles. But there are still many Mossad agents in Syria and in Lebanon assigned to take care of you. So, we have been instructed to escort you to the Lebanese border. From there, it has been arranged for the Lebanese secret service to meet you there and escort you to Beirut.

"Do not forget, we are at war with Israel, and as long as they occupy our Golan Heights, there will be no peace between the Zionist entity and Syria. We are sorry your visit to Syria was so short and, in some ways, frightening."

Then, his voice softening, looking to Leah, he added, "Someday we hope you will return to our country. And now, let us drive to Damascus, that great lady of cities, to gather your possessions, and then proceed to the border. *Allah Maak*! God be with you!"

After François and Leah returned safely to Beirut, shaken, confused, and unsure of what they must do now, they fell into a three day rest period of solitude, still uneasy, but enjoying the beach club, relaxing at the hotel, and engaging in light conversation. Always with Nicola and Antoine nearby.

"I'll have to return to Paris, François, but I really don't want to stay at the embassy very long. Can we meet somewhere very soon?"

"I think Paris would be a great idea some other time, Leah. So I believe we should meet somewhere else. I'll need a few days to take care of some unfinished business. How about joining me for a week in Venice?"

> *For even as love crowns you so shall he crucify you. Even as he is for your growth so is he for your pruning.*
> Kahlil Gibran

CHAPTER 29

Paris

On the morning of the fourth day since Leah returned to Paris, Hanna stepped into François' office.

"I have your papers, sir, as you requested," Hanna said as he walked to the desk, expecting his employer to be seated as usual behind his desk. But he wasn't there. Instead, he was standing still at the floor to ceiling windows across the large office, gazing out at the Mediterranean Sea, his favorite view in the entire world.

"You miss her, sir, don't you?"

François turned away from his fixed position to face Hanna.

"Yes, my friend, I do. I didn't realize how much I would miss her. But I do. My God, how I love her. And now, I worry like crazy for her safety. She's at the Israeli Embassy in Paris which sounds innocent enough, but I feel certain she's still going to be under surveillance by their Mossad agents and their internal investigators."

"All because of that crazy man, Itzak?"

"Yes, Hanna. She is no spy for anyone!"

Hanna did not want to irritate his employer, but felt compelled to reluctantly ask, "How can you be sure, Monsieur DuBois?"

"Because I know her, Hanna. I've known her for twenty years. I know her feelings…her beliefs…her heart. And, we just spent a wild, most incredibly frightening, wonderful week together! It would have made itself known if she was a spy. The first time we've been together in years! And, imagine, we are still deeply in love with each other. Also, we were shot at by the Mossad, and followed daily. Even the Syrians questioned her."

"Yes, sir, I understand."

"But the Syrians saved us from the Mossad."

François sat down at his desk and gave a perfunctory glance over the several stacks of files that Hanna had just given him as requested. But, he couldn't get his mind off the events of the week-long adventure he had spent with Leah. He remembered Beirut, so exciting, so wonderful being with my parents…Sidon and the attack by the Mossad…Tyre…the lush, prolific Bekaa Valley…Douma and the planting of the first seedlings with Marina…Damascus…Palmyra…the Mossad car explosion…the Syrians. All shared with my love, my Leah.

"Ours was an incredible, precious, challenging experience, Hanna."

"Yes, sir, it certainly was, but, permit me to say this," Hanna replied with a smile, "I would much prefer the quiet, boring, not so adventurous times when we work together here doing your business for Credit Suisse. I mean, your Malta trip opened up an entirely new chapter in your life. I think the Israelis believe you are a dangerous man of influence who knows too much, and they consider you a national threat. It is good that our President has provided you with bodyguards at all times. They certainly make me feel safer!"

"Hanna, I wonder how Leah is faring in Paris. I am deeply concerned. The Israelis cannot be happy with the fact that because of her and me, they have lost at least six agents here and in Syria. That's extraordinary. I feel sure they are going to blame us both, especially Leah. And she's in their nest, so to speak."

"Have you heard from her yet today, sir?"

"No, Hanna, not yet. And, I do not dare call her at their embassy. So, all I can do is wait."

"Fortunately, sir, you have a good deal of work awaiting your attention. Perhaps you can devote your time today to clearing your desk, and making calls to keep your mind calm. Frankly, sir, I think you need to take a vacation. You've been under too much stress since June fifth, nearly two months ago. You've been a spy for Lebanon, under surveillance by two governments, shot at, chased, and called on to be a protector for days! Perhaps a few days away to a relaxing, neutral location will do you good."

That's a great idea, Hanna!" François quickly acknowledged. "I'll think about that."

Leah, focusing on her work in the Israeli Embassy, found herself uncomfortable all day long. She worried every time someone walked by her office and looked in at her. *Is there something I should know?* she wondered.

After four days back in Paris, Leah was convinced she could not remain totally dedicated to creating a homeland for her people. *So much has changed. The homeland I envisioned, to which I dedicated so many of my best years, is no longer. Now, instead of a peaceful, safe haven for Jews from all over the world, it is a military state…an occupier of other people's lands, homes, farms…it is not what I devoted myself to build. I turned my back on my first love, my dearest François. Did I make a terrible, terrible mistake?*

After several moments of thought, she abruptly stood up, brushed her skirt smooth, and stepped to her office door. Looking at her watch, she suddenly realized it was after six o'clock in the evening. O, my God, she thought, I hope

François is still in his office. I haven't been able to safely call him.

She left the embassy, hailed down a cab, and asked to be driven to a favorite restaurant near the Sorbonne. Leah spent the entire time looking over her shoulder to see if she was being followed.

In the restaurant, she sought out the pay telephone. She always carried an abundance of French coins in her handbag for the public phones. In the phone booth, she reached for the coins, deposited them, and dialed François' private number.

"*Allo*, François DuBois speaking." François was working late, hoping Leah would soon call him.

"I've wanted to call you every day, but I must be sure I'm not being watched. I'm at a restaurant now. Oh, François, my love, are you safe?"

"Yes, Leah, I am safe," he replied, more than worried about her. "And you, Leah, are you alright?"

"At the moment, François, I am alright. But am I safe? I simply do not know. It is almost impossible for me to relax at the embassy. I don't know who to trust. I have no friends, and, I'm certain there are at least several within the embassy who are aware the Mossad has been chasing you and me. It won't take long for my name to be rumored throughout the embassy. I could become a pariah. Although the work I do is not controversial. I should be virtually invisible in the embassy, but I'm not. Maybe I'm being paranoid, but I think it's only a matter of time before something bad happens."

"I think you are correct, Leah. I think it's a mistake for you to continue going to the embassy. Israel is at war. Politically, it is being ostracized by many nations, it is still pushing, pushing, pushing. I don't think they intend on leaving the lands they've occupied…Gaza, the West Bank, the Golan. As a result, they remain aggressive, paranoid, and duplicitous. They don't want me to live, Leah, because I am a threat to them. They do not want the truth about the USS Liberty to be heard. They continue with lies like Egypt and Syria attacked them first when, of course, Israel started the war with their surprise attacks, just like the Japanese at Pearl Harbor.

"Even now they continue to blame the Arabs, broadcast the Arabs won't make peace, and say that Israel seeks peace."

Then, he thought more about her predicament.

"Leah, I'm sure Itzak is still doing his dirty work. Where is he now?"

"I don't know where Itzak is, François, but we can be sure he is still very angry at us both. The Mossad lost several agents because of us…because of him and his jealousy! I don't know what to do about him. Maybe there is nothing we can do!"

"Maybe we'll be haunted by him and his kind for years, Leah. Dammit! Don't you think it's time you come to your senses? You are not safe there, or in Israel, as long as you don't agree to and support their policies. I worry about you all day long, Leah. I hardly sleep at night because I worry about your safety."

François was growing more frustrated because of her continued involvement with the Israeli government…and not with him. "Soon you are going to have to choose, my love. Soon you must decide what it is you want in your future. And so must I, Leah. So must I. We are being tested. Our love is strong, but how much of this can we take? Our very lives are at stake! I don't think I can take much more, Leah. This is not what I want. You need to choose, Leah. And soon!" For the second time, he was becoming adamant with her.

As Leah held the receiver to her ear, tears filled her eyes as the stress of recent days began to take their toll. She heard François replace his receiver with a click. That sound felt like a knife because never before had François hung up first. He always held his receiver to his ear until he heard her hang up. She began to cry, her shoulders shaking. Leah felt a strong sense of fear, not only for her very life, but for the first time since 1947, for the possibility of losing her love, François.

Leah knew François was right, but, for some reason she couldn't truly explain even to herself, she was reluctant to make a clean break and commit to him and to a new life. She would have to leave her commitment to Israel behind.

My God, what have I done? Since I was so young, François has been there for me, loving me completely, pleasing me. He's my rock, my anchor, my lover. But now, he is surely reaching his limits. I have kept us apart for twenty years. I have even brought on assassins who have nearly killed us both. And for what?

Leah slowly, sadly replaced the telephone receiver, carefully opened the door in the booth, and stepped into the restaurant. Immediately, she saw a familiar face of an internal agent. She turned and entered the ladies restroom where she huddled in a toilet booth and waited, even more frightened now. She sat and alternately paced the room. Finally, she splashed water on her face nearly an hour later, quickly exited the restaurant, hailed a cab, and went home, where she lay in bed, unable to sleep for hours. Finally dozing off, she awoke, exhausted, at day's first light.

Apparently they are not that anxious to get rid of me or they would have killed me by now…or at least questioned me. But it's just a matter of time. I must decide today. I must make the decision I've postponed for so long. I will call François today!

Making certain no one was watching her, she stepped cautiously out of her apartment building onto the cobblestone sidewalk, and carefully, but briskly, walked toward the Israeli Embassy. As she reached the end of the street, she saw the magnificent Notre Dame Cathedral across the river. She decided to visit the cathedral for solitude and peace because her mind and her body were stressed to its limits. She also wanted to honor François and his spiritual beliefs.

I will pray to the God of Abraham, Isaac, and Jacob, and to Jesus for guidance today. I will ask for strength, wisdom, and help in determining what it is He wants of me, and how I can better fulfill His wishes. He is my God of love. I know it, and I know He wants what is best for me.

Frightened, Leah entered the great cathedral of Notre Dame and, as she walked toward the front rows nearest the altar, she looked around the high-ceilinged nave. She saw that the cathedral was mostly empty, being a weekday, so she sat in the first row of chairs and bowed her head and began to pray. She was asking, almost begging, for peace and serenity. As she finished her prayers, an elderly priest came to her and asked softly if she needed to speak with him. She nodded silently "no, thank you," her eyes swelling in tears, although she felt a wonderful sense of peace from his being near to her.

She was so overwhelmed with emotions that her shoulders began to shake as she gazed upward toward the cross above the altar. Her memories raced back to when she was a young girl in Warsaw. At the urging of her frantic mother, she had sought refuge from the Nazis as they invaded the city. "Go, my dearest, go to the Catholic Church," her mother had told her. "The priest will hide you there and you will be safe. Go now, Leah. Go quickly. I must stay here with your father. Always remember, dear child, how much we love you. Now, go! And don't stop running until you are safely in the church with the priest!"

Leah, now praying to the cross as she had done in Warsaw, was visibly shaken and crying aloud for safety for her and François. "Dear God," she whispered, tears running down her cheeks, "please keep us safe from the evildoers who seek to harm us." As she prayed, she was struck by the ironies in her life. Once again, she was hiding in a Christian church seeking safety from her enemies: as a young girl, from the Germans, and now, from the agents of Israel. How can this be? she wondered, heartbroken.

An hour later, Leah decided not to go the embassy, and called in sick. Next, she called François. While sitting in the cathedral, she had finally decided what she must do with her life. As a result, she felt a wonderful sensation of relief, of peace within her.

At the sound of his voice, Leah spoke quickly, "François! François, I need you. I love you. I want only you. I have made my decision. Please come to me now!"

"Leah, where are you? Are you safe? What has happened? he asked, unsure what was happening to her. "What are you saying, Leah? Are you in danger?"

"Oh, François, I believe I am now, and will always be, in danger!" she sobbed. "I can't live like this! But if I must, I want to be with you. It's only been a few days, but I miss you terribly. I am so unhappy. And I know this isn't the place for me."

François, listening intently, measuring each of her words, sensing her anxiety, and measuring her stresses replied, "It is the same with me, Leah! I miss you so much, even though it's only been a few days."

He was becoming almost frantic from his concern for her safety. "Our days together, although dangerous and an adventure, for sure, were wonderful. I love you, Leah. We have to find a way to bring this ridiculous situation to a resolution… somehow."

"Do you still have Nicola and Antoine watching over you?"

"Thank God, yes, I do. Are you absolutely convinced you wish to leave Paris and the embassy, Leah?"

"I…I…cannot go on like this, François," she sobbed. "This is no way for us to live…always being followed or attacked. But if this is our destiny at this time, then we must go through it together."

"Can you meet me in Venice?" he blurted out, assuming that beautiful city would be safe for them, while also being totally different from Paris or Beirut. "Perhaps we can meet there without the world knowing…or maybe not caring!"

"Yes!" she quickly replied. "I can fly there today. When can you join me?"

"I will leave this afternoon. We can meet at the Cipriani Hotel on the island across from St. Mark's Square. We stayed there five years ago. It should be safe."

"I'll go straight there, François. Register under the same name we used in Douma, Leah Chalhoub. Hurry, François!"

*That you, alone and unguarded, commit a wrong unto others
and therefore unto yourself.*
Kahlil Gibran

Chapter 30

Venice, Italy

Leah arrived at the Hotel Cipriani first, her flight landing at Venice's Marco Polo Airport fully two hours ahead of François' plane. She immediately hired a water taxi to the Cipriani Hotel.

Airplanes arrived daily full of summer tourists from all over the world, seeking the opportunity to visit this beautiful, old city on the Adriatic Sea with its renowned canals, picturesque Piazza San Marco, Carnevale masks, jewelry, and exquisite Murano glass, crafted by master artisans.

Businessmen were also frequent visitors to Venice, and, on this particular day, secret agents arrived from at least two countries.

Two Syrian Secret Service agents from Damascus arrived on Syrian Arab Airlines, pursuing their politically driven mission.

Also arriving a few minutes later were Itzak Krakowicz and Ohren Lukor, two Mossad agents from Tel Aviv, on El Al Flight #210. They had been notified by the Mossad in Paris of Leah's sudden flight to Venice. Agents there had followed her to Orly International Airport and questioned the ticket agent. Itzak and his colleague were on a vital mission to eliminate François and, perhaps, Leah. Their anger, and that of the Mossad, was driven by the loss of their agents in Lebanon and in Syria, caused in their view by François and Leah, and that only motivated Itzak with more determination and fury.

"Ohren," Itzak said, with an angry sneer, as they rode in the water taxi from the airport to the city, "we must eliminate François DuBois. His firsthand knowledge and interviews of crew personnel from the American ship Liberty makes him a threat to Israel's very existence. He is an enemy of the state of Israel, and he must die."

Itzak did not share with Ohren his own personal jealousy, his resentment and outrage of Leah choosing François DuBois instead of himself. He simply had to kill his competition, using "state secrets" as his convenient reason.

François' two ubiquitous bodyguards arrived with him on Middle East Airlines

Flight #15 from Beirut. From the airport, François and his bodyguards boarded a courtesy motor launch for the ride to the magnificent Hotel Cipriani, located on the tip of Guidecca Island, directly across from Piazza San Marco. With its convenient, but quite exclusive location, the Cipriani had been chosen by François for its luxurious appointments, service to its patrons, and, above all, its privacy. It was the perfect choice for Leah and François to be alone, to luxuriate, and forget all they had been going through.

At the reservation desk, François told the attendant, "I'm François DuBois. I am joining Mademoiselle Chalhoub...Leah Chalhoub. Can you please ring her room for me?"

"Certainly, sir," he responded politely. "It's ringing, sir."

"*Allo*," Leah spoke into the phone on its second ring.

"She is on the line, sir," the attendant told François as he handed the phone to François' waiting hand.

"Leah?"

"*Allo*, my darling. Are you in the lobby?"

François' excitement grew and his passion reignited as he heard the soft, sensual voice of his lover answer the telephone.

"Yes, I'll be right there. Are you enjoying our suite?"

"Oh yes, it's magnificent, especially the views of the city, and Piazza San Marco directly across the lagoon."

Turning to the attendant, François directed, "I will also need the adjoining room for my two associates, Antoine Kahlil and Nicola Azar. Please register them under their names and charge their costs, as well as Mademoiselle Chalhoub's, to this, my American Express card."

"Absolutely, Signore DuBois. I'll have your bags taken to your room immediately. Please enjoy your stay. Your reservations are for at least one week. Is that correct?"

"Yes, exactly, and thank you."

Moments later, almost too long to suit Leah and François, he arrived at their suite.

"Well, it's about time, François!" she teased. "Every minute seemed like an hour! But I learned they have a special spa and salt water swimming pool here. So, I indulged myself while I waited. And, you know, I swam twenty laps of the pool and got rid of most of my anxiety and stress! It felt wonderful! I'm so glad you suggested the Cipriani and reserved this beautiful suite for us! My body has lost its tensions, and I'm ready for you, my love," she giggled.

"We should be very safe here, Leah, especially with Nicola and Antoine in the adjacent suite. They will be with us all the time. Does that help make you feel more calm, Leah?"

"Yes, François. I've felt so much better since my plane left the ground in Paris. It's been very, very difficult for me there, not knowing what could happen next. I was frightened every day. And I missed you so."

"We are reserved here for a full week, plenty of time to relax, see the sights, including the Doge's Palace and St. Mark's Basilica. I also thought we might enjoy an afternoon cocktail and dinner at a very special place called Harry's Bar."

"Harry's Bar? What a strange name for a restaurant in Venice, Italy! Is it an American establishment?"

"No, Leah, but you are close. It is located on a side street off Piazza San Marco, near the Grand Canal. It has an enduring reputation for hosting renowned celebrities, including Ernest Hemingway, Arturo Toscanini, Aristotle Onassis, Baron Philippe de Rothschild, Charlie Chaplin, and Orson Welles. They also serve a delicious special drink called a Bellini, a blend of peach nectar and champagne. It's delicious and quite a famous delicacy. However, since we have the time, I suggest we relax and be alone here at the Cipriani tonight and tomorrow before we venture out. How does that sound to you, Leah?"

"Well, Monsieur DuBois, are you suggesting we have dinner here in our hotel?" she laughed teasingly. "What will we do here until dinner? And after dinner?" she teased, with a sideways, seductive glance. "What are your intentions, sir?"

"Mademoiselle, I'm going to order a bottle of the finest champagne and some delectable hors d'oeuvres for us to enjoy as we relax here on the balcony and watch the lights come on at Piazza San Marco and the city."

"That sounds very romantic, darling. I love it!"

François immediately did two things. First, he reached for the room telephone and called the suite next door to assure himself that Nicola and Antoine were satisfactorily settled in. Although they were quietly reveling in their luxurious twin suite, both assured François that they were ready to respond to any need of their charges, François and Leah. Feeling more relaxed, François then placed his order with room service.

"I'll be back in a few minutes," François called out to Leah. "I'm going to take a shower, my love."

After two hours relaxing on the large balcony in their terrycloth bathrobes provided by the hotel, they changed into dinner clothes and strolled down to the dining room hand in hand and were escorted to a small, candlelit table. They savored a tasty seafood dinner, accompanied by their favorite Cabernet Sauvignon 1957.

"Let's return to our suite, François. I feel so mellow and relaxed."

They immediately went to bed and cuddled, enjoying each other's company, whispering "pillow talk," and simply releasing themselves of those unpleasant memories they had experienced. As they nuzzled, touched and caressed one another, they could not resist each other and grew passionately excited. He fondled her firm breasts, and she stroked his hard thighs.

"Oh, François, please make love to me tonight. I need you, and I want you now!"

For the next four days, under the watchful eyes of Nicola and Antoine, François and Leah spent relaxed, happy hours enjoying the sights of Venice like veteran tourists. They experienced the intimate joy of holding hands while strolling through the narrow side streets, taking the water taxis up and down the Grand Canal, and sitting in outside cafés watching the people pass by. They were glad to be free of intrigue.

"This is so refreshing, François, and, finally, I feel safe," Leah whispered as they sat side by side on a bench along a narrow canal, gazing at the old buildings that rose from the edges of the canals, while being watched, as always, by Nicola and Antoine.

"What a city, Leah! It is literally built on wood pilings driven into the mud-bottom of these many islands."

"It's so unique, François. How did they do it? And how do the buildings keep from leaning like the Tower of Pisa, or simply falling into the sea?"

"They must have been brilliant engineers and architects is all I can say, Leah. It is remarkable how this city continues year after year!"

"Look at the gondolas and the men who row them in their distinctive striped shirts and straw hats. Let's take a gondola ride one night. It will be so romantic!"

"Let's wait and do it on our last evening here to make it very special," he agreed enthusiastically.

They excitedly awoke on their seventh and final day, having fully shared their love, while indulging themselves in the splendid accoutrements of their fabulous hotel. After breakfast in their room, François looked across the table and, focusing intently into Leah's eyes, asked the difficult question that had been dominating his thoughts for too long, "Well, my love, and I do love you, what have you decided? Are you able to tell me what is in your heart, what you have chosen to do with your life which, as you well know, has a huge impact on my life?"

Then, after an anxious moment of hesitation, he said, "I'm listening, dear Leah."

She smiled, gathered her thoughts and replied, "Well, François, if you haven't read my mind these past glorious days and nights as we made love so beautifully, I will tell you. I have, indeed, come to a monumental decision. In fact, I made that decision before I called you from Paris. While I was in the Notre-Dame Cathedral, it came to me as I prayed for guidance, for peace, and for our continued love and safety. It has been the most difficult decision of my life. But I have become absolutely convinced that I have placed too much love and too much importance on my commitment to building a homeland...Israel...for my people. I believe I have done all I can do. I am now totally, exclusively devoted to you, François," she said, smiling broadly, with joy. "You know I love you with all my heart. And now, you need to know I am committed totally to you and our love."

Then, after a long moment for François to fully understand what she was saying, she added, "That is what I am telling you now and forever."

"Without any reservation, Leah? Without any uncertainty? Are you sure, Leah?"

"Yes!" she said with conviction. "Completely and absolutely! I want to spend the rest of my life with you, my only love, wherever and however you desire. I even want to be Lebanese!" she laughed. "I can even say, François, that I am prepared and want to convert to Christianity, so I will be your total wife, your total partner, your total companion, and your total lover!"

"Then, today and tonight, we celebrate," François declared happily, enthused and filled with great relief.

Looking lovingly into each other's eyes, they reached across the breakfast table and touched each other's glass as a toast, symbolically completing their promises to each other, smiling in anticipation.

"Tonight, Leah, we will, in our hearts and minds, be one! We can now, together...finally...build a whole new life, one for which we have waited twenty years to begin. The future is ours. Ours to share, my love!"

They spent much of that morning being spoiled at the hotel spa, both having massages and steam baths, and then napping in their lounge chairs on the terrace, feeling the sun's warmth and the light breezes on their glistening bodies. Leah even had her hair coiffed and her nails manicured.

Then, early in the afternoon, they took the hotel courtesy water taxi to Piazza San Marco to spend the rest of the day shopping in the many little boutiques surrounding the piazza.

After leisurely strolling among the many tourists, they decided to enjoy a snack at one of the many restaurants on the piazza with outdoor seating. As they sat at their small metal table, Leah exclaimed, "François! Look at all the pigeons!" She smiled and gestured, "There are so many! Should we get some food and feed them?"

"Leah," he warned with a laugh, "let the tourists' children feed the pigeons. Watch how they swarm around those tossing bread morsels and peanuts to the pigeons. They won't leave you alone once you begin." Then, he laughed again, "Some of them will tangle your hair as they fly in to share the food, or poop on you! Let's just watch, darling."

"Is the piazza always so crowded?" she asked, as her eyes scanned over the many tourists. Then, the worst that could possibly happen, did happen.

"Oh, my God, François! Look! Over toward the entrance to St. Mark's Basilica! Do you see two men standing there, in dark glasses?"

Turning his head, François looked and asked, "And?"

"I believe one of them is Itzak! Oh, my God! Is there no place we can go?" Her body began to shake from fear. "Where can we be safe?" She twisted her body away, hoping to hide her face.

"Damn! You're right!" François replied. "Where are Nicola and Antoine? Can you see them?"

François stood up and looked around, thinking, Where are they? When François looked back at Leah, who had also stood up, clearly anxious to leave, his eyes returned to where Itzak had been. He and his partner were gone.

But the Mossad agents had made their point.

Leah and François suddenly realized that Itzak and his companion were in Venice. And now they would be forced to worry about Itzak and his intentions. Itzak wanted them to suffer, to become stressed and nervous…wondering…always watching over their shoulders.

Just then, Nicola and Antoine, who had been lurking behind two nearby columns while watching over their charges, had also noticed the two suspicious men who clearly were not tourists, and were trying to be less than conspicuous. And they saw them leave their place and walk past the cathedral to the waterfront.

"Antoine? Nicola? Are we safe?"

"Yes, sir, you are protected. We saw mademoiselle's gesture and focused on the two. They are the Israelis, correct?"

"Yes, they are Mossad agents, and I fear they are after both of us. I think it's time for us to leave Piazza San Marco and go to Harry's Bar. We'll be safe there. It's nearby on Calle Vallaresso. Let's go now."

It was a short walk from the piazza to Harry's Bar at San Marco 1323. Upon entering the restaurant, Leah noticed that the long wooden bar immediately along the left side of the dining area was crowded with patrons. Most of the first floor was filled with small, three-legged tables for two, four, and a few for larger seatings. On the back wall, beyond the bar, she saw a sign noting the toilettes and stairs to the second floor. The restaurant was simple, with an art deco interior featuring marine motifs on the walls.

"Antoine, we will be here for a while."

"Yes, sir. Nicola and I will be just outside. We will locate secure spots for us for when you exit in the event there is a problem and our Mossad friends return."

"We are safe here, Leah. I don't believe Itzak knows we are in here, so let's just relax as much as we can and enjoy a famous Bellini. After dinner, we'll return to the Cipriani."

"I am nervous, François, but I am determined we will share our lives in Lebanon…together!" Aside from the haunting knowledge of Itzak's presence, she was feeling a sense of joy as she excitedly envisioned their future together…for the rest of their lives.

"We have Antoine and Nicola, and tomorrow we return to Beirut and truly begin our lives together. I am so happy you've decided the way you have. Leah, I promise I will do everything in my power for you to never to regret your decision. You are my sun, my moon, my life, Leah, and while I want us to enjoy this evening, as we planned, I cannot wait to get you back in our suite and make love with you tonight...all night," he added with a twinkle in his eye. "That way, you'll have an idea of what your life will be like in Beirut!"

"I already know, darling," she giggled with a wink. "I too can't wait to wrap my arms around you later tonight. And I am looking forward to being Mrs. François DuBois, a Lebanese citizen!"

They held hands as they chatted, sipping from their small glasses of a very tasty and intoxicating Bellini. They were both on emotional highs, filled with thoughts of enjoying each other's love for many years to come, safe in Beirut.

"Leah, they say that Harry's Bar is known for three things: simplicity, quality, and a smile."

As they enjoyed this quiet moment, a slight, elegant, elderly gentleman dressed in an expensive tailored three-piece suit, perfectly fitted to his small frame, came to their table. He reached out his hand to François and said in impeccable English, "Welcome to Harry's Bar. I do believe you have been here before. May I welcome you with a gift for you two lovebirds?"

Then, gesturing with both arms, he continued with a broad smile, "Other guests have been watching, as have I, and are pleased to see you share your love for each other here in my restaurant. Are you on your honeymoon here in Venice?" he asked with a warm smile. "Many couples come to Venice to enjoy their most romantic days...and, may I say," he smiled wider, "share their first nights together as a married couple in our beautiful city with so many exciting opportunities. It is known for its romance, isn't it? Just a moment, please." He then turned and signaled the bartender to send two more Bellinis to their table.

"We love it here, sir. Are you the owner of this establishment?"

"Indeed I am, sir. Permit me to introduce myself. I am Giuseppe Cipriani, the proprietor of Harry's Bar."

François couldn't help but smile as he asked the obvious question many had asked Signore Cipriani before.

"I am François DuBois, and this is Leah. We are from Beirut. Now, let me understand, sir, that you, Giuseppe Cipriani, own a prominent, internationally known restaurant and bar called Harry's Bar. How then, sir, did your wonderful establishment become named Harry's Bar?"

Leah, intent on hearing Signore Cipriani's response, eagerly leaned forward, chin on her fist and elbow on the table, and a broad smile on her face.

"It is a story I love to tell, Signore DuBois, one which I hope you and your lovely companion will enjoy."

He took a seat at their table and smiled, with a great deal of pride, recalling happily, "I was a bartender when I was younger, during the exciting 1920s, at the

Hotel Europa. During those days, a rich, young American from Boston named Harry Pickering frequented the hotel and the bar. We became very good friends. Harry always enjoyed himself at the bar. We discussed many things, including his life and his wealthy and prominent multi-generational Boston family. And I told him of my dreams of owning my own bar one day. We were both young, and grew to become dear friends.

"Suddenly, in late 1929, Mr. Pickering stopped coming to Venice, to the Hotel Europa, and to the bar. He finally came by a several months later and I asked him where he had been. He told me he was broke because his family had learned about his drinking habits and cut him off financially. He needed money, so I loaned him 10,000 lira, about $5,000 US. After all, he was a very good friend and had been very generous with me.

"Six months later, in 1930, Mr. Pickering returned to the hotel bar, ordered a drink and then he gave me my 10,000 lira back! He said to me, 'Thank you, Signore Cipriani, for your loan. Here is your money back. And to show you my appreciation, here's 40,000 lira as well, enough for us to open a bar together. We'll call it Harry's Bar.' I was so excited! He had made my life's dream come true!"

He spread his arms wide in a grand gesture as he concluded, "And that's the story of how I opened this wonderful bar and restaurant. God has been good to me."

"What a marvelous story, Signore Cipriani," Leah exclaimed with a huge smile and joyful laugh, clapping her hands. "I loved hearing it!"

"Yes, it is a fascinating story," added François. "But I would wager you have another incredible story to tell us. You see, Signore Cipriani, like many visitors who seek the finest way of life, we are residing at the Hotel Cipriani. Is it yours?"

With another broad smile, Giuseppe Cipriani laughed aloud. "You, Signore DuBois, are a genius. Many people do not connect this bar with the Hotel Cipriani. But you did, and now, I am obligated to tell you another story of how God has been good to me."

And so, he began…with Leah and François, bending forward, eagerly listening…

"After the war, in the early 1950s, Harry's Bar was enjoying its halcyon days, and I was able to think about a new adventure. I was always attracted to the island named Giudecca. There was a piece of land on the island where a farmer kept his pigs to fatten so he could make salami. Next to it was an abandoned work yard. The whole area was overgrown with wild undergrowth. But from there I could view that wonderful lagoon and the island of San Giorgio. I thought it was a perfect place for a hotel. That was my vision, but I couldn't raise the money to build the hotel. Everyone thought I was a crazy man. No one else in Venice thought it was a good idea.

"Then, one evening, God smiled on me again. Lord Iveagh, the owner of Arthur Guinness, Son and Co., Ltd., the famous Irish brewery, came here for dinner. I told him about my idea of a luxury hotel on the island of Giudecca. Lord Iveagh loved Italy, especially Venice. The next day, although it was foggy, rainy, and the land on Giudecca was muddy, he insisted we walk the site. Afterward, he said, 'Count me in.' And that's how we became partners. I contributed the land, the name, and the work to oversee the construction. Lord Iveagh provided the money. We both wanted to build an elegant service-oriented hotel. I'm happy to say that the hotel opened in 1950, and we are still fifty-fifty partners."

Leah and François were overwhelmed by Signore Cipriani's visit to their table. His eagerness to share his history and his two life stories with them completely replaced any fear or stress they had felt since they realized Itzak was in Venice.

"Let's have a bottle of your finest champagne, Signore Cipriani," declared François with a smile, overjoyed with his new friend and more relaxed now. "We have another excellent reason to celebrate. Leah and I have decided to get married and live in Beirut."

"Ah, I would wager that you, too, have a story to tell," replied Signore Cipriani.

Leah responded, saying, "Oh, Signore Cipriani, indeed we do."

"Tell me, then, how did you two meet?"

François eagerly dove right in, smiling at Leah's twinkling eyes, and described their first meeting and subsequent love affair as students at the Sorbonne immediately after World War II.

"That's beautiful, Signore DuBois," Signore Cipriani replied with gusto. "I hope you both have a wonderful, full, loving marriage for years to come. I will have my son, Arrigo, who is our bartender this evening, bring you a bottle of our best champagne as my special gift to you. One day, Arrigo will own Harry's Bar. And that makes me very happy!"

During their delicious dinner, Giuseppe's special for the evening, they reveled in their good fortune to have shared so much with Signore Cipriani, recapping their idyllic week in Venice and their hopes and dreams for their life together in Beirut.

"I am so happy, François. I love you so much, and I can't wait until we are in Lebanon, building, finally, a life together."

"Leah, my love, this has been the most wonderful week of our lives and, I hope, just a prelude of what is in store for us for the next thirty or forty years!"

"Oh, François, may I ask you, aside from your parents, have two people so deeply in love ever lost so many years to make up for…and so much to look forward to? I can't wait, dearest. I'm so excited, I feel like a young girl!"

"Shall we try a gondola ride before heading back to the hotel? We can catch one right here, only a few steps to the dock."

"Oh, yes. Let's do it, François. That would be so romantic!"

After François gestured to their waiter for the check and paid it, he stepped to the entry door and looked for Antoine and Nicola to escort them to the nearest water taxi and gondola dock. Only Nicola was watching the door.

"Where is Antoine, Nicola?" he asked, a touch of concern in his voice.

"There," he pointed to a dark balcony across the vanalt on the second floor. "He is watching the street and this door. We are prepared for anything, Monsieur DuBois. You are safe if we are careful. And," he added, "there are two Syrian agents at the dock, waiting to protect us there."

After finding Signore Cipriani to thank him and extend best wishes, they embraced and went to the door, Leah waving gracefully to the proprietor as the door opened.

"Are we safe, François?"

"Hold onto my arm, Leah. Nicola is right beside us, and Antoine is watching us from above. We have to walk only a very short distance to the dock even if we are to catch the courtesy water taxi to the hotel. It's just thirty feet to the end of the building, and then, another thirty feet to the dock. Let's go now. We'll walk briskly. Ready, Nicola?"

"Ready, sir. I just signaled Antoine and the Syrians. They are ready also."

With trepidation and a growing concern, Leah, who feared Itzak's raging jealousy, was more worried for François than herself. She huddled close to her love until they reached the end of the building. It was late and it was dark. Shadows cast their eerie scene. An eery darkness with a bit of fog covered the walkway making it difficult to see movement. They saw only a few pedestrians in the distance. The bustling activity and traffic had disappeared just an hour earlier. "We're almost alone, François. I don't feel very safe. I'm frightened."

"Hold tight, Leah. We're nearly there."

And when Love speaks to you,
Believe in him, Though his voice
May shatter your dreams as the
North wind lays waste the garden...
Kahlil Gibran

Chapter 31

Venice: The Encounter

Each step became more and more deliberate as they walked through the shadows toward the San Marco open terminal. There, the water taxis and gondolas were waiting for the evening's last patrons and tourists. Leah's hand nervously gripped François' hand even more tightly. After they passed the protective end of the building, she anxiously glanced to her left, searching for any threatening movements, hoping to see none. They were now, briefly, only a few feet in the open, unprotected area by the front building on Calle Vallaresso.

"Let's hurry, François," she whispered nervously. "Let's go straight to the hotel by their private launch and save the gondola ride for another time, say our first anniversary. Isn't that a good idea, François?"

"Yes, Leah," he agreed quickly. "Without knowing where your friend Itzak is, we should go directly to the Cipriani. We can celebrate without fear in our suite. Now, let's get into our private launch to the hotel, just over there."

They neared the Hotel Cipriani's private landing stage at Piazzetta San Marco.

It was at that precise moment, with apprehension and fear, Leah, frightened, again looked to her left, and barely spotted two men backed against the building in a recessed doorway, only thirty feet away. The larger one she recognized as Itzak, her very jealous and angry adversary, and a man emotionally out of control.

"Leah!" he shouted in anger.

"Itzak! No!" she pleaded as she watched him pull his pistol from inside his jacket and aim it directly at them.

"No, Itzak! No!" she screamed.

She could see his eyes ablaze with fury and his veins standing out on his neck, reflecting his seething rage.

"It is too late, Leah. You and your friend have humiliated me for too long. He is a threat to Israel and cannot live!"

It took just three seconds. As Itzak spoke, his index finger, responding to his frenzy, tightly squeezed the automatic pistol trigger, igniting the explosive charge in each bullet. Five shots rang out…Pop! Pop! Pop! Pop! Pop! The silencer kept the sound muffled, but the missiles streaked toward François' head and midsection. Immediately, Leah, instinctively responding to Itzak's intent, leaped in front of François to protect her lover. Three bullets immediately struck Leah's body. One entered her heart, another found its target in her left lung, a third one struck her temple.

"Oh, my God," she exhaled, as she was brutally thrown down to the ground by the impacts.

Two missiles struck François. One entered his right shoulder. The other grazed his temple.

Blood from both spewed in every direction as they both responded to the impact of the bullets and fell hard onto the stone walkway.

Leah's head slammed down severely onto the stone walk, while François landed on his back, knocking him unconscious.

Immediately, but too late to protect them, Nicola and the Syrians opened fire at Itzak and Ohren, his accomplice. Their pistols, also with silencers, found their prey. Four shots entered Itzak's brain and heart; four entered his partner's body. Itzak fell backward, cracking his head on the cobblestones. Within seconds both were dead.

Suddenly, two more shots rang out. Nicola turned to see Antoine clutch his chest and fall from the second floor balcony into the canal, landing facedown. Startled, he raced to Francois' fallen, limp body.

The Syrian agents watched it happen. One had fired the additional two shots; the other asked him, "Are they dead?"

"Yes, Antoine, Itzak, and Ohren are finished."

The two then rushed to join Nicola at François' side.

"Why did you kill Antoine?" Nicola screamed to the Syrian agents from his crouch beside François.

"We have known for a long time that Antoine has been an undercover agent for the Mossad. He has not been able to hide his anger at the Palestinians, mostly Shiia, taking over his city of Tripoli and the south of Lebanon. He was convinced they are organizing to take over the Lebanese government and the Syrian government was financing their cause. He deeply resented Syrian intrusion into Lebanese politics and sided with the Israelis. For some time we have been watching him, and believed Ms. Wolsinski was to be his accomplice. We were convinced that she and he were conspiring to kill Monsieur DuBois.

"We were sent to eliminate that man Itzak and Madame Wolsinski and ensure Monsieur DuBois' safety. But then we determined she was not an accomplice.

"I shot Antoine as he was aiming directly at Monsieur DuBois. I couldn't allow him to be killed."

"My God," Nicola replied, "I am shocked. Antoine certainly fooled all of us."

"He was very good, but, in the end, his anger against the Muslims in the south turned to rage. He was very dangerous to Lebanon's welfare and had to be stopped."

Nicola bent down and checked François' pulse, the two Syrian agents by his side.

Nicola knew it was in François' and his best interests to get him out of the area as quickly as possible. He was his responsibility, now he had to assume that there may be more Mossad agents nearby.

One of the witnesses, a gondola operator, saw the entire, but very brief, shocking shootings. Alarmed, he ran into Harry's Bar and announced what he had seen. Very quickly, the young bartender grabbed the telephone and called the police who then notified the hospital. Cutters were sent on their way within seconds from the nearby police station and the Venice Municipal Hospital.

It took only a few minutes for the cutters to arrive, the first with two policemen, the second with two young emergency technicians on night duty.

Nicola and the Syrians, not wanting to become involved with the police, stood aside while watching over Leah and François, frustratingly unable to protect them or remove them from the scene.

François, unconscious and unaware of all the commotion around him, nor Leah's condition, began groaning on the ground, as blood emerged from his wounds. Leah, in deep trauma and critically wounded with profuse bleeding in her brain, lay very still on her back with blood streaming from her head and chest.

The police were directed by witnesses to the two Mossad agents because they were the first to fire their pistols. The witnesses also urged the hospital emergency technicians to rush to where François and Leah were prone on the stone walkway in the midst of growing pools of blood.

Giuseppe Cipriani rushed out of Harry's Bar and hurried over to their bodies. As he looked down, tears overflowed his eyes onto his cheeks.

"They were so in love!" he exclaimed in disbelief. "How could this happen to two such lovely people? We were together just moments ago as they told me of their profound love for each other. Now that is no longer possible. Their future was to be so wonderful and joyful. Now, it appears they have no future. May they rest in peace." He crossed himself in respect. "Dear God, this is terrible. She was so beautiful, so kind. He was full of life and so in love with her. Oh, how I hate such violence!"

The young EMTs checked François injuries, and found them to be serious, but not life-threatening. They carefully put him on a stretcher, preparing to take him to the cutter, then to the city's hospital Emergency Room.

Quickly directing their attention on Leah, they knelt down beside her, but found no pulse, no breathing, and no sign of life.

After several minutes of trying to revive her, one of the EMTs declared, "I believe she is dead. It's so sad. Do you agree, Antonio?"

"Yes, I checked her too, and she has no pulse, no breath. We are too late. We'll have a second cutter take her to the morgue. The hospital is no place for a dead person."

Just then, the police came to the EMTs and told them, "The two men over there and the man in the canal are dead. You are not needed by them. We'll take them to the morgue."

"Can you also take this woman to the morgue? We'll put all four on stretchers for you."

And that is what the police did. Leah, Itzak, her mortal enemy, Ohren, his fellow agent, and Antoine ironically, were taken together by cutter to the morgue as François, in shock, not realizing what was happening, was taken by cutter to the Municipal Hospital. Alone.

Nicola and the Syrian agents watched the entire scenario, recognizing they could be of no help to Leah, except to understand that she was declared dead by the hospital medics. Because they were deeply concerned there could be more Mossad agents in the city, Nicola wanted to take François out of Venice as soon as possible and back to Lebanon where he could assure his safety.

Avoiding the police, the Syrian agents silently slipped away into the shadows to watch the activity and determine whether more Mossad agents were in the area.

Nicola followed the cutter carrying François to the hospital and, in time, would find a way to have him discharged so he could safely fly him back to Beirut. He would then have to instruct them as to what to do with Leah's body.

Meanwhile, Leah's body arrived at the Venice city morgue and was immediately met by the pathologist on night duty. He quickly had her riddled body wheeled into his examination room where he began examining her wounds under very bright lighting. As he began removing her clothing, slightly jostling her, he was shocked to hear her moan very softly, and begin to faintly breathe intermittently.

"My God," the doctor blurted aloud, "This woman isn't dead!" He immediately placed an oxygen mask on her face and called in another doctor. "Come see this woman who was just brought in…I believe she was incorrectly pronounced dead at the scene of a shooting in the city. But I cannot confirm she is dead. She has a very faint pulse, although so weak that it is almost not there, and her breathing is very irregular. It's certainly abnormal, and for a time, she does not breathe at all."

"I can see that she has severe brain damage," remarked the second doctor, examining her head wound, "and it appears she has significant intracranial bleeding, which is causing her to have the symptoms of arrhythmia or striking oligopnea, low or absent breathing. But, most definitely, she is not dead!"

"We must rush her to Municipal Hospital so she can be treated immediately. She could suffer heart failure and further brain damage, perhaps death, if the bleeding continues."

"Certainly, she does not belong here in the morgue! Let's get her out of here into a cutter and to the hospital. I'll call the Emergency Room over there so they can prepare the staff and set up an operating room. She needs immediate attention and surgery."

Leah, unconscious, barely alive, hardly breathing, was placed on a stretcher, blanketed for shock, and taken by cutter to the Emergency Room, arriving at least twenty minutes after François was transferred from the Emergency Room to a private room.

The staff in the ER, trained for almost all possibilities, went into action, having been alerted by the morgue's pathologist about her condition. They acted quickly, removing her clothing, shoes, and all jewelry. Then, while locking her belongings in a locker, they dressed her in a hospital gown. They did their best to stabilize her before rushing her into the Operating Room. For a few minutes, the doctors met and discussed her situation, trying to determine if she could even survive the surgery she needed…brain surgery, and surgery on her heart and her lung. It would be risky at best.

"Can she survive the surgery, doctor?" the ER doctor asked the surgeon.

"I can't be sure. She is critically injured, and has a very low possibility of survival, but we have no choice but to do our best to try to save this woman's life. And we must strive to do her no harm. God bless her. She has suffered terribly. We must first stop the bleeding in her brain or she'll never come out of her coma. Clearly, she has had a lot of cranial damage. We can all see the symptoms in her abnormal breathing, and her faint pulse. I believe she's suffering from Cheyne-Stokes syndrome. She could slip into arrhythmia or periods of apnea, even the rapid breathing of tachypnea. The anesthesiologist will have his hands full, that's for sure."

"Well, we really have no choice, doctor. Let's go to work and do the best we can. Hopefully, we can at least save her life."

"Yes, but we have no idea what condition she'll be in after all this."

For the next several hours, the doctors carefully performed brain surgery, repaired her lung and heart damage, and stopped the bleeding.

In his private room at Municipal Hospital, François grabbed Nicola's arm and frantically asked, "Where is Leah? Is she alive? Is she being taken care of?

Tell me!"

"Monsieur DuBois, I am so sorry. We had no time to stop them before they ambushed you. We did not see them until it was too late. But I can tell you that I and the Syrians immediately shot and killed both Mossad agents. We did not know if there were more, but we were prepared if there were."

"But what about Leah? Is she alright?" he asked again, his voice growing weaker as the pain medication began to take effect.

Not yet wanting to break the news of Leah's death, Nicola continued, whispering nervously, "Madame was seriously injured. We do not know her condition."

Nicola sighed with relief as a nurse entered the room to tend to Francois' bandages and give him pain medication.

"Please let him rest for a while," she advised.

About an hour later, Nicola, still sitting silently beside François' bedside, noticed he had awakened.

"Where is Leah?" François whispered.

Nicola took a deep breath, and looking directly into François' eyes, told him, "I'm very sad to say, Monsieur DuBois, but Mademoiselle Chalhoub is no longer alive. She received three bullets in her chest and her head. The medical technicians said she was dead, so the police took her to the morgue along with the two dead Mossad agents and Antoine."

"Leah is dead?" François screamed frantically, his face distorted from the pain, tears welling in his eyes. "How could this be? How is it I'm alive and she is not? I cannot live without her," he cried. "Nicola, how can this be? They were after me! Those goddamned Mossad agents! And Antoine is dead too?"

"She saved your life, Monsieur DuBois. When she saw the Mossad agent about to fire, she leapt in front of you and got between you and the agent. She was struck by the bullets meant for you. She was very brave. She saved your life," Nicola said as he lowered his head and sadly continued, "but it cost her own life, I am sorry to say."

"And what about Antoine?" François asked, painfully trying to absorb this horrific turn of events.

"The two Syrian agents killed my partner because he was an undercover agent for the Mossad. They had been watching him for a very long time. How he got past the interview inspection process is frightening. He apparently embraced the right wing Maronite views toward the influx of Palestinians and what they, especially the Shiia, are doing in the south. The Syrians, under President Assad are financing the Shia, his enemy, which made Israel his friend. At first, they told me, the Syrians thought Madame Chalhoub was a co-conspirator with Antoine. They believed Madame and Antoine were conspiring to kill you here in Venice. They were assigned the task of killing Antoine and Madame. But they notified us the Syrians had determined Madame was indeed not an ally of Antoine nor the

Israelis. They realized, almost too late, that she was innocent."

Nicola's eyes were filled with sadness as he watched François DuBois suffer, tears flowing down his cheeks.

"Where is Leah, Nicola?"

"I am so sad and sorry to say, but, she is at the morgue, sir."

"At the morgue?"

"Yes, sir. I didn't want to have to tell you, but because of her mortal injuries and no signs of life, the emergency medical team pronounced her dead at the scene. I am so, so sorry, sir. I know how much you loved here. I was very fond of her too."

Then, worried about the future, Nicola quickly said, "We must get you to Beirut as soon as the hospital will release you. Perhaps tomorrow? You are still in danger. There may bemore Mossad agents coming for you even now."

Tearfully, François asked Nicola again, "Leah is dead? Are you certain? That cannot be!"

Nicola lowered his head and nodded yes. "I am so sorry, Monsieur DuBois. We grew to admire Mademoiselle Chalhoub so much. But you can rest assured the Mossad agents and Antoine died painful deaths. They did not last long."

"But, I must find her before we leave Venice, Nicola! I cannot leave her here alone."

"But, Monsieur DuBois please understand," Nicola replied anxiously, "we are certain there are more Mossad agents here in Venice, and they want you dead. You must understand we cannot stay. I am responsible for getting you back to Beirut alive."

"But, Nicola! I must be certain Leah is truly dead. And how can I be assured that she has a decent burial if indeed, she is dead. Don't you see what a horrible position I am in?"

"I understand you have a very difficult choice to make because you loved her so much. But, we are told Madame is dead. The doctors were certain of that, and now, I must look after the living. Don't you see, sir? We have very little time to get you out of Venice."

"Yes, Nicola, I understand your responsibility," Francois sobbed, in great distress. But I cannot leave her here without making proper burial arrangements! You say they were certain, absolutely certain? You are sure? Absolutely sure, Nicola?"

"Yes, sir, they were sure, and the morgue told us she would receive a good, Christian Venetian burial.

"Now, sir, please. We must go before the Mossad discover your whereabouts."

"Then get me to Beirut on a flight as soon as possible. I cannot bear staying in Venice without Leah. We will leave as soon as I am released from the hospital. I must do something for Leah!"

*All these things shall do unto you
that you may know the secrets of your heart.*
Kahlil Gibran

Chapter 32

Venice

Leah remained in a deep coma for nearly three weeks. She had carried no identification with her that evening, so no one knew who she was. And no one had called the police or the hospital looking for a missing person.

François, convinced his love, his very reason for living, was gone, returned to Beirut so depressed he couldn't return to work. He felt dead himself, believing he had no reason to live another day. As a result, he took an indefinite leave of absence and drove into the mountains to Douma to recuperate and heal his mind and body. But he could not get beautiful Leah out of his mind.

She's gone, but she'll never be gone from my heart or my mind. We were finally going to be married, sharing the rest of our lives together. Oh, Lord, it is so cruel! Why did she have to die? Why her and not me?

He went home to *Beit* Chalhoub and spent his many lonely hours meditating in the fruit orchards up on figerie, gazing at the sea as he and Leah had, remembering, and tending to his Uncle Milhelm, who couldn't fully understand his nephew's deep depression and sadness.

François and Marina took long walks and, one day on the mountaintop, they oversaw more plantings of the cedar seedlings on the mountain. That day he went to visit the special seedling he and Leah planted together, and kneeling down, remembering, tears streaming from his eyes, blurring his vision, he began tending the fragile seedling, caressing its soft, young needles, dressing the soil around its roots, adding stones that circled their tree, praying, thinking of his beloved. With a deepening sense of loss, he again gently touched their symbolic little tree. *I will never forget you, Leah, my love, my very life. This young plant will grow into a strong, resilient tree symbolizing our enduring love.*

Marina did her best to console her cousin, seeking to keep Francois' mind occupied with positive subjects. But nothing seemed to help him heal. He wasn't ready.

Then, one day, she asked lovingly, "François, do you recall I asked you 'who is Leah' during your first visit here with Leah?"

"Yes, Marina," he replied sadly, pausing for a moment, "I remember. Actually, cousin, I was not totally certain I knew all I needed to know about her at that time. There were false accusations that she might be a spy for Israel, but that became clear later not to be true. I have loved Leah with all my heart for nearly twenty years. She was a peaceful person, and, I must be totally honest about her and tell you, years ago she left Paris…and me…to go to Palestine to help build a homeland for her people."

"I can see that you love her dearly, François. What matters to us is that you both love each other so deeply."

"Thank you, Marina. I know it might be difficult to understand, but the day we were shot, she declared not only that she wanted to marry me, she wanted to…" his shoulders shuddered at remembering, tears flowing onto his cheeks, "…she wanted to become a Christian and a Lebanese, become a part of our family, Marina. She was my love, my soul, my partner for life, and hopefully the mother of my children."

He stood for several minutes, crying openly looking to the west and gazing on the sparkling waters of the Mediterranean Sea.

Then, looking into Marina's eyes through the tears flooding his own eyes, he said in a weak whisper without hesitancy, "Marina, that's who Leah was."

Milhelm, still in his bedroom during François' recent visit, asked for Francois. After watching his miserable nephew suffer so much, he looked deeply into François' moist eyes and held his hand as he counseled, "My son, you must not allow yourself to sink so low. We pride ourselves on our resilience, our tenacity. *Habibi*, dear one, I recognize you think you have lost your beloved Leah forever. But how can you be sure? You must go and find out for yourself. You have a life to live, and I am sure she would not want you to be so unhappy. She would tell you, I am certain, that you should never give up. Maybe she needs you! You must stop focusing on your own pain and do something yourself. Look ahead. Stop dwelling in the miserable abyss of depression and uncertainty. We can support you. We can pray for you. But in the end, I have to tell you that you must reach deep inside and take control of your own life. We cannot do it for you.

"*Y'eini*, with faith, God's love and in His embrace, you can find her. It truly is up to you, François. My advice to you is to do it now. Return to Venice. Find her. Be sure and find proof. Life is filled with good things and bad. You and Leah have had beautiful times together, and you have all those wonderful memories. Embrace them, recall them, enjoy them. They bring you vitality. It is one thing to suffer a potential loss. It is quite another in how you deal with it.

"You are not alone. We all suffer tragic losses. But you must go on. François, you have been dead long enough. You know your father's story. Follow his path and, like him, you must never give up! *Habibi*, go and find your love, your Leah!"

"You are so wise, Uncle Milhelm, and I must confess you are right, as always!" he said suddenly, coming out of his depression, nearly shouting, "I can't leave her alone in Venice! I don't even know where she is, or whether she is really dead! I only know what the EMTs told Nicola, and what he told me! I must be certain. How stupid I've been! I have to immediately return to Venice and find her. If she's dead, I'll bring her here and bury her beside our cedar seedling. And if she's alive…Oh, my God! What if she is alive? I must find Leah and bring her back to Lebanon. And I must go immediately or I cannot live my life. I must see for myself if she is dead or alive!"

Nearly three weeks after the shooting, Leah, with excellent care and regular visits from the medical staff, remained in a deep and dangerous coma. The doctors were unsure of her prognosis. But, her vital signs were becoming stable, and her body continued to heal. Fortunately, there appeared to be no compelling reasons why she would or would not have any significant lasting impairments. But no one knew for certain.

"She has recovered remarkably, doctor. Your surgeries were quite successful. I think she has a very strong will to live and must realize she has much to live for. She certainly is a fighter. She has never given up, has she?"

The surgeon, nodding to the affirmative, with a somber face replied, "We are very pleased with her progress. The massive doses of diuretics have helped relieve the pressure on her brain. And the bullet to her brain, in the end, ironically provided a means of relieving pressure on her brain. There may be permanent damage to a small part of her brain, but her motor skills, speech, and memory could possibly return." Then," he added, "I expect that in more time, the improving relief on her brain could enable her to come out of her coma."

François left the family house and immediately drove up the mountain drive, then down to Tripoli, then along the coast to Beirut. He proceeded directly to the airport south of Beirut and caught the next plane out to Milan, and a connecting flight to Venice. He was very anxious and committed to determining Leah's fate.

It took François two days in Venice to locate and question the appropriate authorities and receive credible verification by the morgue pathologist that an unknown woman was indeed taken there.

"Yes," the pathologist told François as he read from his records, "a woman, whose name we could not locate, was shot and believed dead. She was critically wounded with, at best, a twenty percent chance of survival. She had no pulse, was not breathing, and was in a deep coma when she was brought to the morgue. Fortunately, the coroner suddenly found a very faint pulse and had her transferred to the hospital Emergency Room. I cannot give you any reason to be hopeful, but you should inquire at Municipal Hospital. I wish you good luck."

Turning on his heel, François quickly left the morgue and caught a water taxi to the hospital.

After questioning the senior administrator, he was able to verify that indeed, a woman, whose name the hospital did not know, was admitted several weeks before, late at night, suffering from multiple gunshot wounds and severe cranial damage. François was told that the woman arrived in a coma, and, as far as the official knew, she was still in critical condition and in a deep coma. She had not spoken a word since her arrival.

"I don't know, and cannot tell without conferring with her doctors, if she will ever come out of her coma, and, if so, what will be her condition."

"Thank you, sir. Thank you very much," he replied with gratitude and concern.

François was filled with hope, without any positive reason other than his renewed optimistic nature, and his faith, inspired by his Uncle Milhelm. Yet, he realized the serious condition that this unknown woman, perhaps Leah, was struggling with from moment to moment. He crossed himself and quickly said a silent prayer for her survival.

Then he anxiously inquired of the head nurse, "I wish to go directly to her room and see if this woman is my Leah. May I?"

"I see no reason why you cannot, although she remains in the Intensive Care Unit. Are you family?"

"Yes," he lied, thinking, *I would have been.*

The nurse then instructed her visitor how to reach the woman's room.

François, ecstatic with joy to learn that Leah, if it really was Leah, could still be alive, stepped to the door and literally ran to the elevators. His passion and anxiety were almost too much to control.

She's alive! I know it! This woman has to be Leah! Oh please, dear God, let her be Leah!

Arriving at the ICU nurses' station, he was directed down the hall to her room.

Only moments before François' arrival, a nurse came into the woman's room to check on her. She was stunned to see her eyes begin to slightly flutter.

"Mademoiselle?" she asked in a soft voice in Italian, "can you hear me?"

At the sound of a friendly voice, her eye lids barely fluttered. The nurse rushed to her station and called the doctor, then rushed back to the patient's bedside.

The doctor appeared and, after checking her vital signs and analyzing her eyes, looked at the nurse and softly said, "Hopefully, she's coming out of her coma."

"Thank God," replied the nurse as she crossed herself.

Then, bending down to her face, the doctor asked, "What is your name?"

The patient, hearing his voice, wanted to respond, but could only moan weakly, "Le .. Le...Leah. My name is Leah." Then, after a moment, she added softly and slowly, "I . .I...need...François."

"François? François who?"

"François, my love...where is François," she murmured.

As she was calling for him, Francois appeared in the doorway, out of breath, his legs weak, his hands moist, and his body shaking. He was exhausted, but lovingly and happily grateful as he looked into the room and saw Leah...her head, still swathed in bandages, on the pillow...her beautiful face almost radiant.

It was the most wonderful sight in the world to him, blurred only by the tears that welled in his eyes and flowed down his cheeks as he rushed to her bedside and spoke to her lovingly, "I am here, Leah, my beloved, and I will never ever leave you again."

Leah, hearing his familiar voice, but barely able to focus on her beloved François, began to cry softly. Convinced that François was with her at last, she slowly stretched out both her arms to him, and for the first time in weeks, broke into her wide, joyful smile, beckoning him to come to her.

www.ingramcontent.com/pod-product-compliance
Lightning Source LLC
Chambersburg PA
CBHW070646160426
43194CB00009B/1601